A TIME OF PASSION

Also by Charles R. Morris

The Cost of Good Intentions: New York City
and the Liberal Experiment—1960–1975

A TIME OF PASSION

AMERICA 1960–1980

Charles R. Morris

A Cornelia & Michael Bessie Book

HARPER & ROW, PUBLISHERS, New York

Cambridge, Philadelphia, San Francisco, London

Mexico City, São Paulo, Sydney

FIRST EDITION

Designer: Sidney Feinberg

Library of Congress Cataloging in Publication Data

Morris, Charles R.

   A time of passion.

   "A Cornelia and Michael Bessie book."

   Includes bibliographical references and index.

   1. United States—Social conditions—1960–1970.

2. United States—Social conditions—1970–

3. United States—Social policy. I. Title.

HN59.M66   1984   973.92   82–48675

ISBN 0–06–039023–9

---

84 85 86 87 88 10 9 8 7 6 5 4 3 2 1

In memory of my father

CONTENTS

Foreword   *ix*

I. PRACTICAL MEN, PRACTICAL PLANS   1

II. THE POWER OF IDEAS   22

III. POLITICS AT THE EDGE OF MORALITY   48

IV. REVOLTS AND REVOLUTIONS   70

V. TWO WARS   89

VI. VIOLENCE   109

VII. NIXON   129

VIII. THE COLLAPSE OF THE KEYNESIAN
      CONSENSUS   157

IX. THE HEAVENLY CITY OF THE
    LIBERAL PHILOSOPHERS   182

X. RATIONALISM RESURGENT   210

XI. MATURITY   226

Bibliographical Notes   243

Index   259

FOREWORD

It is axiomatic that an author doesn't explain his book, but I'll break the rule. This book happened because I wanted a better understanding of the momentous changes that took place in America between 1960 and 1980. I wanted to find out for myself, as best I could, what the real changes were, separate from the turbulence, the fury, the atmosphere of passion, that suffused the twenty years. And, I suppose, I wanted to decide to what extent my perception of vast upheaval stemmed merely from the fact that I was twenty in 1960 and forty in 1980.

Since the book is primarily a personal exploration, the events I've chosen to emphasize are the ones I most wanted to learn about. I spend time on the background to the war in Vietnam, on what Keynes said, and on the civil rights movement, because I felt I needed to know more about them in order to understand the period. I have also included a number of personal anecdotes, not because the facts of my life warrant autobiography—they don't—but to help make my point of view and biases clear. For example, I was anxious to put the War on Poverty into a broader context because I was involved with it in its early days. By the same token, I devote little space to the impact of television or computers, simply because I don't feel I have anything particularly useful or original to say about them. I trust the choice of topics will not appear idiosyncratic, however, for there are consistent themes and variations that play throughout the twenty years: in particular, I think the period demonstrates how much styles of thought, the mental filters we use to interpret the world, what we *think* is happening, affect real outcomes.

An author invariably imposes on friends. Extended conversations with Evan Davis and Tony Terracciano helped clarify my ideas and shape key chapters. In addition, Jon Weiner, Diana Murray, Carol Flynn and Greg Farrell all provided thoughtful comments on the manuscript. My thanks to Robert Zevin for sharing a working manuscript of his book, *The Greater Good.* It was a privilege to have Mike Bessie as an editor. Jackie Yudelowitz was a competent and expeditious typist. Finally, and above all, I'd like to thank my wife, Beverly, and my three children, Michael, Kathleen, and Matthew, for their affectionate tolerance and support throughout the project.

Although writing a book is supposed to be an onerous enterprise, this one was an almost unmitigated pleasure. I hope the reading of it is as enjoyable as the writing was.

A TIME OF PASSION

I

PRACTICAL MEN,
PRACTICAL PLANS

The 1960 presidential election seemed eerily devoid of issues. It was the first in which I voted, and the lack of ideological clash was a disappointment. In the election chronicles, the turning points are almost always technical ones—packaging, polling, advance work. Richard Nixon's use of "Lazy Shave" instead of real makeup during the first televised debate, so his heavy beard made him look jowlish and glowering under the hot lights. John Kennedy's adroitly publicized phone call to the wife of the imprisoned civil rights leader, Martin Luther King. Nixon's theory of pacing and peaking, and Eisenhower's too-late entry into the campaign. Lyndon Johnson holding Texas for his party. The mismatch between Nixon's brutal schedule and his physical stamina. Chicago precinct captains eking out Illinois by rounding up 90 percent of the Democratic voters—or stuffing the ballot boxes to make it look that way.

Both men searched valiantly and unsuccessfully for substantive issues. They both made the mandatory swashbuckling noises about the Russians. Kennedy stressed the "missile gap," while Nixon reminded the voters that he had "stood up to Khrushchev" in their famous "kitchen debate." Kennedy was more willing to spend federal dollars than Nixon, but both favored better education, better health care, and a better environment. The positive personal impression Kennedy made in the television debates counted heavily, but on substance the debates were bloodless and boring. Nixon summed up, "I know Senator Kennedy feels as deeply about [the issues] as I do, but our disagreement is not about the goals for America but only about the means to reach those goals." Later, the two men clashed enthusiastically over whether America should go to war for the sake of Quemoy and Matsu, two forlorn pieces of rock off the China coast. They repeatedly brought up the issue throughout the rest of the campaign, grateful they had found something to argue about. In desperation, Arthur Schlesinger, Jr., a Stevenson Democrat who switched early to Kennedy and was later a presidential assistant, printed at his own expense and circulated among his liberal friends pamphlets with titles like *Kennedy or Nixon—Does It Make a Difference?*

The result seemed finally to turn on style. Kennedy's claim to the presidency did not rest on his experience, his knowledge, or his position on the issues, but on atmospherics—his youth, his vigor, his charm, his wit, his grace, even on his bobby-sox sex appeal. As Murray Kempton, the liberal New York *Post* columnist, summed it up, "Kennedy represents something fresh, something innocent of all the sins and mistakes [of the past] . . . our hope for the future."

One school of political theorists—Daniel Bell, Seymour Martin Lipset, Edward Shils—saw the lack of substantive debate in American political life as the "end of ideology." The great nineteenth- and early-twentieth-century political ideologies, Marxism and Fabian socialism, had run their creative course, leaving politics in the hands of administrators, the "managerial revolution" that James Burnham and Peter Drucker had been predicting. They saw it for the most part as a malaise of the spirit, a symptom of lack of content in the political dialogue, carrying the risk of turning the nation over to organization men, soulless, "other-directed" bureaucrats.

The "end of ideology" theorists, of course, turned out to be wildly wrong. In a few short years, the political contentions that had been murmuring below the placid surface of the Eisenhower years burst into the open, full-throated enough for any ideologue. In any case, the fading of Marxism and socialism could hardly have been of such moment, for they never held sway in America as they did in Europe. The importance assigned to the decline of two alien ideologies reflects American intellectuals' fascination with European thought more than it does a real problem in American politics.

Beneath the technical surface of the campaign, in fact, there was an underlying issue, although it was difficult to express except stylistically. I remember arguing the merits of the two candidates with my father— I was for Kennedy, he for Nixon. He was a working-class Irish Catholic from South Philadelphia, but his roots went back to Boss Bill Vare's Republican machine (probably the only big-city Republican machine in the country). It would have been hard for him to vote Democrat, even for a breakthrough Catholic candidate. We argued without heat, for we both seemed to recognize that the choice had to turn on intuition rather than any precisely definable policy stances. What Kennedy was offering, although I wasn't able to articulate it in the debates with my father, was an *attitude* toward American government, a sense of omnicompetence that had been missing during the Eisenhower years, a style of problem solving—cool, pragmatic, nonideological to be sure, but brimming with confidence that the world could be made a much better place than it was.

Kennedy expressed the thought vaguely, but catchily, with his slogan that he would "get the country moving again." Schlesinger, in one of his pre-election pamphlets, said it more elegantly, if no less vaguely.

> The choice in 1960 is whether . . . we are going to recover control of our national life and national destiny and resume the movement to fulfill the real promise of American life, a promise to be identified not by the glitter of our wealth but by the splendor of our ideals.

Rather later, Theodore H. White put it even more grandly.

> I doubt whether Kennedy himself sensed the hinge he turned in American history. . . . He was of a new generation of Americans who saw the world differently from their fathers. [They were] brought up to believe, either at home or abroad, that whatever Americans wished to make happen, would happen . . . and a whole generation of new Americans was about to follow them to political command and influence.

Kennedy was acutely aware that he was the adventurous alternative, and he and his entourage self-consciously adopted a coolly heroic mien. It was a style that easily lent itself to parody. Schlesinger assigns to his chief all the virtues the New Frontiersmen so ardently desired for themselves.

> The mistrust of rhetoric, the disdain for pomposity, the impatience with the postures and pieties of other days, the resignation to disappointment . . . his contempt for demagoguery, his freedom from dogma, his appetite for responsibility, his instinct for novelty, his awareness and irony and control; his imperturbable sureness in his

own powers, not because he considered himself infallible, but because, given the fallibility of all men, he supposed he could do the job as well as anyone else.

The British journalist Henry Fairlie reacted caustically. To his eyes, Kennedy and his men were simply playing out adolescent fantasies, recreating a romantic image of the World War I pilot-hero—silken-scarved, grimly smiling, gaily meeting the greatest danger, ice-cool in the face of death. Fairlie's barb has the sting of truth: Kennedy himself had been an avid reader of the John Buchan novels—the archetypically cool British hero.

But extremes aside, the Kennedy promise of pragmatic problem solving struck deep chords in American culture, resonating of turn-of-the-century philosophical pragmatism and realism, and beyond that, of the experimentalism of Jefferson and Franklin. What the "end of ideology" theorists seemed not to recognize was that the pragmatic style did not necessarily reflect the absence of governing ideologies; it was itself a positive position, a "principled aversion to general principles," an almost ideological anti-ideology all its own. For Kennedy and his academic advisers like Schlesinger and the economist John Kenneth Galbraith, it was a commitment to a method, to a process for handling data and making decisions; it was an ideological belief that rational men supported by rational inquiry could decide wisely, allocate equitably, and govern benignly.

The position was so deeply ingrained by 1960 that it had become a cliché. Nixon made the same claims for himself that Kennedy did: that he was "pragmatic," "tough-minded," "nonideological." The Nixon he presented in his book *Six Crises* was the cool problem solver, finding the solution that fit the situation. Nixon may have lost the election simply because he was never convincing in the role. The cool control seemed too easily strained; and a candidate who quibbled over "means, not goals" hardly seemed so pragmatic. In an important sense, the election came down to who could best be trusted to deal pragmatically with whatever problems arose—which is why it is so difficult in retrospect to find any substantive issues in the campaign.

Theodore H. White's judgment that Kennedy's election marked an historic turning point must surely be wrong. Kennedy's promises had been made before, certainly by the two Roosevelts. The discontinuity was Eisenhower—a President shrewd enough to know when the country was on a winning streak, and self-disciplined enough to keep his hands out of the machinery. If anything, Kennedy marked the end of a tradition, not the beginning of a new one, and was late to sense the coming changes in the country's mood. It was Kennedy, after all, who said in 1962 that there were no great ideological issues left, that the only problems facing the country were "technical problems, administrative problems"—this just before the country almost drowned in a tub of ideological ferment. Kennedy had such wonderful star quality that he might have assumed the leadership of any movement he chose, had he survived; but it is hard to make the case that he was at the head of a parade. Rather, I think, Kennedy's election was the culmination of a fifty-year tradition of expansive pragmatism, one that perfectly suited an America of limitless opportunity and that expressed precisely the spirit of restless optimism Kennedy was seeking to evoke in his campaign.

The Pragmatic Style

Practical politicians don't usually seek their inspiration in the writings of dead philosophers. But philosophic concepts exercise greater influence than we know. They slip gradually into the common parlance until they become the slogans that govern our everyday attitudes. John Maynard Keynes made the point in a slightly different context.

> Practical men, who believe themselves quite exempt from any intellectual influences, are usually the slaves of some defunct economist.
> . . . I am sure that the power of vested interests is vastly exaggerated compared with the gradual encroachment of ideas.

The word "pragmatism," so beloved by Kennedy and his aides, was the name of the philosophic system worked out by William James, brother of the novelist Henry, and doyen of the turn-of-the-century philosophy department at Harvard. At about the same time James published his book *Pragmatism* (1907), John Dewey was working out a similar set of ideas at the University of Chicago. The two exercised a profound influence on the next fifty years of American thought and are the intellectual source of the pragmatic and "realist" strain in American political assumptions.

Neither James nor Dewey was a reclusive cap-and-gown philosopher who buried his ideas in dusty academic tomes. James had a sparkling, wonderfully lively writing style and was a smash-hit lecturer on the intellectual circuits. He consistently filled thousand-seat halls when he spoke; Harvard had to move his Lowell lectures on pragmatism to a larger hall to accommodate the overflowing crowds. A lecture tour through Europe late in his life was something of a triumphal procession, and he was in such heavy demand as a speaker that he never had time to complete a systematic exposition of his ideas. James came to philosophy late in his life from a career in medicine, physiology, and psychology. Even before he began publishing his ideas on pragmatism and "radical empiricism," he enjoyed a respectable fame for his psychological researches, which were truly distinguished. He knew most of the leading men of his day—he was called "Teddy Roosevelt's favorite philosopher"—and was a good friend of Justice Oliver Wendell Holmes, the patron saint of the legal realism movement, which was closely allied with pragmatism. Never shy about pressing his ideas, James was a relentless publicist for his "pragmatistic church"—as Dewey said, "an apostle seeking the conversion of souls."

Dewey was more of an academic philosopher than James, but no less the polemicist. For more than forty years after James's death in 1910, Dewey thumped the pragmatist tub, pouring out an almost endless stream of books and articles on education, social reform, industrial organization, war, peace, philosophy, and the law. His columns in the *New Republic* for decades were as intellectual mother's milk to a generation of liberal reformers and statesmen. Walter Lippmann's *Drift and Mastery* (1913), for instance, is permeated with Dewey's ideas. The Greek root of "pragmatism" meant "action." James said that he was concerned with *prospective* philosophy; the past was of little interest— "Give us a matter which promises *success*" (his italics). Dewey continually hammered away at the point. He was a philosopher with a mission: "Philosophy recovers itself when it ceases to be a device for dealing with the problems of philosophers and becomes a method for dealing . . . with the problems of men."

The common kernel in James and Dewey—Dewey always insisted on differences in detail—was that a concept's truth could be tested only by measuring its impact in real life, by testing for its "cash value," in James's famous phrase; or as he put it in *Pragmatism:* "Either a concept is useful because it is true or it is true because it is useful. Both phrases mean exactly the same thing." The intensely practical bent of pragmatism was quintessentially American*—the "philosophic expression of commercialism," Bertrand Russell sneered—and one that banished ab-

---

*James was wryly self-aware on this point. Americans, he said, are the only nation who would name "a prodigious star group" after "a culinary utensil."

solutely the absolute ideas cherished by philosophers on the European continent, like Truth, Beauty, or the Divine Order. Interestingly, James seems to have arrived at his pragmatist ideas after an extended spiritual depression as a young man. It was his way of reconciling his scientific observations with his lifelong interest in religion and mysticism. "On pragmatic principles," he could say, "if the hypothesis of God works satisfactorily in the widest sense of the word, it is true."

James's dichotomy between "tender-minded" and "tough-minded" philosophers caught perfectly the virile, open-minded, frankly experimental spirit of the Progressive era. Tender-minded thinkers were "Rationalistic, Intellectualistic, Idealistic," while the tough-minded were "Empiricist, Sensationalistic, Materialistic." "Tough-minded," of course, was one of the favorite clichés of the New Frontier. The "rationalism" that James and Dewey persistently attacked was the European love of abstraction, the fatal insistence on arguing from first principles instead of building up a picture of reality from gritty fact after gritty fact. James, again, said, "In this real world of sweat and dirt, it seems to me that when a view of things is 'noble' that it ought to count as a presumption against its truth." Even the great British empiricists, Locke, Hume, and Mill, were only "half-hearted empiricists" in James's view. Dewey applauded Thorstein Veblen's attacks on British economics as too abstract and a priori. Veblen scoffed that such a creature as John Stuart Mill's "economic man" never existed, while Jeremy Bentham's utilitarian "hedonic calculus" was simply ridiculous.

The more deeply intellectuals were involved with practical affairs—as political scientists, social reformers, historians—the more readily they embraced pragmatism. Narrow academic philosophers had no time for someone who wrote as well as James. James's "pragmatistic church" was an irreverent one, of "a happy-go-lucky, anarchistic sort" that delighted in stripping away the cant and pretense that surrounded established institutions, and was the perfect intellectual underpinning for the Progressive reform movement. Charles Beard's *An Economic Interpretation of the Constitution* (1913), celebrated by activist Progressives, showed that the founding fathers were merely pursuing their economic self-interest when they embarked on their feat of nation-building. Its very lack of awe made Beard's work a pragmatist landmark. Lack of awe and an open-minded readiness for change was a common thread running through Veblen, Beard, Dewey, and James, the trust-busting sallies of Roosevelt and Wilson, and the realist movement in law; and a half century later, it was just the attitude Kennedy was trying to convey with his campaign slogans of energy and motion.

Pragmatism was a powerful influence on American legal thought. The Warren Court's 1954 school desegregation decision, *Brown* v. *Board of Education*—and particularly the Court's use of sociological evidence—culminated fifty years of development of American "legal realism." The movement's motto was Holmes's thoroughly pragmatist dictum that "the life of the law is not logic; it is experience." And his dissent in *Lochner* v. *N.Y.* (1905) was a sacred text. Beard called the dissent a "flash of lightning in the dark heavens of juridical logic"— although Holmes himself was somewhat embarrassed by accolades from left-wing Progressives. In *Lochner* the Court ruled that state regulation of overtime hours violated employees' liberty of contract. Holmes's dissent contains his famous grumble that "the Fourteenth Amendment does not enact Mr. Herbert Spencer's Social Statics," and the pragmatist axiom that "general propositions do not decide concrete cases." He goes on to argue that because of the complexities of modern societies, government was required to, and indeed did, regulate life in a variety of ways. The Court, in his view, had an obligation to transcend empty canons, understand the reality that lay behind a law, and only then decide whether the law was reasonable. The stress on understanding reality was a constant with Holmes, and Dewey cheered his statement that "for the rational study of law, the man of the future is the man of statistics and the master of economics."

The heady success that attended America's involvement with World War I was a formative experience for pragmatist intellectuals, in the same way that World War II conditioned the outlook of Kennedy and his aides. To Dewey, pragmatism was not just a way of cleaning out cumbrous philosophic abstractions, but a method for achieving social mastery and control. He argued that the war was the final demonstration that

> it is possible for human beings to take hold of human affairs and manage them to see an end which has to be gained, a purpose which must be fulfilled, and deliberately and intelligently go to work to organize the means, the resources, and the methods of accomplishing those results.

Dewey was convinced that advances in social science made a "political technology" possible for the first time, and even before the war was over, he was hatching vast schemes of social reorganization and industrial improvement. Interestingly, his focus on method and his insistence on setting practical tests for ideals like "morality" or "freedom" was already provoking some thoughtful observers to raise the same challenges that were posed to Kennedy's intellectuals in the mid-1960s, particularly in the debates over Vietnam. The following was written in 1917 by the pacifist Randolph Bourne:

> The war has revealed a younger intelligentsia, trained up in the pragmatic dispensation, immensely ready for the executive ordering of events, pitifully unprepared for the intellectual interpretation or the idealistic focusing of ends. . . . They have absorbed the secret of scientific method as applied to political administration. They are liberal, enlightened, aware. They are touched with creative intelligence toward the solution of political and industrial problems. They are a wholly new force in American life. . . . There seems to have been a peculiar congeniality between the war and these men. It was as if the war and they had been waiting for each other. . . . What is significant is that it is the technical side of war that appeals to them, not the interpretative or the political side.

It was simply not true, of course, that the political technology Dewey sought for was at hand, not in 1917, and as the failures of the Great Society demonstrated so convincingly, not even a half century later. One of the ironies of the pragmatists' drive for control was how easily it caused them to slip into the very rationalism they inveighed against so strenuously. The rationalist's failing is to become so dazzled by the elegance of his own theories that he is unable to perceive conflicting facts. Dewey rhapsodized that the social sciences had progressed to the point where men could make "intelligence and ideas the supreme force for the settlement of social issues." But the technocratic mastery he yearned for required a theory of society—what motivated people and what would change them. Dewey and his disciples were convinced that they had constructed such a theory. And, for all their "religious devotion to the facts," when it came to a choice between the pragmatists' cherished theories of social uplift and the depressing facts of stubborn reality, they almost always chose their theories.*

*Charles Beard's economic interpretation of the motives of the Constitution's framers—the flagship of pragmatic scholarship—is an outstanding example of the rationalist trap. Beard spun his theories of motivation out of the most fragmentary data, but he was convinced that

The 1920s saw a vast upspringing of social improvement schemes, from settlement houses to asylums. The burgeoning interest in city planning was characteristic. Robert Park and his University of Chicago students were sure that they could control the physical environment in such a way as to benefit the physical health, the morals, the social and spiritual well-being of a city's inhabitants. The social-engineering bias was identical in its rationalist premises to the concepts of Lyndon Johnson's Great Society forty years later. Society was like a machine. With enough research, you could understand how the parts fit together—"model" it, in latter-day jargon—then by adroitly manipulating the social inputs, you would produce predictable improvements in the outputs: people would be healthier, friendlier, more industrious. Individuals could be managed and developed the same way. It was in the 1920s that Karl Menninger developed his clinical approach to curing criminality: a criminal was simply maladjusted, the product of a poor learning experience. Shrewd modification of the prison environment would produce a useful citizen.

All of these ideas enjoyed a renaissance in the late 1950s and early 1960s. The state of California adopted detailed sociological indices to predict the criminal futures of delinquent youth. In 1964, *Time* magazine devoted a cover story to the "new" discipline of city planning. When Lyndon Johnson preached the "Great Society" in 1965 and proclaimed a "War on Poverty," whether he knew it or not, they were Dewey's phrases, and he was using them with almost exactly the meaning Dewey gave them in his writings of the 1920s.

Depression and another world war swept away the practical opportunities for benign social engineering. But the pragmatic intellectuals never discarded their agenda, and the pause allowed them time to fill a gaping theoretical hole. Dewey had always been frustrated by the impersonality of economic forces, by the apparent inability of men to manage the economy precisely to their own purposes. "The immense assemblage of minute and wonderfully interwoven acts" of economic science, he lamented, produce "a net result that is irrational." But during World War II, American economists enthusiastically imported from England the ideas of John Maynard Keynes, who seemed finally to have mapped out the blueprint to the economic machine and to have

---

further research would support his views. In fact, it doesn't, and it is quite likely that Beard's thesis is simply wrong. His book tells us more about the mind of a pre–World War I Progressive than it does about the minds of the founding fathers.

shown the detailed connections between government policy and continued prosperity. The prospect of scientific management of the economy opened up new intellectual vistas, and put Dewey's vision of a social "transfiguration" within reach for the first time.

The Age of Keynes

John Maynard Keynes was the *beau ideal* of the New Frontier—brilliant, witty, an elegant academician, a journalist and publicist, patron of the arts, adviser to governments, successful investor and businessman —the very model to which Kennedy's men aspired. Keynes was a Cambridge don, son of another great political economist, and born to that uniquely English upper-middle-class tradition of service and achievement. His earliest academic work was in mathematics and probability theory—although he mocked the pretentious use of mathematics in economics literature, and his own writings were always a model of lucidity. With the ease befitting his class, Keynes made a fortune as a foreign exchange arbitrageur, according to legend spending an hour each morning in bed in his dressing gown, studying the rate tables in the *Financial Times* and dictating his instructions over his breakfast tea. His social life was centered in the Bloomsbury Group—the Woolfs, the Bells, Lytton Strachey—literary, glittering, vaguely androgynous, always outrageous, and he was actively involved in the development and management of several English theater and dance companies.

Keynes spent most of his life battling official idiocies. He burst into prominence in 1919, when, as the Treasury's financial representative to the Versailles treaty negotiations, he became disillusioned with the small-minded vengefulness of the allies, and published *The Economic Consequences of the Peace,* full of acid sketches of the principals at the negotiations. The book accurately predicted the disastrous consequences that would follow upon the impoverishment of Germany, became a best-seller, and made Keynes famous. In the 1920s, he lobbied strenuously against England's return to the gold standard at the prewar gold/pound parity. In a series of essays, later collected under the title *The Economic Consequences of Mr. Churchill,* Keynes argued that with the changed economic circumstances of England and America, the old parity would price British exports out of their overseas markets. When Winston Churchill, then Chancellor of the Exchequer, followed the near-unanimous advice of the British financial community—who *knew,* by Gad, what a proper monetary standard looked like—and restored the old parity, there was a collapse of British exports and a devastating recession, just as Keynes had predicted.

Keynes published his magnum opus, *The General Theory of Employment, Interest, and Money,* in 1936. He then returned to the Treasury as a wartime consultant, publishing in due course *How to Pay for the War.* Keynes recommended a policy of enforced savings through mandatory payroll deductions to permit the vast expansion of government debt required to finance armaments without runaway inflation. (Parts of the scheme were in fact adopted by the British government.) Following the war, Keynes threw his energies into the cause of international monetary reform, lobbying energetically on both sides of the Atlantic. Although his detailed recommendations were too radical for actual adoption, they were a powerful influence on the discussions that eventually culminated in the Bretton Woods agreements of 1944. Bretton Woods established the dollar as the international medium of exchange —the reserve currency—and fixed the value of all other major currencies in terms of the dollar, a system that functioned for twenty-five years until Richard Nixon dismantled it in 1971. Keynes was seriously ill even before Bretton Woods and exhausted himself the following year negotiating with the United States for postwar loans to Britain. He died of heart disease in 1946.

Keynes's achievement must be measured by his influence on subsequent generations of economists rather than by his academic output. He never produced a finished body of economic theory in the tradition of, say, Alfred Marshall, and his worldwide reputation rests almost solely on the ideas expressed, or hinted at, in the *General Theory.* Keynes was a polemicist, and was constantly revising his ideas to fit immediate political requirements. A quip ran: "Three economists will hold four views on anything—at least two of which will be Keynes's." The *General Theory* itself was a tract for the Great Depression, and Keynes would have been appalled to see it elevated to the status of a biblical text. Under the spur of attacks by conservatives like Friedrich Hayek, Keynes always intended to supply a technically rigorous exposition of his views, but the press of his public activities never allowed him the time.

The powerful appeal of the *General Theory* was that for the first time it presented a view of the economy as a problem that intelligent men could understand whole and manipulate to a national purpose. As the economist Robert Lekachman admiringly put it in 1966, the high point of Keynes's reputation in America, "If Keynes can be said to possess an ideology, it was a confidence . . . that intelligence in human affairs is both essential and possible"—precisely the impulse that inspirited Dewey's intellectuals and the pragmatists of the New Frontier. Before Keynes, the iron laws of classical economics were blind, impersonal forces, like gravity. Classical economists optimistically postulated a benevolently self-regulating economic machine. If more people want to buy corn, the price of corn will rise and call forth more production, and vice versa. Labor is a commodity like corn; absent unclassical union obstructiveness, wages will move to the point where the available labor supply is fully employed. Supply creates its own demand: the income generated in the production of goods is enough to buy them. In short, if government, if unions, if monopolies, would only foreswear mucking with the economic machinery, the economy will hover at a state where all its resources are fully employed, with a steady rate of growth limited only by the pace of technological advancement.

The Great Depression thoroughly demoralized professional economists. It made the "signal failure of the classical doctrine," in Keynes's words, and "the lack of correspondence between . . . theory and the facts of observation" only too patent. The classical corrective mechanisms clearly didn't work, and Keynes was scornful of economists who blamed high unemployment on unions and high wages. Too many men were looking for work at almost any price; the jobs were simply not there.

Keynes shifted the terms of the argument by looking at the problem of total employment. He postulated that total employment must depend, obviously, on the overall level of economic activity, or total spending. But total spending included both spending for consumption and spending for investment. Keynes reasoned that as the country got wealthier, people would begin to save a greater proportion of their income and spend a smaller proportion on immediate consumption. If entrepreneurs did not actively convert the savings into new investment, the savings would lie idle, and total spending would eventually drop, causing total employment to fall. Keynes speculated that an investment shortfall could easily start a vicious cycle, the kind of dreadful downward spiral that characterized the Great Depression. If total employment fell because of a lack of investment, total wages would also fall. The fall in wages would reduce total spending even further, causing pessimistic entrepreneurs to reduce their investment again, which would induce an even greater fall in employment, and so on.

The key, therefore, was investment. But Keynes, as opposed to most economists, had lifelong experience of the financial markets. He knew that investment did not depend on classical equilibrium models, but on what investors thought would happen in the *future,* on the robustness of expectations, or, as he put it, on the "animal spirits" of the entrepreneurs.* He could find no reliable rule for predicting the state of those expectations. History seemed to show, in fact, that investment fluctuated erratically, and probably irrationally. Durable investments, in particular, which Keynes regarded as the most important, depended on the state of very long-term expectations, and were thus wholly subject to "the dark forces of time and ignorance." The conclusions Keynes drew from this were profoundly pessimistic. As a community industrialized, full employment would depend on ever higher rates of investment, which in turn depended on a "fickle and highly unstable" state of investor expectations. There was no mechanism to assure a benign outcome; indeed, rather the opposite tendency could be assumed. And, given the tenderness of investor expectations, if the initial position turned out badly, everything would conspire to make it worse.

Keynes saw a way out of the dilemma. If government would take upon itself to ensure a level of investment sufficient for full employment, a process Keynes called "a somewhat comprehensive socialization of investment," the problem would be solved. In other words, if government would estimate the amount of investment required to sop up existing unemployment, borrow that amount from the public's savings, and employ it actively—probably in schemes of public works—all the happy laws of classical economics that ensured growing wealth could begin to operate again. Keynes stressed that he was not advocating socialism; he had too much experience with the incapacities of the official mind. He was merely advocating for the first time what later came to be known as "countervailing fiscal policy": government should borrow and spend in times of slack resources, and, as Keynes himself proposed in *How to Pay for the War,* run a surplus by one means or

*The key role of expectations was a fundamental for Keynes, but the point was almost completely submerged by mainstream Keynesians in the 1950s and 1960s, who forced Keynesian theory into mathematical equilibrium models—it's hard to put "animal spirits" in a computer. The point is relevant here, not as an argument in economics, but as another example of the rationalist trap. If the facts are too messy for the theory, it's the facts, not the theory, that are cleaned up.

another to absorb excess purchasing power when the economy threatened to overheat.

The desirability of increased government spending during times of depression seemed perfectly obvious to Keynes, but it was staunchly resisted at all levels of the government and the financial community, provoking him to heights of polemical frustration.

> Pyramid-building, earthquakes, even wars may serve to increase wealth, if the education of our statesmen on the principles of the classical economics stands in the way of anything better. It is curious how common sense . . . has been apt to reach a preference for *wholly* "wasteful" forms of loan expenditure. . . . For example, the form of digging holes in the ground known as gold mining, which adds nothing whatever to the real wealth of the world . . . is the most acceptable of all solutions. . . . If the Treasury were to fill old bottles with banknotes, bury them at suitable depths in disused coal mines which are then filled up to the surface with town rubbish, and leave it to private enterprise on well-tried principles of *laissez-faire* to dig the notes up again (the right to do so being obtained, of course, by tendering for leases on the note-bearing territory), there need be no more unemployment and with the help of the repercussions, the real income of the community, and its capital wealth also would probably become a good deal greater than it actually is. It would, indeed, be more sensible to build houses and the like; but if there are political and practical difficulties in the way of this, the above would be better than nothing.

Keynes's sarcasm about pyramid-building or "even wars" proved prophetic, for the Western democracies shortly spent their way out of depression by making armaments. Few politicians saw the connection between wartime financial policies and Keynes's theories, of course, but to a growing band of academic economists, the wartime prosperity was a demonstration tantamount to the observations of the bending of light during the solar eclipse of 1919 that vindicated Einstein's theory of relativity. The postwar rebuilding of Europe was another vindication. Keynes himself, in fact, had expected a major depression to follow the war because he believed the capital required for reconstruction would not be forthcoming from wrongheadedly thrifty governments. But the United States provided the investment capital in the form of massive loans in roughly the amount, as it turned out, that Keynes had estimated would be required. His academic reputation grew.

As university economics departments embraced Keynesianism, economists were at the same time gaining influence in government. Several of Roosevelt's key advisers were impressed with Keynes's analysis of the Depression and arranged a meeting between him and the President. The meeting was hardly a success—neither Keynes nor Roosevelt understood what the other was talking about. Keynes also made an impression on Walter Lippmann, who consulted Keynes from the early 1930s, and helped publicize his ideas among American liberal intellectuals, just as he had Dewey's. Lippmann and Keynes, in fact, helped draft the final American position on cutting loose from the gold standard in 1933. The incident is an example of the behind-the-scenes influence of Lippmann. Not only did he help draft the proposals, but in the succeeding weeks, he used his daily column to advertise their wisdom.

Keynesian ideas came into their own with Kennedy's election. In the first place, a whole generation of younger economists had been extending the Keynesian approach into the new discipline of "macroeconomics"—the study of the economy as a whole and the interaction between total employment, government policy, and the activities of the private sector. It is easily forgotten, for instance, that when Keynes was writing, there were virtually no readily available statistical data to track overall economic performance. The U.S. Department of Commerce published the first national income statistics only in 1936 and the first gross national product report in 1942; the two were not combined in a presidential budget message until 1945, and statistical reporting was even slower to develop in England. By 1960, of course, the full panoply of modern economic statistics was available to policymakers, and economists had developed enough expertise to use them as the basis of detailed recommendations. It would have been hard for politicians to ignore them completely.

More important, the Keynesian promise of actively controlling and managing the national economy was irresistible to a man of Kennedy's instincts. His entourage of intellectuals, mostly Harvard-trained Keynesians, did nothing to discourage him. Repeatedly, in the weeks between the election and the inaugural, Kennedy and his advisers arranged meetings with economists so he could learn how to achieve a 5 percent annual rate of economic growth. One can reconstruct the meetings:

Kennedy simplistically asking for the talisman, and the economists hedging and evading, but not quite willing to admit that their science wasn't all *that* good at giving anything but the most general advice.

There was another attraction as well. To Kennedy's intellectuals, Keynesian theory was delightfully counterintuitive. To get richer, it was necessary to spend, not to save. The principles that governed the family budget didn't apply to the national budget. The average man felt he was falling behind when he slipped into debt; but borrowing might be the best and fastest road to the country's advancement. Keynes himself enjoyed that aspect of his theory. There was an edge of wry humor in his Depression radio broadcasts when he urged the British to stop being thrifty: "Oh, patriotic housewives, sally out tomorrow early into the streets and go to the wonderful sales. . . . You will do yourself good . . . you are setting on foot useful activities." Intellectuals like counterintuitive solutions. The fact that businessmen and bankers were so slow in catching up to the new theory just added to the fun. What's the use of being smart, after all, if the answers you produce are the same ones that anyone else would have come up with?

Kennedy's pragmatist instincts and his fascination with the technical details of governing were enough to excite his interest in Keynesian economics; but his insistence on getting "the country moving again" had a larger purpose, for he was convinced that America was losing out in the competition with the Soviet Union. Anti-Communism was good politics, of course, for it converted Eisenhower's complacency into defeatism and Kennedy's impatience into patriotism. But it also provided a standard for measurement. Precisely because pragmatists disavowed European notions of final ends and absolute goals, they needed a competition to see how well they were doing.

Anti-Communism

Kennedy's anti-Communism ran deep; for all his Harvard sophistication, he was still an Irish Catholic. To the mass of Catholics in the 1950s, as with Protestant fundamentalists in the 1980s, Communism was not just the enemy, but a satanic enemy, the Antichrist. Kennedy's father was a good friend of Senator Joe McCarthy and a contributor to his 1952 campaign, when "McCarthyism" was already a swear word among liberals. Robert Kennedy's first job in government was with McCarthy's investigative subcommittee. John Kennedy himself seems to have disapproved of McCarthy's more extreme tactics, but he never spoke out against him. And it would have been impossible for him to maintain his roots in Boston Irish politics and his friendship with Catholic prelates like Cardinals Cushing and Spellman, without espousing a staunchly anti-Communist line.

But there was also a powerful strain of anti-Communism among American liberals and left intellectuals—although it has been obscured by liberal and intellectual opposition to McCarthyism and later by the academic leadership of the Vietnam War protests. American leftists flirted with Communism in the 1930s, but were disillusioned by the Hitler-Stalin pact, the repression in Eastern Europe, and the gradual revelations about Stalin's purge trials. Jews, in particular, were repelled by the persistent strain of anti-Semitism in Soviet policy. Journals like *Commentary, The New Leader,* and *Partisan Review* were taking a hard anti-Communist line by the late 1940s, although their editorial staffs later divided bitterly over whether fighting Communism took priority over fighting McCarthy.

The rigidly militant anti-Communist posture of the United States during the 1950s—when the world was halved between "Commie rats" and all others—is usually associated with the names of Republicans like John Foster Dulles, Francis Walter, and William Knowles, but the anti-Communist strategy itself was the creation of the Democrats. It was fear of Communist expansion in Europe that spurred Congress into funding the Marshall Plan, and it was George Marshall's State Department intellectuals—George Kennan and his policy-planning staff—that first enunciated the doctrine of "containment." Walter Lippmann criticized Kennan's ideas severely in a series of columns that gave the "Cold War" its name, but even Lippmann was questioning Kennan's tactics, not the fundamental anti-Soviet cast of his policy recommendations. A left fringe among socialists and revisionist historians, like Michael Harrington and William Appleman Williams, long argued—on the whole unconvincingly, I think—that the Cold War originated in American rather than Soviet policy, but they commanded little support until well into the 1960s. Mainstream Democrats, from blue-collar workers to labor intellectuals and the Stevensonian left, were solidly anti-Communist as a matter of first principle.

By 1960, reflexive anti-Communism was reinforced by real fear. If the United States was in an economic competition with the Soviet Union, as Kennedy insisted, it was surely losing. The average annual

GNP growth in the United States during the 1950s fluctuated between 1.5 percent and 2.5 percent, while the Soviet economy was rollicking along at rates double, triple, even quadruple that. Khrushchev's boasts that "we will bury you" and "your grandchildren will live under Communism" didn't seem completely farfetched.

It is important to understand the depth of the fear. My own impressions may be magnified by parochial schooling. In the 1950s, the nuns painted frightening pictures of Stalin, much as English nannies terrified their charges with tales of "Boney" a century and a half earlier, and my friends and I were genuinely anxious about Russia. Once a week—public and parochial school students alike—we spent five minutes crouching under our school desks with our faces hidden in our arms to practice warding off a Russian atom bomb blast. Whether or not the Soviets were "objectively"—as the Marxists say—a threat to America in the 1950s, the unfolding pattern of events, to a nation insecure in its new world role, was sinister in the extreme. The threat of a Communist takeover in France and Italy after the war. The fall of China. Spies. Fifth columns and disciplined Communist cells. Russia's nuclear weapons. The invasion of South Korea. "Human waves" of Chinese rolling back MacArthur's troops. The Iron Curtain. The tanks clanking into Budapest. The persisting crisis in Berlin. The "winds of change" in Africa and Asia. The spreading red and pink on the maps in *Life* magazine and *Reader's Digest.*

The Russian launching of a Sputnik satellite in 1957, more than anything else, was a blow to American self-confidence. It called into question not only America's technological and military leadership, but its moral fiber, its internal discipline, its ability to organize large projects. America was soft; its youth shied away from hard subjects like science and math; college students majored in liberal arts instead of engineering. To Kennedy and his aides, the problem called for a national response. It was an opportunity to demonstrate how a pragmatic and results-oriented leadership could cut through the welter of local restrictions and outdated curricula, overcome the lack of imagination, install new teaching concepts (like the misconceived "new math"), raise the level of physical fitness, and produce a generation of young people that was fully competitive with the Russians.

Global politics had even greater intellectual appeal than Keynesian economics—a broader canvas, more subtlety, less technical aridity. In college, around 1960, courses on international relations were the biggest campus draw. There were the tongue-curling pleasures of knowing whether Souvanna Phouma, Souvanaphong, or Phoumi Nosavan was temporarily on top in Laos; there was the grave discipline of memorizing Herman Kahn's twenty-seven or forty-five stages to thermonuclear incineration; there were the moral satisfactions and continental sweep of plans to upgrade the "human capital" of Africa and Asia.

As Kennedy gradually focused on the contest with global Communism as the ultimate test of pragmatic competence, foreign affairs began to dominate his campaign speeches and he assumed, more and more, a tone of strident militancy.

> I think to be an American in the next decade will be a hazardous experience. We will live on the edge of danger.

> I think the American people are willing to undergo whatever is necessary for the world's best defense. They want to know what is needed—they want to be led by their Commander-in-Chief.

> The world cannot exist half-slave, half-free.

> Across the face of this globe, freedom and Communism are locked in a deadly embrace.

> The fight is between Red imperialism and the world of the freemen.

> This is no ordinary enemy, and this is no ordinary struggle.

> We must move forward to meet Communism, rather than waiting for it to come to us and then reacting to it. . . . We must move outside the home fortress, and we must challenge the enemy in fields of our own choosing. We must indeed take the initiative again—we must start moving forward again—at home and abroad.

Arthur Schlesinger, Jr., the card-carrying Stevensonian liberal in the Kennedy circle, lumped together social progress and production of military hardware as though they were the homogeneous product of a society run on principles of energetic pragmatism.

> [If Kennedy is not elected] we will fall farther and farther behind the Soviet Union in ICBMs and the fight for space; we will witness the deterioration of American education and the quality of American life; we will see a continued failure to make adequate provision for our children and our future. . . . The choice is stark and impera-

tive: either a continuation along these lines of least resistance, until we drift into minor-power status and oblivion; or a recovery of national purpose and an exercise of "national leadership."

The campaign threads were pulled together in Kennedy's inaugural:

Let every nation know, whether it wishes us well or ill, that we shall pay any price, bear any burden, meet any hardship, support any friend, oppose any foe to assure the survival and success of liberty.

We paid dearly for that promise, but the speech met with general approbation, and there is no doubt that Kennedy's militarism helped him gain his razor-thin election victory. My own view is that the militarist mood expressed a general fear that we were really falling behind. The contest between Communism and capitalism was not going to be about philosophy but about performance—and performance was what America was all about.

And so the experiment was launched: a President in the pragmatic liberal tradition of the two Roosevelts and with the intellectual heritage of Dewey and James; but the first to be possessed of the tools Dewey could only dream of—the computer, national data centers, Keynesian macroeconomics, modern quantitative analysis, new theories of organization and control; and unequivocally the first President who truly believed that technology gave him the reach to manage events. We know, of course, how the experiment ended. The Kennedy-Johnson administrations may have been the last of that pragmatic liberal line, or the last for a long time. Their reach was too short, their grasp too unsure, and events too unmanageable. Neither people, the economy, nor other nations were so plastic as they hoped.

The sense of failure and defeat that was the legacy of Kennedy's and Johnson's New Frontier makes it difficult to recapture the hopefulness of the moment—leaving aside the nonsense written about Camelot. But Kennedy expressed an impulse that ran deep in American culture and intellectual life. The opportunity to give it free rein was, for a time, thrilling.

II

THE POWER OF IDEAS

John Kennedy assumed the reins of power, Arthur Schlesinger assures us, with "incomparable dash," "zest," and "gaiety." In Schlesinger's eyes, the new administration's "sense of possibility had its gayest image" in a White House party for Jackie Kennedy's jet-setting relatives, the Radziwills.

> Never had girls seemed so pretty, tunes so melodious, an evening so blithe and unconstrained. The President, who rarely danced, moved from one group to another, a glass of champagne in his hand . . . while the music played lightly on. The glitter of that night remained in slightly ironic memory for a long time.

A nostalgic haze beclouds Schlesinger's memories of the Kennedy years, but he captures the euphoria of the New Frontier, the sense of hopefulness and imminent achievement. Kennedy wanted to be a strong President; he intended to dominate the administration and dictate the flow of events in ways that Eisenhower never did. He said to the national press club that he rejected a "restricted concept" of the presidency. The needs of the day demanded that the President be

> the vital center in our whole scheme of the government . . . [that he] place himself in the very thick of the fight, that he care passionately about the fate of the people he leads, that he be willing to serve them at the risk of incurring their momentary displeasure . . . [that he] be prepared to exercise the fullest powers of his office—all that are specified and some that are not.

Kennedy selected his closest aides in his own image. They were young—David Bruce was disqualified for secretary of state because he was sixty-two—and they were versatile—the archetypal New Frontiersman could

> turn from Latin America to saving the Nile monuments at Abu Simbel, from civil rights to planning the White House dinner for Nobel Prize winners, from composing a parody of Norman Mailer to drafting a piece of legislation, from lunching with a Supreme Court Justice to dining with Jean Seberg—and at the same time maintain an unquenchable spirit of sardonic liberalism and an unceasing drive to get things done.

Kennedy himself was a legitimate war hero, and most of his men had command experience in wartime. They had been bomber pilots, and guerrilla leaders; they had been on the beach at Normandy or had suffered in Japanese prison camps; a surprising number had served in the Office of Strategic Services, the forerunner of today's CIA, where they had planned bombing strategies, broken codes, disrupted enemy communication, and plotted espionage. Kennedy's men were used to winning. Most of them had spent some time in government service after the war and had savored firsthand the successes of the Marshall Plan and the reconstruction of Germany and Japan. They had helped manage the conversion from a wartime to a peacetime economy without depression and had been part of the worldwide expansion of American industrial and financial might.

They understood the power of ideas. A number of them, McGeorge Bundy, Walt Rostow, Kermit Gordon, were university professors, and even the few businessmen, like Robert McNamara, were at home with intellectuals. The Marshall Plan, after all, had started with an idea. Ideas could transform the world; it was just a matter of finding the Archimedean fulcrums. All of this strikes us now as arrogant or fatuous, jaundiced as we are by the experience in Vietnam. But when Kennedy claimed that his ill-fated Alliance for Progress "would develop the resources of the entire hemisphere, strengthen the forces of democracy, and widen the vocational and educational opportunities of every person in all the Americas," the experience in Europe and Japan seemed to confirm his optimism. When he told a task force on Africa to advise him "in regard to raising the educational level, the fight against disease, and improving the available food supply," he had every confidence that if he could just find the right lever, he could lift Africa out of its mire. His

staff aide Walt Rostow had written a book on economic development
that showed how it was done.

It is doubtful whether Kennedy himself believed all the New Frontier rhetoric. Aides report that he was embarrassed by the slogan, at
least once the campaign was over, and his cabinet appointments, in
contrast to those of his personal aides, were generally cautious. He
reappointed Allen Dulles at the CIA and J. Edgar Hoover at the FBI.
Douglas Dillon at Treasury was a Wall Street stalwart and had served
in the Eisenhower State Department. Dean Rusk at State was very much
a man of the foreign policy establishment. Kennedy's slow start on
domestic problems, like the economy and civil rights, dismayed many
of his liberal supporters. Kennedy liked keeping his options open and
enjoyed playing his young enthusiasts off against the older hands.

There was consensus, however, on the importance and the nature of
presidential power. If there was a philosophic break with the Eisenhower administration, it centered around the notion of power: Kennedy
really expected to run the country. The pragmatic liberalism that was
the inheritance of Dewey and that inspired his aides required prescrip-
tive management from the top, organizing and allocating resources to
comport with policy. Kennedy was fascinated with the problem. He
gave a prominent place in his preinaugural planning to Richard Neu-
stadt, an academic student of presidential power, and was genuinely
worried about his ability to motivate the bureaucracy to carry out new
activist policies. He needed, and recognized that he needed, new concepts of management, techniques that would extend his reach and make
control practical. He found the answers he was looking for when Robert
McNamara, his secretary of defense, brought the Pentagon to heel, and
demonstrated both the style and the method of bureaucratic mastery.

The Department of Defense is the free world's biggest bureaucracy.
It was created after World War II to coordinate the policies of the
Army, Navy, and Air Force and weld a common national defense
strategy. The stresses of the job drove the first secretary, James Forrestal, to suicide. His successors made little headway in imposing order on
the sprawling military establishment. Under Eisenhower, their role was
more or less limited to arbitrating interservice disputes. When
McNamara took office, he found that there was no strategic consensus
among the services—the Army, for instance, was prepared for a long
war of attrition, and the Air Force for a quick war of annihilation.
Procurement policy was competitive, with each service racing to build

the most glamorous new weapons, regardless of strategic requirements. There were serious deficiencies in basic readiness—airlift capability, divisions at strength, spare parts, trained reservists, functioning equipment.

None of it daunted McNamara. He was a Harvard MBA, had been briefly a Harvard assistant professor, teaching statistical control techniques, and a lieutenant colonel in the Air Force during World War II; he joined the Ford Motor Company after the war and, just a year older than Kennedy, had risen to the presidency of the company only weeks before the inaugural. He was not an expert in defense, but he considered himself a specialist in managing large organizations, and he was familiar with the work of an emerging group of defense intellectuals at the RAND (Research and Development) Corporation and its growing progeny of defense-oriented research institutions.

The brief heyday of the defense wizards in McNamara's Pentagon was also the high point of liberal pragmatism in American government. It was the defense intellectuals' achievement, and McNamara's temporary triumph, to bring public practice fully into conformity with technocratic theory. The defense intellectuals, men like Herman Kahn, Thomas Schelling, Stephen Enke, Charles Hitch, and Alain Enthoven, were mathematicians, physicists, and economists, but they shared a common interest in the theory of choice. They were fascinated by developments in game theory and computerized optimization techniques, like linear programming, that allowed a practitioner to select mathematically the most desirable outcome among a range of complex alternatives.

As Hitch explained it, a rationalized policy process requires first that goals be specified, preferably in a quantified way—such as the square miles of enemy territory that should be destroyed—then that alternative methods be developed for accomplishing the mission—air attack, infantry assault, missiles. Next, a model must be developed that simulates actual conditions—in this instance, the nature of the enemy response, the imperviousness of his defenses, the effect of weather conditions on mobile equipment. Finally, a success criterion must be specified—speed, economy of lives, protection of the civilian population—or, if there are several criteria, they must be assigned quantitative weights or ranks. The practitioner then simulates the mission on his computer and presents the policymaker with the alternative most likely to produce the desired result. It was heady stuff. And, because it was easy to show that the existing American defense posture was irrational, it put the military men on the defensive and gave McNamara the upper hand almost from the day he entered the Pentagon.

McNamara's contribution was to convert the defense intellectuals' theories into an ongoing management process, using a technique called the Program Planning and Budget System, or PPBS. Budgeting in the Pentagon was still something of a rudimentary art in 1961. General MacArthur had thought that the notion of a military budget was "silly": you spent what you had to spend. Under Eisenhower, the budget was just an accounting process. The individual services would develop their plans and submit their spending estimates to the White House through the secretary. If the numbers were too big (they always were), the secretary would convey the bad news back to the services, which would then proceed to lop off their lower priorities.

McNamara reversed the procedure, budgeting from the top down, and holding the purse strings tightly in his office. The heart of PPBS was to recast the budget in terms of *outputs*. In PPBS parlance, an output was an expected result, an input a means to the result. The items in a conventional military budget—soldiers, airplanes, ships, rifles, ammunition, supplies—were *inputs* and made no sense except as they related to the accomplishment of a specific set of military objectives. McNamara and his analysts defined eight fundamental missions, or basic military outputs, including, for example, the "Continental Air and Missile Defense" mission, designed to protect the United States and its land-based missiles from an assault by the enemy; the "Strategic Retaliatory Forces" mission, supposed to weather a nuclear assault and deliver a disabling attack in riposte, and the "Airlift and Sealift" mission, charged with delivering American military forces in specified quantities to likely points of contention overseas.

The Pentagon analysts—primarily Hitch and Enthoven and their staffs—then specified the requirements of each mission in terms of likely "scenarios." If a nuclear attack came, what direction would it come from, with what firepower, with how much warning? If U.S. troops had to intervene elsewhere in the world, where would the trouble likely occur, how many flare-ups could reasonably be expected at one time, how many troops and what kind of equipment would have to be moved, how long would they have to be supplied? Once the likely scenarios had been selected and the mission requirements specified, budgeting became a process of reasoning backwards from the mission requirements to specific numbers of troops, planes, artillery shells, spare parts, and so on, right down to the numbers of nuts and bolts that should be in inventory.

The process seems straightforward enough, but it hit the Pentagon with the force of a thunderclap. All the pet projects that had been for years in the private preserves of the service chiefs were suddenly dragged out into the white glare of McNamara's relentless scrutiny, subjected to the unremittingly logical analysis of the systems intellectuals, stripped of their lazy rhetoric to expose their underlying irrationalities, the confusions of purpose, the overlappings and the duplications, the lack of any integrating strategic and tactical overview. Hardest to take was the lack of respect for old-line military wisdom. In the civilian view, the generals had no experience with warfare in the nuclear age, and scientists were probably in a better position to understand the technical requirements of modern weapons and command and control systems. McNamara, for his part, never doubted that his methods could be extended across the entire range of government problems, particularly those of managing the economy. He commented casually to Walter Heller, Kennedy's chief economic adviser, "Your fellows and mine should get together and see what we can do."

Despite grumblings from the service chiefs and their friends in Congress, McNamara swept all before him. His appearances on Capitol Hill were performances of dazzling virtuosity. Evincing total mastery of grand strategy and tactical detail, his briefings were crisp, comprehensive, and candid. (Early on, he stated bluntly that the "missile gap" that had been a key issue in Kennedy's campaign simply didn't exist.) The overwhelming majority of Congress were delighted. McNamara was laying out for the first time a reasoned view of military doctrine, a clear statement of policy assumptions, and closely argued justifications for his recommended spending levels. Kennedy had made shoring up the nation's defenses his top policy priority, and he got everything he wanted from McNamara. Congress approved sharp increases in military spending, and by 1965, McNamara could claim that he had presided over a 100 percent increase in strategic nuclear weapons, a 45 percent increase in combat-ready Army divisions, a 33 percent increase in tactical fighter squadrons, a 60 percent increase in tactical nuclear weapons stationed in Europe, a 75 percent increase in airlift capacity, a 100 percent increase in ship construction, and a 600 percent increase in counterinsurgency capabilities.

PPBS became something of a fad. In 1965, President Johnson ordered all federal agencies to apply the method. I was working in an antipoverty agency at the time, and shortly afterward in the New York City Budget Bureau, and in each case we dutifully, and laboriously, tried to recast our planning and budgeting to fit within the PPBS format. A minor PPBS industry sprang up around university political science and public administration departments; professors and ex-bureaucrats conducted seminars and hired themselves out as consultants to instruct the uninitiated in the arcana of the new management techniques. The exercise was not totally without value. The conventional budget objectives of a city school system, for instance—smaller class sizes or more reading specialists—are just inputs: they are justified only to the extent that they improve the performance of the children. Ideally, an education budget should start with the increments of educational improvement one wishes to buy, and reason from there to the additional teachers or reading materials needed to produce the desired results. Focusing on results was a helpful corrective: every large bureaucracy sheltered operations whose purpose had long since been forgotten.

The education example, of course, makes plain the weakness in the method and how easily pragmatic intellectuals could slip into the rationalist trap. For the fact is that no one really *knows* very much about how teachers and texts affect reading performance. Smaller class sizes might help, but perhaps only because they allow the teacher to keep order. Or perhaps what really matters is the personal qualities of the teacher. But PPBS demands that problems be forced into a quantifiable framework—which may actually obscure the central issues. It is the error Whitehead called "misplaced concreteness"—trying to apply a category of thought to a situation where it isn't appropriate. Hitch himself admitted that the "scenarios"—the war games that "modelled" putative military encounters—almost always required drastic oversimplifications to permit quantitative analysis of the outcomes. A battle had to be won by occupying the enemy's territory; otherwise the computer had no way of knowing which side was ahead. The seriousness of the problem was not appreciated until Vietnam, when the conventional quantitative measures turned out to be useless. By grasping at numbers —like the percentage of the countryside that was "pacified"—the analysts managed to misunderstand completely what was going on.

The ascendance of the intellectuals pointed up a second problem at the heart of liberal pragmatism, one that would become more evident as the Kennedy-Johnson programs shifted their focus to economic and domestic issues: the technocratic approach to government had a fundamentally antidemocratic bias. When Kennedy said that a President had to lead beyond where the voters wanted to go, he meant it. To the defense intellectuals, the complexities of military balance in the nuclear age were quite beyond the ken of the common man, just as the favored economic policy was usually the counterintuitive one. There had always been a tendency toward *étatisme* in the left wing of the Democratic party, a position shared with the socialist parties of Europe, and one urged upon Kennedy with unflagging zeal by liberal intellectuals like John Kenneth Galbraith. The airy webs of ratiocination spun by the metaphysicians in the Pentagon were distinctly elitist playthings. And the Defense Department was a particularly fertile ground for hypertrophied rationalism—for as long as the nation was at peace, the elegant theoretical formulations would never be subjected to the rigors of real-world testing.

The ultimate military failure in Vietnam shouldn't obscure the magnitude of McNamara's achievement. Viewed strictly as an exercise in the management of large-scale enterprise, McNamara's taming of the Defense Department must rank as one of the virtuoso cabinet performances of all time. In his hands, PPBS—instead of being the dry-as-dust technical discipline hawked by the management consultants and academics—was a brilliant bureaucratic ploy. By shaping the department around a series of broad strategic missions, he broke the grip of the individual services over military programs. Each service was assigned a role in the basic missions, and their individual contributions could only be pulled together by the Office of the Secretary. McNamara's introduction of systematic analysis was a whole new departure in itself. And skimming through the pages of a *Harvard Business Review* from the 1960s provides a measure of his contribution to management theory. Virtually all the techniques of management control now routinely used by large businesses—project management, PERT, critical path analysis, matrix management, management by objectives, computerized management information systems—were either invented, developed, or refined in McNamara's Pentagon—one of the few cases where government was the technical mentor to private enterprise. It was, at least for the time being, a signal confirmation of the pragmatist faith and shored up Kennedy's confidence that he had the men and the means to get the "country moving again."

The New Economics

McNamara's management triumphs were gratifying, but to John Kennedy, "getting the country moving again" meant spurring economic growth. During the campaign, he had pounded again and again at the lackluster performance of the economy under Eisenhower. The recession that set in during 1958 and persisted until just before the election undoubtedly contributed to his narrow victory over Nixon, who was saddled with the defense of Eisenhower's policies.

Although the *Wall Street Journal* and Richard Nixon were prepared to defend the Eisenhower years as ones of remarkable stability and broad advancement ("You never had it so good"), there was a near consensus among professional economists that the nation was slipping into the worst of all worlds—slowly stagnating production, high unemployment, and high inflation to boot. Growth was slow during the best of the Eisenhower years and was virtually imperceptible after 1958. Unemployment, which had been just over 4 percent when Eisenhower took office, had gradually crept up to 5.5 percent by the start of his second term, reached a postwar high of 7.5 percent in 1958, and was still hovering around 7 percent by Kennedy's inauguration. Inflation, which had been tamed with some difficulty after the Korean War, was on the rise again, averaging 1.4 percent per year during Eisenhower's second term, with monthly peaks as high as 2.5 percent—a worrisomely high rate for a nation not yet exposed to the double-digit excitements of the 1970s and the 1980s.

Growth was an imperative for Kennedy. In the first place, traditional Democratic concern for the unemployed made better economic performance mandatory. Even more important, Kennedy's ambitious goals for expanding U.S. defense efforts would not be achievable without the increased tax revenues that would accrue from accelerated growth. His intellectual advisers, moreover, particularly Galbraith and Schlesinger, were pressing ambitious ideas for sharply increased social spending—on education, health, recreation, resource development, income security—to "right the social balance," as Galbraith put it. Galbraith's *The Affluent Society,* an eloquent brief for an expanded public sector, was a national best-seller in the year before the election. The clinching argument, finally, was the rapid advancement of the Soviet Union, surging ahead at a growth rate of about 7 percent per year. Projections of the U.S. and U.S.S.R. growth rates—all analysts agreed that such projections were silly, but persisted in making them anyway—showed that by the year 2000 the Soviets would have a gross national product almost triple America's, just as Khrushchev had been promising.

Kennedy's personal understanding of current economic theory was casual at best, but he brought a high-powered team of academic economists to Washington and challenged them to come up with the answers he needed. The Council of Economic Advisers was chaired by Walter Heller of the University of Minnesota, with Kermit Gordon of Harvard and James Tobin of Yale as the other two members. David Bell, the budget director, Seymour Harris, adviser to the Treasury, and Galbraith, ambassador to India and gadfly-at-large, were all Harvard economists. Schlesinger, a Harvard historian with a strong interest in economic issues, was a convenient translator. Although there were some important policy disagreements within the group, they shared a common outlook on the larger issues. They were all trained in the Keynesian tradition and believed strongly in the efficacy of government deficit spending to spur the economy in times of slack. In particular, they viewed Eisenhower's single-minded pursuit of a budget surplus in the low-growth years of 1959 and 1960 as senseless and destructive. They were committed to an interventionist strategy and to the technocratic faith in government's ability to manage a national economy, and they were envious of the *dirigiste* national planning that was taken for granted in Europe. Finally, they believed in forecasting. They were convinced that national statistics and their own understanding of the economic machine had progressed to the point where they could accurately identify trends and problems and adapt government policy to produce the most desirable outcomes.

Through at least the first five years of the Kennedy and Johnson administrations, they turned out to be splendidly right. National economic policy from the first quarter of 1961 through the beginning of 1966 was an unmitigated success, an almost unalloyed triumph of Keynesian principles—it was simply the best five-year economic record in the nation's history, an economist's El Dorado. Kennedy's 5 percent real growth target was met and exceeded by 1963, and the growth rate for the entire period was in excess of 4.5 percent. Unemployment dropped from almost 7 percent to less than 4 percent, the "full-employment" target. (Some "frictional" unemployment—people changing jobs, new labor force entrants—was unavoidable.) At the same time, the rate of inflation slowed to only 1 percent a year; by the end of the period, consumer prices were stable, and wholesale prices were actually dropping. Long interest rates stayed low, and there was a boom in capital spending. The average person's real income increased by a third, and corporate profits doubled. The increase in national output exceeded $200 billion, creating seven million new jobs. Kennedy and Johnson were able, all at the same time, to increase social spending sharply, pay for the fastest peacetime military buildup ever—bigger in real terms even than Ronald Reagan's 1980 armament plans—and make substantial across-the-board tax cuts. The first-power pretensions of Russian chauvinists like Khrushchev were buried as deep as the economic dogmas of conservative orthodoxy.

By 1965, the "new economics," the "new economists," and even Keynes himself were a media event. *Time* magazine told how the academics came to Washington, pragmatically analyzed America's problems, overcame congressional hesitancies and conventional doctrine, and brought scientific management to economic affairs. Schlesinger extolled Kennedy as "the first Keynesian president." Seymour Harris spoke of economists as "therapists"—wise doctors who diagnosed the country's ills and prescribed effective remedies. Heller's review of his own record may be forgiven a touch of smugness.

> The critics . . . told us that the economy would reach full employment . . . without government stimulus, indeed that such stimulus would simply run off in inflation. It didn't. Late in 1962 they told us that a $2½ billion tax cut was all the economy could stand, that a tax cut of several times that amount was not only unorthodox but bizarre, and would generate "simply enormous deficits." It didn't. Late in 1963, the critics told us that structural unemployment . . . would frustrate the expansionary impact of the tax cut and bring inflation long before the 4 percent unemployment target was reached. It didn't. And in 1964, we were warned that too big a tax cut, coupled with too little tax withholding in 1964, would overheat the economy in 1964 and cool it off early in 1965. It didn't.

In 1966, with critics confounded and doctrinaires of the left and right routed, Heller could state with some confidence that economic management was now a question of "flexibility and finetuning," vindicating Kennedy's 1962 Yale speech that banished ideology and reduced politics to problems of "practical management."

The sweeping triumph of economic policy and the consequent media hype tended to exaggerate both the unanimity of the intellectual policy consensus and the extent of the break with past policies. There was, by this time, really nothing new about planned deficit spending, although most politicians in 1960 still considered it a novelty. The liberal wing of the Democratic party had actually adopted the Keynesian synthesis by the mid-1940s, and the Employment Act of 1946, shepherded through Congress by Senator Paul Douglas, a professional economist, explicitly recognized the demand-management role of the national government. The business-oriented Council on Economic Development adopted in 1947 a policy statement that recommended federal budget-balancing over the course of the business cycle—deficits during times of slack and surpluses as the economy overheated—effectively the Keynesian countercyclical prescription. Eisenhower's Treasury secretaries tended, like George Humphrey, to be unreconstructed fiscal conservatives, who believed that government surpluses were a mark of good performance, much like business profits; but his economic advisers—Arthur Burns, Raymond Saulnier, Gabriel Hauge—were sophisticated technical economists in full command of current macroeconomic theory. Eisenhower's drive for a surplus at all costs in 1960 was certainly ill-advised, but it was uncharacteristic of his administration. Even Galbraith praised his 1955 economic report for its "considerable grace and ease in getting away from the clichés of a balanced budget"; and Eisenhower's fiscal 1959 budget deficit was bigger than any incurred by Kennedy.

The new administration's loose allegiance to "Keynesianism" left wide scope for disagreement on specific issues. Kennedy himself instinctively mistrusted the enthusiasms of some of his advisers. He loved the stimulus of exchanges with his resident professors, and was heartened by their monumental self-assurance, but he was decidedly timid about embracing their policies. When the 1961 Berlin crisis untracked his spending estimates, he seriously considered asking for a tax increase—to Heller's despair, for there was still considerable slack in the economy. In 1962, he insisted on balancing his proposal for investment tax credits with tax increases to offset the revenue losses, thereby nullifying their stimulative effect. The "supply-side" emphasis itself—some fifteen years before that particular shibboleth was born—was inconsistent with the received liberal interpretation of Keynesian doctrine, with its emphasis on the primacy of consumer demand (although not with Keynes's own writings). Predictably, of course, the tax credit proposals passed Congress and the revenue-generating schemes didn't, confirming James Reston's observation that "conservatives and liberals both like money more than they like theories."

Some of the policy differences among Kennedy's advisers were sharp. An influential wing of liberal academicians were "structuralists," who believed that because of automation and the heritage of poverty in Appalachia and among blacks, unemployment would not respond to measures that increased general demand. It was the line of reasoning that later led to Lyndon Johnson's antipoverty programs. The dogmatic Keynesians deplored Kennedy's caution and his respect for the politically achievable. Walter Lippmann, for instance, who had been a Keynesian when Kennedy was still in prep school, attacked his "Eisenhower fiscal orthodoxy." Galbraith and Schlesinger railed against the emerging policy of tax cuts and lamented the lost opportunities for expanding public sector spending. Stimulating the private sector, Galbraith snorted, would just produce more deodorant, more television programs, and more "mauve and cerise automobiles."

Kennedy finally committed himself only in mid-1962. In April of that year, he had shocked the business community by using the considerable powers of his office and his unmatched talents as a propagandist to force the rollback of a steel price increase that he considered inflationary. In May, there was a sharp break in the stock market—the "Kennedy crash"—that a number of analysts ascribed to lack of confidence in the President's economic management. With the economy beginning to sputter and the markets nervous, Kennedy decided to go all out for growth and set his advisers to work on the comprehensive package of tax reductions that was finally enacted in 1964. The decisive break with orthodoxy that so fascinated the media was not that tax reductions would cause deficits, but that Kennedy refused to apologize for them. More technically, Kennedy was proposing deficits while the economy was still on the upswing and was willing to incur deficits over the entire course of the business cycle, if that much stimulation was needed to employ the nation's resources. It was a daring package, but at the same time a shrewdly contrived one; for as Reston had cynically predicted, businessmen and conservative congressmen, when given the opportunity to keep more money, eventually swallowed their scruples and supported the tax cuts. In the course of a single presidential term, the "new economics" became the conventional wisdom.

Viewed from a distance of twenty years, the remarkable fact about Kennedy's economic policies is not that they were successful for so long, but that contemporary observers were so disposed to give the administration all the economic laurels it claimed. Kennedy did not, after all, initiate the 1961 recovery, for it was under way even before he took office. The 1962 tax package, Kennedy's major early economic achievement, was not the one he wanted. Congress passed only the tax cuts and declined to legislate the offsetting revenue increases that he asked for. The persisting strength of the economy through 1962 and 1963 surprised the economists. Kennedy's assistant Ted Sorensen, seeing a glum gathering of Heller and his colleagues, quipped, "There they are, contemplating the dangers of an upturn." The crowning accomplishment of the new economics, the 1964 tax cut, was hardly the exercise in fine-tuning that it was touted to be. In mid-1962, when they committed themselves to the tax cut, Kennedy and his advisers could have had no precise idea of what the state of the economy would be or what effects the cuts would have two years later, when they were finally enacted. Kennedy's public spending increases were undoubtedly stimulative, but they were not truly part of an economic program. Three-quarters of the increases were in the military sector, and Kennedy was committed to his military programs almost without regard to their economic effects.

The notion that Kennedy and his advisers were engaging in scientific economic management was a media myth—although the administration did all it could to encourage it, and probably half believed it. The ponderous American policy-making process simply didn't lend itself to fine-tuning; policy could never follow neatly the dictates of theory. More important, even if the policy process could have been tamed, the fit between the Keynesian theoretical apparatus and the real world was not nearly so precise as Kennedy's men confidently proclaimed. Empirical evidence could be found to support almost any argument anyone cared to make. Rapid growth followed the huge wartime deficits, and Eisenhower's drive for a surplus in 1959 caused a recession, as Keynesian theory would have predicted. But a tax cut in 1948, on the other hand, was followed by a recession; most of the Korean War inflation occurred despite an increasing budget surplus; and, after the war, inflation abated as the budget moved into deficit—all rather the opposite of what a Keynesian would have expected. The 1954 recession coincided with a rising full-employment surplus—consistent with theory—but it was milder than the 1957–1958 recession, when the budget was moving into deficit. In 1964, the budget was actually running a sizeable full-employ-ment surplus, which should have been a drain on the economy, but growth was accelerating more rapidly than ever. There is not even consistent empirical evidence to support Keynes's view of the Depres-sion, the centerpiece of his theory. Milton Friedman, for one, has chal-lenged the Keynesian analysis sharply, while impartial scholars can find little to support either the pure Keynesian or the pure Friedmanite position.

The unfortunate reality is that, despite its occasional pretensions, economic theory has yet to catch up to the complexities of the real world. The deficiencies of theory were dramatically demonstrated in the 1970s, when economists were persistently unable to forecast with accu-racy not only the *rate* of economic change, but even the *direction* of the change. From the pinnacle of public esteem in 1966, the economics profession very quickly fell into something approaching disgrace. And this despite the fact that in the later period economists had access to far better data and far more sophisticated computer models and had devel-oped far more experience in translating theory into policy.

Kennedy's economists, in short, were very lucky. Economic policy-making was a pleasant enterprise in the 1960s. *All* the industrialized countries were growing rapidly—most more rapidly than the United States. World trade was expanding strongly. The real cost of energy was falling sharply, boosting productivity. The world was reaping the be-nefits of the postwar flowering of technology. Only malignly incompe-tent management could have shut America out of the boom. But it is so typical of the period that politicians and intellectuals, despite all the gaps in the evidence, were prepared to leap to the conclusion that their economic theories were the source of the boom. The powerful intellec-tual appeal of the Keynesian synthesis overrode the insufficiencies of the data. In the administration's mix of pragmatism and rationalism, in other words, the rationalist strain predominated. The rationalist is enamored of theoretical constructs. When facts are missing, his theory supplies them. At the extreme, theory reshapes facts that are uncon-forming. The self-assurance of Kennedy's economic advisers stemmed from their confidence in their theories, not from their grasp of the facts, for sufficient facts didn't exist. They adopted the pose of tough-minded pragmatists, flying in the face of conventional wisdom on balanced budgets, for example; but, in truth, they were defeating dogma with doctrine.

The adventure into the new economics illustrates the contradictory tendencies within American pragmatism, dating back to Dewey himself. On the one hand, the pragmatist is a realist, who discovers and deals with the world as it is, unfettered by doctrine. On the other hand, there is the drive toward mastery, and mastery on a large scale requires theory, a worldview, a grasping whole of the structure of the machine. The intellectuals Kennedy brought into government aimed at mastery and were prone to construct theories and act on them. The rationalist tendency was reinforced as theory appeared successful; and the astoundingly good performance of the economy lent it powerful impetus.

Rearming and bringing the economy under control were two of the three challenges Kennedy had posed for himself. The third was to block the expanding circle of Communist influence, particularly that portion spreading south from Russia and China through the deltas and jungles of Vietnam and Laos.

Vietnam

Interpreting the history of U.S. involvement in Vietnam comes down to choosing epistemologies; the reality of the long war is so protean, so elusive—a prism of shadows. The shifting transparencies of perception and illusion, in an important sense, are the real facts of the war. Even today, some thirty-five years after the beginning of our involvement in Vietnam and twenty years after Kennedy committed combat troops, it is still difficult to arrive at any comfortable conclusions. Vietnam continues to be an ideological battlefield. The authors of the innumerable books on the war tend to be partisans of particular realities—although I suspect the actual facts are too complex to support any consistent ideology. It may be true, for example, that the leaders of the insurgency were never part of an organized global Communist conspiracy; but on the other hand, once in power, they turned out to be as cruel and despotic as the most rabid anti-Communist could have predicted.

The narrow point that is relevant here is how the rationalist mind-set was conducive to increased involvement in the war. It is a point that has been made before, most notably by David Halberstam, and also one that has been exaggerated, again most notably by Halberstam—but it warrants repetition nonetheless. Kennedy's economic policy-making demonstrated the sway exercised by the Keynesian doctrine over his intellectual advisers, despite the thinness of its empirical support. There, at least, subsequent economic outcomes seemed to confirm the theory. Vietnam illustrates the remarkable power of doctrine over rationalist minds even when the facts are actively opposed. In order to place Kennedy's step-up of the war in perspective, a brief sketch of the major events that led up to the expanded American commitment will be helpful.

After the Japanese surrender in World War II, the French immediately attempted to restore their prewar colonial empire in Southeast Asia, with the passive approval of the Americans and the active assistance of the defeated Japanese armies. Military resistance to the French came from the Communist Vietminh movement, under the leadership of Ho Chi Minh, who for thirty-five years had been traveling the world, as far afield as New York's Harlem, organizing opposition to French colonial rule in Vietnam. In 1945 and 1946, Ho wrote a series of letters to President Truman requesting support against the French and citing the American anticolonial tradition. (America was at the time pressing the British hard to divest their colonies.) The letters were never answered; and a number of scholars lament that an irretrievable opportunity was lost to align the United States on the side of a legitimate anticolonial liberation movement. Ho was driven into the arms of the Russians and Chinese, and America was left predictably mired on the wrong side of an historical struggle.

As always, it is a question of epistemologies. In the late 1940s there were strong advocates for the vision of Ho as a grass roots nationalist, but it seems almost inconceivable that Truman could have embraced him. Ho, after all, was an avowed Communist, who had spent years training in Moscow. He was an associate of Stalin and an admirer of Mao. From a thirty-five-year perspective, we can dismiss the actual dangers of a postwar Communist hegemony, but Truman and Secretary of State Dean Acheson could hardly be so casual. France and Italy were tottering on the brink of a Communist takeover, and the brutal imposition of Communist rule in Eastern Europe left few illusions. The American ambassador to Vietnam had seen Bulgaria and Poland succumb to Soviet power. China fell to Mao in 1949; North Korea launched its attack across the 38th parallel in 1950; Communist insurgents threatened in Malaya and the Philippines. Vietnam was a stepping-stone to India and the entire subcontinent of Asia, or so it most plausibly seemed. U.S. policy may well have been wrong, but the contemporary system of reality hardly admitted an alternative. In any case, by 1949, Ho was openly avowing a hard Stalinist line; whether he would have acted otherwise given a different American policy response is an intriguing but unanswerable question.

The French at first accepted Ho's rule in the North, but with the help of British troops, displaced the Vietminh in the South, and installed a government under Emperor Bao Dai, who had been a local ruler under French control in the 1930s and a Japanese collaborator during the war. Bao Dai's government was to be part of the "French Union"—he had some nominal local authority, but military affairs, foreign relations, and finances were firmly under French control. Bao Dai offered the premiership to Ngo Dinh Diem, a staunch Catholic, who had resigned a prominent post in the prewar colonial civil service in protest against the government's subservience to the French. Diem refused the post and exiled himself to Catholic retreat houses in America, from which he lobbied vigorously for an independent and anti-Communist Vietnam, making a favorable impression on Dulles, Eisenhower, Cardinal Spellman, and John Kennedy, among others.

Neither the French nor Ho gave up their design of ruling a unified Vietnam, and the pattern of tension, skirmishes, and terrorist incidents soon gave way to all-out war, culminating in the stunning French defeat at Dien Bien Phu in 1954. America was deeply implicated in the French war effort. With the fall of China and the outbreak of war in Korea, the United States viewed the French effort in Indochina as a critical line of defense against Communist expansion in Asia. America picked up the bills, supplied "civilian" supply pilots, and, by some accounts, agreed that there would be no unilateral ceasefires in either Korea or Indochina without prior French-American consultations.

When the Korean ceasefire did take place in 1953, there was a sharp increase of Chinese and Soviet supplies to the Vietminh, which added considerably to the pressure on the French garrison at Dien Bien Phu. As the disaster there began to take shape, the French importuned the Americans for direct air support, but were rebuffed by Eisenhower, after a bitter debate that foreshadowed the policy divisions within the United States ten years later. Dulles, Vice President Nixon, and Admiral Arthur Radford, chairman of the Joint Chiefs of Staff, favored American air assistance to knock out the Vietnamese artillery ringing Dien Bien Phu and to interdict the Vietminh supply lines. Winston Churchill and his foreign minister, Anthony Eden, were adamantly—callously, in French eyes—opposed, because they were hopeful that a Geneva conference scheduled later in the year would reach a political settlement in both Korea and Indochina. Within the American military, Matthew Ridgway, the Army chief of staff and commander in Korea, was strongly opposed—air interdiction of supply lines had failed in Korea, and American air support, he thought, would inevitably lead to ground combat. (It took another fifteen years for American advocates of air power to assimilate those lessons.) Congressional leaders were also opposed to American involvement, particularly without strong support from the British.* In the end, however, the decision not to go in was Eisenhower's; for there seems little doubt that, had he been personally committed to intervention, he could have carried the Congress with him. Less than a year after the ceasefire in Korea, he simply didn't have the stomach for another Asian war. I don't think it's necessary to infer from this that Eisenhower was taking a long view of Communist development in Asia—in effect siding with the 1960s dovish attitude toward Vietnam. The Pentagon opponents of intervention, for example, and there were a substantial number, did not seem to doubt that America would, sooner or later, be at war with Communist China; but they thought that Vietnam, for a host of logistic and strategic reasons, was the wrong place for that fight. To the French, the American failure to intervene was perfidious.

The Geneva conferees, Great Britain, France, the United States, the Soviet Union, and Communist China, carved out a solution so unsatisfactory to all sides that it was probably the best that could have been hoped for. The conference formula created two independent Vietnamese states, divided at the 17th parallel, with the North under the control of Ho and the South under Bao Dai; the assumption was that the country would be unified two years later after national elections. *None* of the conferees ever signed the agreement—they merely "took note" of its provisions—and the United States specifically refused to endorse its terms because in Dulles's view it conceded too much to the Communists. There is some recent evidence that North Vietnam accepted the agreement only after heavy pressure from the Chinese, who were worried about Western military activity on their southern borders.

The most hopeful development from the American point of view was

*Lyndon Johnson, then majority leader of the Senate, forcefully opposed intervention except under conditions of allied support that were for all practical purposes unattainable. But when Dien Bien Phu fell, Johnson attacked Eisenhower for having "needlessly weakened" America in the eyes of the world.

that Diem finally agreed to accept Bao Dai's offer of the premiership and returned to Vietnam right after the Geneva conference. Once in the country, he quickly superseded Bao Dai, and by a referendum the following year was declared president with virtually dictatorial powers. At about the same time, Eisenhower issued the relatively open-ended commitment of American support that was later used by both Kennedy and Johnson to justify continued American intervention. The United States, according to Eisenhower, would "assist the government of Vietnam in developing and maintaining a strong and viable state capable of resisting attempted subversion or aggression through military means."

The American hopes that Diem could create a non-Communist buffer state in South Vietnam were not completely baseless—Diem seemed to enjoy considerable popularity, and Ho Chi Minh's support in the South was shaky. But the swirl of intrigue made dreams of stability implausible. For one thing, the French continually undercut Diem, fomenting trouble among the Hoa Hao and Cao Dai religious sects and covertly supporting the Binh Xuyen gangsters who were overrunning Saigon. (The French, now out of power, and more worried about their commercial interests than Communism, were apparently placing their bets on Ho.) To add to the instability, about 800,000 Vietnamese moved from the North to the South when the war ended; most were Catholics fleeing a Communist regime, but there were also a sizeable number of Vietminh—now Viet Cong—cadres bent on sedition. The United States, to keep the pot stirring, dispatched Colonel Edward Lansdale, who had achieved guerrilla-fighting fame in the Philippines, to instigate espionage against the North.

The American intelligence services and professional diplomats never shared the high regard for Diem that their political masters had. In 1955, a drumfire of complaints had about convinced Dulles to withdraw support from the pudgy mandarin, when suddenly Diem, with surprising energy, won control of Saigon by defeating the Binh Xuyen in a sharply contested military action, and then followed up by breaking the rebellion of the religious sects. With Diem's sudden reversal of form, Dulles's earlier pro-Diem judgment was vindicated, the professionals' complaints were stilled, and the American commitment became almost irrevocable. The victory over the Binh Xuyen, however, was probably the high point of Diem's career. From there on, he became ever more isolated and unpredictable, withdrawn into a narrow circle of the Catholic elite, and almost totally dependent on his Machiavellian brother, Ngo

Dinh Nhu, and his brother's wife, Madame Nhu.

The origin of the insurgency in South Vietnam engendered one of the fiercest controversies of the mid-1960s—whether the antigovernment subversion was a Communist conspiracy organized from the North or an indigenous rebellion against a squalid and oppressive dictatorship. As is so often the case when the subject is Vietnam, both sides were right. Diem's paranoia, his increasingly erratic behavior, and the corruption of his entourage caused widespread disaffection and outright revolt, particularly among the leaders of the country's Buddhist majority. A 1959 U.S. intelligence report said, "The people were ready for rebellion." At the same time, by 1959, the North was sponsoring a full-throttle campaign of terror and destabilization. Immediately after Geneva, Ho seems to have concentrated on consolidating his power in Hanoi. But when it became apparent that Diem had no intention of permitting the South to participate in a unification election, the North Vietnamese politburo decided to resort again to guerrilla warfare, relying at first on the cadres that had moved South in 1954, but progressively infiltrating military leadership, instructions, and weapons. By the time Kennedy took office in 1961, the Diem regime was crumbling on all sides; intelligence estimates foresaw total collapse only months away unless some action was taken to halt the rot.

To Kennedy, the most symbol-conscious of Presidents, South Vietnam was a crucial symbol. Eisenhower had impressed upon him the potential seriousness of a collapse of anti-Communist forces in Southeast Asia. In the month of Kennedy's inaugural, Khrushchev announced that the world advance of Communism would be accomplished by means of "wars of national liberation"—just like the one in Vietnam. Early in his administration, Kennedy consented to the neutralization of Laos, and feared that a similar course in Vietnam would prove that America's allies were easy prey to subversion. The crisis in Berlin—which nearly developed into a shooting war—made the new foreign policy establishment hyperreactive to signs of Soviet aggressiveness. The debacle at the Bay of Pigs sent them scurrying for a foreign policy success.

Although international power politics predisposed Kennedy toward intervening in Vietnam, the evolving military doctrine of the administration made such a commitment almost inevitable, whether in Vietnam or someplace else. The central tenet of the Kennedy-McNamara military policy was the principle of "flexible response." It was not a new idea, but was first enunciated in a famous policy memorandum—NSC-68—developed during the Truman administration. The containment of Communism implied resisting Communist expansion along a number of fronts, the reasoning went, and so required a military capability that was flexible enough to respond to low-level "brushfire" threats in undeveloped countries as well as to a major conventional assault in Europe. Eisenhower had scrapped the policy because he thought it was too expensive. Since America had overwhelming nuclear superiority over the Soviet Union, he preferred to rely on the doctrine of "massive retaliation." In the simplest terms, if Soviet aggressiveness threatened vital American interests, America would threaten to incinerate the Soviet Union.

Eisenhower's policies, viewed strictly in military terms, were indefensible. The threat of massive retaliation was never credible in the first place, at least so long as the Soviet Union maintained its aggressiveness below some threshold of direct danger to the United States—as demonstrated by American powerlessness during the invasion of Hungary in 1956. More important, the major premise of "massive retaliation" dissolved as the Soviets developed the capacity for all-out thermonuclear retaliation against the United States. A policy that offered only a choice between doing nothing and vaporizing half the world, America included, began to look like no policy at all. But Eisenhower genuinely believed that America's economic strength was the key to its security, and that an excessive military buildup could place the economy at risk. Throughout the "missile gap" controversy of the 1960 campaign, he pleaded, with little success, for "balance," for "adequate, not excessive" defenses, and ended his presidency by issuing his famous farewell warning against the influence of a "military-industrial complex."

Increased military spending was the centerpiece of Kennedy's campaign, and he had been advocating a "flexible response" military strategy in congressional speeches since 1954. The hostilities in Indochina were an obvious testing ground for the new principles—and if he had any personal doubts, his choice of advisers seemed calculated to dispel them. In the fall of 1961, he sent General Maxwell Taylor, his personal military adviser, and Walt Rostow, the deputy director of the National Security Council staff, on a fact-finding mission to Vietnam to develop a course of action for the administration. Taylor was Kennedy's favorite general—sophisticated, athletic, fond of classical allusions, in the self-consciously intellectual style of the New Frontier. He had been Army chief of staff during Eisenhower's second term and, when he retired, wrote a book, *The Uncertain Trumpet,* that was an eloquent critique of the rigidities of the Eisenhower military doctrine and a call for, among other things, an American counterinsurgency capability. When he went to Vietnam for Kennedy he had just been named to direct a White House committee to come up with ways to defeat Communist guerrillas.

Rostow was an MIT economist, a man of great force and energy, with the splendid self-assurance that was the hallmark of Kennedy's closest aides. He had a sweeping mind that, as one diplomat put it, "constructed theories—often with perception and ingenuity—but once the pattern of his belief was established, some automatic mental filter thereafter accepted only reinforcing data." Rostow's grand teleologies had an oddly Marxist flavor. In his view, America was moving into a new phase of an historic struggle with Communism that would be decided in the underdeveloped world. When the pragmatic principles of economic development Rostow had spelled out in his book *The Stages of Economic Growth: A Non-Communist Manifesto* were applied throughout the underdeveloped world, Leninist and Maoist ideology would be smothered beneath a surge of peasant prosperity. But security was the first requisite for growth: part of America's historic mission was to secure the underdeveloped world from Communist military incursions. Rostow was fascinated with guerrilla warfare, seeing it as a key intellectual problem in development economics; and he had strong views on military tactics—an OSS bombing strategist in World War II, he had "an almost mystic faith" in the efficacy of air power.

With Taylor and Rostow leading the fact-finding mission, the outcome of their report was never in doubt. They recommended unequivocally that Kennedy expand the war, and Kennedy essentially followed their recommendations. From 500 advisers in late 1961, the American presence grew over some fifteen months to more than 16,000 troops— with most of the original contingent billed as "flood relief workers." President less than a year, Kennedy was well along the path to the "land war in Asia" that Eisenhower and Ridgway had been so wary of.

There was precedent for the notion that a Western military force could defeat Communist guerrillas on the ground in Asia. The British had cleared the Malayan peninsula of guerrillas after World War II, under the leadership of Sir Robert Thompson, who was later brought in as an adviser in Vietnam. And Kennedy's guerrilla expert, Edward Lansdale, now a brigadier general, had coordinated the successful campaign against the Hukbalahap guerrillas in the Philippines. In both instances, the government forces fought the guerrillas on their own terms in the jungle, cut off sources of outside supplies, and gradually developed defensible safe zones for the indigenous population, until they had isolated the insurgents and could hunt them down almost cadre by cadre. Pessimists—including most of the intelligence community—pointed out that the similarities with Vietnam were superficial; in the Philippines and Malaya, there were no friendly borders for sanctuary or supplies, the guerrillas had no outside assistance, and the government leadership on the spot was far stronger, with much better support among the local populace than the tottering Diem regime. But professional pessimists were not likely to receive a sympathetic hearing in the early days of the New Frontier.

The decision to intervene showed the most arrogant and unattractive face of the new administration's rationalist pose—no matter what allowances are made for the counterinsurgency precedents, for domestic political demands, or for Khrushchev's international swaggering. The self-congratulatory effusions of the insiders are beyond parody. Here is Rostow, the newly-anointed guerrilla expert, addressing a class of Green Berets at Fort Bragg:

> We are determined to destroy this international disease [guerrilla warfare]. This requires, of course, not merely a proper military program of deterrence, but programs of village development, communications and indoctrination. . . . I salute you as I would a group of doctors, teachers, economic planners, agricultural experts, civil servants, or those who are now leading the way in the whole southern half of the globe in fashioning the new nations.

And McNamara (to his credit, the most reluctant of the born-again warriors):

> When the day comes that we can safely withdraw, we expect to leave an independent and stable Vietnam, rich in resources and bright with prospects for contributing to the peace and prosperity of Southeast Asia and the world.

The administration's penchant for the counterintuitive was a trap. With the exception of Kennedy insiders like Taylor, the military men were quite clear from the beginning on what was required to win in Vietnam. As early as 1961, the Pentagon figured they would need more than 200,000 combat troops to ensure a victory; and the intelligence reports left little doubt that, if America wanted to win the war, it would require a major commitment and a thoroughly Americanized effort. Kennedy wanted to hear none of that. He was privately scornful when General Lemnitzer, chairman of the Joint Chiefs of Staff, explained why a pattern of escalation and response in Laos meant that America would have to commit more than 100,000 men and possibly use tactical nuclear weapons if the goal was a military victory. The New Frontiersmen would win the war by giving the South Vietnamese "the élan and style" they needed to win, by giving them a "shot in the arm" that would "spark real transformation" of the South Vietnamese army. Kennedy and his aides seemed to think that by sheer power of intellect they could locate just the right button, the strategic lever, touch it with just the lightest force, and redirect the river of events. Doubters were not "tough-minded," not "pragmatists," or as Schlesinger, another instant guerrilla expert, snorted:

> The professionals, infatuated with the newest technology and eager to strike major blows, deeply disliked the thought of reversion to the rude weapons, amateur tactics, hard life and marginal effects of guerrilla warfare.

As it turned out, throughout 1962 and into 1963, the administration appeared to be right again. The sudden influx of men and equipment, especially helicopters, surprised the Viet Cong and caught them just as they were shifting from classic guerrilla tactics to the more conventional stand-and-fight methods perfected at Dien Bien Phu. To stand and fight against American firepower was to invite slaughter. Although there were some dissenting dispatches from the more independently minded newspaper reporters, the overwhelming impression from field reports was that the war was going very well. Terrorist and other insurgency incidents dropped sharply; the Viet Cong stopped collecting taxes throughout large areas of the country; a strategic hamlet program was under way to create safe zones on the Philippine and Malayan models; virtually all of McNamara's quantitative indices were looking positive. In late 1962, U.S. forces in Vietnam were actually reduced by a thousand men; the rationalist approach to war seemed every bit as successful as its most confident practitioners had expected it to be.

Contemporaries, of course, were far from adjudging the Kennedy administration an unmitigated success. His congressional program, for instance, was in serious trouble just before he died. But the particular problems that the administration's band of pragmatic intellectuals had set themselves to solve appeared to be coming along very well indeed —reform of the Pentagon, reform of the economy, and, at least until late in 1963, resistance to the insurgency in Vietnam. Such a resounding demonstration of the power of theory had the perverse effect of entrapping the intellectuals within the confines of their own mental constructs, a consequence of no small irony for an administration that took such pride in its realism. The singular ability of the national security planners to resist for years the evidence of failure in Vietnam is only the most spectacular example. McNamara's ability to convince himself and the Congress that he was actually saving money at the Pentagon while defense costs were skyrocketing was of the same order of illusion.

A basic problem was the procrustean tendency to force issues to assume the favored shape of mathematical optimization models, and the related susceptibility to false quantification. The world is not populated by economists; but the administration's policy reflex—whether the issue was Vietnam, civil rights, or poverty—was to assume that all problems were solved by a process of marginal trade-offs among rational men, and that any result could be achieved by a consistent skewing of marginal incentives. There was an even more serious problem, although it wasn't immediately obvious. It was essentially the same one that Randolph Bourne had raised about Dewey's young adherents in 1917. The penchant for ordering the world in neatly arrayed theoretical models—for defining interest groups, economies, even entire nations, as so many problems of input-output analysis, as Rostow delighted in doing— tended to preclude a moral dimension in policy-making. Morality emerges in the face of the unmeasurable or the unknowable. But when outcomes can be predicted with confidence, and their desirabilities calculated and ranked in advance, transcendent concepts easily become superfluous. A set of policy predilections more strikingly unsuited to the problems of the mid-1960s can hardly be imagined.

III

POLITICS AT THE EDGE
OF MORALITY

When John Kennedy took office as President, although he seemed hardly aware of it, the country was already hovering on the edge of an explosive racial confrontation, one that would test his principles of pragmatic political action and find them wanting. The history of race relations in the United States is a story of sin and retribution, of prolonged transgression and embittered expiation. The institution of chattel slavery was a crime against the most fundamental principles of the American experiment. For two centuries, the deep guilt lurking in the white subconscious was betrayed by the ferocity of the recurrent reactions against exposure of the evils perpetrated upon blacks. Civil rights movements and violent repression alternated in the South in a hundred-year rhythm—before the Revolution, at the time of the Civil War, and again in the 1960s.

The evidence is sketchy, but as far as the colonial records show, the first black slaves were not treated very much differently from contemporary European indentured servants. The English settlers were notoriously bigoted against all manner of men and don't seem at first to have singled out blacks for special obloquy. Freed blacks were apparently commonplace, particularly once they had converted to Christianity; in fact, an influential body of theological opinion held that conversion made manumission mandatory. There are records from the seventeenth century of blacks who rose to sufficient prominence to own slaves themselves. The exoticism of the blacks, however, and their heathenism, gradually served to set them apart from European servants. An effort in the mid-seventeenth century to attract more Europeans to colonial service probably helped worsen black conditions—there was no need to apply the incentives to blacks since they were brought involuntarily in the first place. The large-scale cultivation of rice and indigo, work which the Europeans generally refused, sealed the position of blacks as a separate caste. By the last third of the seventeenth century, there was spreading use in the colonial statutes of the word "slave" in its modern sense—a perpetual and hereditary status uniquely applicable to blacks.

The eighteenth century was dominated intellectually by the natural rights movement—a philosophy antithetical to human slavery and the inspiration of the early abolitionist movements that failed in the United States and were successful in much of Europe. The theory of natural rights was official dogma in the United States, and Jefferson and his thoughtful Southern contemporaries, like St. George Tucker, were acutely aware of the contradiction. Tucker stated it forcefully.

> Among the blessings which the Almighty has showered down on these states, there is a large portion of the bitterest draught that ever flowed from the cup of affliction. . . . Whilst we were offering vows at the shrine of liberty . . . we were imposing upon our fellow men, who differ in complexion from us, a *slavery,* ten thousand times more cruel. . . .

But his mind boggled at the problem of correcting the evil. Deportation and colonization, Tucker reasoned, would surely consign the former slaves to starvation, and was anyway impracticable. And since the law explicitly recognized the right of property in slaves, he was sure that the compensation required to make up the loss to former owners would be immense. Emancipation leading to civil equality was likewise unthinkable, for "if it be true, as Mr. Jefferson seems to think, that the Africans are really an inferior race of mankind," the admission to full citizenship "may eventually depreciate the whole national character."

The basic conundrum was implicit in the Lockean trinity of natural rights—life, liberty, and *property:* for by the nineteenth century slaves had become an immensely valuable capital asset in the Southern economy. Eli Whitney's invention of the cotton gin is often blamed for making the Southern slave plantation an economically viable enterprise, but much more important were the emergence of large-scale textile manufacturing in England and the marvelous suitability of great expanses of the American South for cotton agriculture. Before Whitney's gin, new strains of cotton had already been developed that could be ginned (have the seeds removed mechanically) on an industrial scale with current technology. By the 1830s, slavery was fundamental to the South's economic well-being. Even the areas that did not specialize in cotton, like Virginia, made immense profits after the closing of the foreign slave trade by breeding slaves for export to the rest of the South.

The most recent generation of economic historians has established that throughout the middle of the nineteenth century, the South was enormously successful, viewed strictly on its own terms as a specialized extractive economy. The white standard of living was not as high as in the North, but was considerably higher than in the West or Midwest, and the sustained rate of economic growth was the highest in the country. The thinking Southerner, in modern jargon, lived with a cognitive dissonance: the area of the country that perhaps had contributed the most to the natural rights principles of the American Revolution found that its continued well-being depended on the most brutal denial of natural rights to fellow humans. That dissonance lies at the heart of the virulent racism that developed in the South during the nineteenth century: if blacks were subhuman, slavery was not a contradiction at all. And it accounts for the viciousness of the reaction against blacks when Southern whites regained political and economic control after the end of the post–Civil War Reconstruction. The degradation of blacks confirmed Southern whites' superiority over their former slaves and served, retrospectively, as a perverse justification of the suicidal struggle for secession.

Over the decades, a quasi-official mythology developed to explain away Southern apartheid—the Sambo myth, the stereotype of the shiftless, happy-go-lucky, but loyal black, whose cozy world in Scarlett O'Hara's "big house" was destroyed by rapacious Union troops and fanatically vengeful Reconstructionists. The antebellum researches of Ulrich B. Phillips, a Yale historian, dominated Southern historiography in the first half of the twentieth century, and most school textbooks presented the Phillips picture of the benignly paternalistic slaveholder, whose plantation was a losing proposition because of the charming incompetence of his slaves. The stereotype was more damaging than any amount of discrimination could have been and had repercussions far beyond the South. My own recollection of blacks from the 1940s and 1950s—I was raised in Philadelphia—are dominated by "Amos and

Andy," by the Bing Crosby song about happy blacks "slapping their feet" on the levee, and by a whole generation of Stepin Fetchit entertainers—the black retainer in the "Stu Irwin Show," for instance, a 1950s television situation comedy about a white family whose servant, Willie, lived in the basement, rolled his eyes a lot, and when he saw a coffin, fainted, to general hilarity.

With hindsight, we can speculate why the country's racial problems came to a climax in the 1960s: the increasingly youthful population of blacks; the millions of blacks achieving relative prosperity in the North and communicating back to the South that there was an alternative to feudal submission; the experience of World War II—skin color fades under fire; and the feedback effect upon blacks' own accelerating expectations from each small victory at the racial barriers. Rather to Kennedy's surprise, civil rights came to dominate the latter part of his short administration, swept away his marginalist preconceptions, and catapulted issues of personal freedom and social morality squarely to the center of the political stage.

The Politics of Civil Rights

Civil rights was hardly a central theme of Kennedy's politics in 1960, although in company with most Northern liberals, he was certainly in favor of equal rights in the abstract. The first civil rights skirmishes were fought far away from Massachusetts and for the sake of causes that to liberals were mother's milk. In 1954, the *Brown* decision took the uncommon step of overturning an old line of Supreme Court "separate but equal" cases and outlawed segregated school systems. In 1955, Rosa Parks, an elderly black woman whose feet hurt, refused to move from her seat in the front of a Montgomery, Alabama, bus. When she was arrested, the black community responded with a successful bus boycott that propelled Martin Luther King, Jr., a young Baptist minister, into national civil rights leadership. In 1957, Eisenhower, in the face of the apish antics of Arkansas governor Orville Faubus, had to resort to federal troops to enforce the right of a handful of black students to attend a Little Rock high school. In 1960, a group of black college students refused to leave a Greensboro, North Carolina, lunch counter when denied service—the first of the 1960s "sit-ins." The successive conjuncts of that new suffix became a barometer of the decade's mounting strains—sit-ins, teach-ins, lie-ins, and finally yip-ins.

As one Southerner put it, despite his conventional liberalism, Kennedy was "no hellraiser or Barnburner" on civil rights. He enjoyed early Southern support in his 1956 floor fight for the vice presidential nomination, when Southern delegates sought to punish Tennessee's Estes Kefauver for his heterodoxy on racial issues. Kennedy voted with the Southern bloc to weaken a crucial section of the 1957 Civil Rights Act and earned the lasting enmity of the national office of the NAACP in consequence. He enjoyed the strong support of the NAACP in Massachusetts, however, and could make a good case that the 1957 compromise was necessary to pass any bill at all. Kennedy spoke in favor of the *Brown* decision—Eisenhower disapproved of it—and he supported Eisenhower's decision to use troops in Little Rock, although he criticized the episode as an example of bumbling management.

Kennedy's presidential campaign was a study in ambiguity. Since his strategy was based on carrying the "solid South" and the big Northern cities, he had to fashion a rhetoric that would appeal to white Southerners and Northern blacks at the same time. Garnering the Northern black vote turned out to be easier than expected because Nixon conceded it from the outset. (A peculiar decision: the Republican platform contained its strongest civil rights section ever, and Eisenhower had made important inroads into the urban black vote in 1956.) Kennedy's campaign had a strong civil rights section staffed by committed aides, and young black politicians like Andrew Hatcher clearly had access to the inner circle. The Democratic civil rights platform was even stronger than the Republicans', if only by inadvertence. Robert Kennedy, the campaign's floor manager, had intended the strong platform statement as a bargaining counter but got confused in the heat of the convention and instructed his aides to ram it through, much to his brother's discomfiture.

In the South, Lyndon Johnson soothed fears about the strong civil rights plank—ironically, Johnson was probably more instinctively sympathetic with the black underdog than Kennedy—and ladled out good down-home talk on whistlestop tours in his "Cornpone Special." ("What has Dick Nixon ever done for Culpeper?") By the fall, segregationist senators like Mississippi's James Eastland and John Stennis and Georgia's Richard Russell were passing the word that the Kennedy-Johnson team could be trusted to respect Southern racial sensibilities. While there is no evidence that the Kennedys ever made such representations, they certainly did nothing to discourage them. The ambivalence of the strategy is illustrated by the famous phone call to Coretta King. Martin Luther King was sentenced by a Southern judge to four months at hard labor in a rural prison farm for a trivial offense related to a demonstration. It occurred to Harris Wofford, Kennedy's chief civil rights aide, that a sympathetic phone call to King's nearly hysterical wife—she rightly feared for his life—would be a decent gesture. Wofford and Sargent Shriver, who agreed with the idea, were careful to corner Kennedy away from his campaign technicians to press the notion. When Robert Kennedy found that the candidate had made such a call, he was outraged, snarling to Wofford that he had just cost them three Southern states. In fact, the call received little adverse notice in the South, but was heavily publicized in the Northern black media along with the reaction of Martin Luther King, Sr.—a wonderful excursion into meta-bigotry: "I don't want a Catholic, but I'll take a Catholic or a Devil himself if he'll wipe the tears from my daughter-in-law's eyes. I've got a suitcase full of votes . . . for Senator Kennedy."

It would be a mistake of emphasis, however, to attach too much significance to the civil rights aspects of the campaign. For Kennedy, it was clearly a side issue, a problem to be managed and contained, but hardly a central theme like the economy or America's international vulnerability. If he had a major worry in the South, in fact, it was his Catholicism, not his stance on civil rights. Postelection analyses showed that black voters in a few key urban states may have made the difference in the outcome, but in such a close election, the same could have been said of any marginal group of voters, whether urban blacks, Jews, working-class Irish, suburban Protestants, or Texas dirt farmers. For what it's worth, in the long debates on the election with my father, I don't remember either of us ever thinking of civil rights as an issue that distinguished the candidates, or, for that matter, ever thinking of it as an issue at all.

Kennedy's civil rights record, during his first two years in office, was as ambivalent as his campaign strategy. On one level he was forceful and effective. The scale and breadth of his appointments of blacks to high public positions was unprecedented—Robert Weaver as the nation's chief housing official; Carl Rowan to a top international public affairs post; Frank Reeves and Andrew Hatcher on the White House staff; Clifton Wharton to an ambassadorship; Louis Martin to an influential party position; and perhaps most gratifying to the old-line civil rights organizations, Thurgood Marshall, the NAACP's preeminent civil rights litigator, to the U.S. Court of Appeals. Lyndon Johnson was placed in charge of a cabinet committee to promote nondiscrimination in hiring. The Civil Rights Commission, an independent fact-finding body, was refurbished and energized. Prominent blacks were conspicuously introduced to the Washington social scene. Top administration officials just as conspicuously resigned their memberships in segregated clubs. Kennedy himself was accessible and charming to civil rights advocates and used his opportunities for pro-civil-rights propaganda with characteristic deftness—publicly congratulating a school district for adopting a desegregation plan, for instance, or lending his presence to the announcement of a nondiscrimination plan at Lockheed's Georgia factory.

But civil rights leaders were never sure if Kennedy was with them in a crunch. When he let it be known that he wouldn't propose a comprehensive civil rights bill—in effect, repudiating the Democratic platform—Clarence Mitchell, the NAACP's chief lobbyist, snorted that "the New Frontier looks like a dude ranch with Senator Eastland as the general manager." And Kennedy dithered embarrassingly over issuing a housing antidiscrimination order. During the campaign, he repeatedly charged that Eisenhower could end discrimination in federally supported housing "with a stroke of the pen." But once in office, he couldn't bring himself to issue an order: he worried that irritated congressmen would block Weaver's appointment; he was afraid that he would lose Southern support for his economic program; experts told him that a broad order would depress home construction and knock $6 billion off the GNP. Finally, after a sardonic mail campaign sent him thousands of pens and bottles of ink, Kennedy signed the narrowest possible order, so narrow that he was at first afraid that Weaver might resign in protest. To Kennedy, the ambivalence was not a contradiction; his commitment to civil rights was genuine, but not all-or-nothing. Problems were solved at the margin; everything was subject to trade-offs through a kind of metaphysical cost-benefit analysis. Making deals with segregationists wasn't wrong, particularly if you were convinced that you were the superior bargainer.

In the two major civil rights crises faced early in the administration, in fact—the Freedom Rides and the confrontation at the University of Mississippi—Kennedy's essentially tactical approach served him well. The Freedom Rides grew out of a 1960 Supreme Court decision striking down segregation in interstate bus terminals. The following spring,

CORE (the Congress of Racial Equality) decided to test the ruling by sponsoring group rides of blacks on bus routes throughout the South. The first convoy of blacks weathered isolated attacks until they reached Birmingham, where they were badly beaten by a white mob. The local police made no move to stop the beatings, because as Chief Bull Connor explained, the Mother's Day holiday had left them shorthanded. The beatings attracted national publicity, and when the Freedom Riders vowed to continue despite the dangers, the administration was forced to intervene to uphold federal law. Robert Kennedy spent several days trying to reach the Governor of Alabama, who refused his phone calls and persisted in making inflammatory statements ("Alabama isn't the Congo," and the Freedom Riders were "fools" who "would find all the trouble they're looking for"). After another group of riders was savagely beaten in Montgomery, and one of his own staff aides hospitalized, Kennedy finally dispatched federal marshals—in street clothes, not uniforms—to protect them. A highway escort was arranged to see the riders safely to Mississippi, the last stop, but Kennedy implicitly accepted that Mississippi authorities would arrest the riders as soon as they disembarked. His objective was only to prevent mob violence.

The administration responded in the same vein in 1962, when Governor Ross Barnett of Mississippi ("The Negro is different because God made him different to punish him") refused to honor a federal court order to enroll James Meredith at the state university. Robert Kennedy, in the vain hope that the problem would be resolved locally, spent days in fruitless telephone conversations with Barnett, who was whipping mobs of students and hangers-on into a frenzy. At one point, in fact, the federal judge overseeing the case sharply criticized the Justice Department for its delays. Four separate times Barnett, backed by the glowering mob, turned Meredith from the university doors, until Kennedy finally called in a force of five hundred marshals to control the mobs and implement the order. Meredith was enrolled, but a virtual insurrection ensued. For a time the marshals were in serious danger—more than a third of them were injured, twenty-eight by gunfire, and two bystanders were killed—until a contingent of army troops forced their way through the acrid clouds of tear gas and imposed an uneasy peace.

Ted Sorensen congratulated the President after the Mississippi confrontation: "In contrast to your predecessor, you are demonstrating how many graduated steps there are between inaction and troops." The comment is revealing of the Kennedys' criteria for success in civil rights enforcement. Forceful intervention was to be used only as the very last resort, and only when local officials had so egregiously flouted the law and so outrageously incited to violence that fair-minded Southerners would have to concede the necessity for federal action. And since the Kennedys were strongly committed to gradualism in breaking down racial barriers, principle was readily sacrificed to tactics to keep local incidents from getting out of hand. The Justice Department did not intervene when Mississippi arrested the Freedom Riders, even though the action clearly violated the requirement for desegregated terminals. On the other hand, by working with Southern officials behind the scenes over the next two years, Robert Kennedy and his civil rights aides contended, they succeeded in substantially eliminating segregation in interstate facilities without bloody confrontations.

A policy of broad political accommodation within a context of steady progress made a great deal of sense from a pragmatist problem-solving perspective; but it could also lead to serious problems if the other side didn't play by the rules. With only a slight twist of fortune, a lot of marshals could have been murdered in Mississippi, and the Kennedy performance would have appeared irresponsibly inept. More insidiously, the tactical accommodations could undercut the broader strategic objectives. Under Robert Kennedy, the Justice Department adopted a litigating approach to equal rights enforcement. As rights were secured by the courts, particularly the right to vote, the department reasoned, blacks would gradually acquire the political and economic power to chip away at racial barriers on their own. But in order to satisfy powerful Southern senators, the two Kennedys acquiesced in the appointment of five outright segregationists to key federal judgeships in the Deep South.* Between them, the five decided more than a hundred civil rights cases brought by Kennedy's own civil rights attorneys. They consistently found against the plaintiffs, often in flagrant violation of the Constitution or settled principles of law, and contributed mightily to the lawlessness of hard-line Southern communities. To the young activists who were risking their lives for equal rights in the Deep South, they were a continuing mockery and threat, a palpable symbol of where the ad-

*They were: Judge William Harold Cox, sponsored by Senator James Eastland of Mississippi; Judge E. Gordon West, sponsored by Senator Russell Long of Louisiana; Judge Robert Elliot, sponsored by Senator Herman Talmadge of Georgia; and Judges Clarence Allgood and Walter Gewin, sponsored by Senators Lister Hill and John Sparkman of Alabama. Cox may have been the worst. A sample of his jurisprudence: "I'm not interested in whether the registrar is going to give a registration test to a bunch of niggers on a voting drive."

ministration *really* stood. The blunt obstructionism of Southern justice poisoned idealism and fed the corrosive sense of isolation and alienation that ultimately impelled some of the country's most promising youth, and perhaps Kennedy's most natural constituency, toward nihilistic disgust and despair.

Reality

In the sleek and marbled world of official Washington, a world of limousines, linen tablecloths and fresh-cut flowers, men and women who spoke smoothly, who thought clearly and consecutively, whose métier was reasoned debate, set about solving the civil rights problem. They put it first into historical perspective and political context. They weighed the effect of improved voter registration, of integrated schools, and of Southern economic development. They tried to divine the pace of change that could be accepted by "good" segregationists like Arkansas's William Fulbright, but which would not alarm "bad" segregationists like Eastland or Virginia's Howard Cannon. The strategy that emerged was a subtle and gently gaited one. The Justice Department pursued its litigation. The President provided his words of encouragement. But there would be no legislation. No affront to cultural sensibilities. No social upheaval.

But on the front lines of the civil rights struggle in Mississippi and Alabama, in rural Virginia, and in the baked-clay farming counties of Georgia, there was a reality far from the crystal water glasses and carefully modulated discussions in Washington. It was a reality hard-eyed, sinister, and obstinate. It was padded footfalls and stark fear in the night. It was burly men in unmarked cars and torched farmhouses. It was an aura of violence that hung in the air like the scent of magnolias.

Reality was Terrell County, Georgia, where voting rights organizers from the Student Nonviolent Coordinating Committee (SNCC) were beaten again and again, their meeting house burned down and their residence bombed. Where Jack Chatfield, a SNCC worker, was told by local whites that they would "send him home in a box" and then badly wounded him with rifle fire. Where the violence was presided over by Sheriff Zeke Mathews, whose men beat to death James Brazier, a local black involved in civil rights work, and who then snarled at his terrified widow, "I ought to slap your damn brains out."

Reality was Danville, Virginia, where police with submachine guns rounded up voting organizers; fractured demonstrators' skulls; and hauled marchers before the local judge, who sat on the bench with a gun strapped around his waist, and who sentenced marchers to jail for "inciting the colored population to acts of violence and war against the white population."

Or Camilla, Georgia, where Mrs. Slater King, five months pregnant and carrying a three-year-old, was knocked down and kicked unconscious when she tried to visit young civil rights workers in jail. Her baby was born dead. Later, a deputy sheriff broke SNCC worker Bill Hansen's jaw and Sheriff Cull Campbell administered a bloody beating to the local black attorney, then bragged to reporters: "I knocked the hell out of the son of a bitch, and I'll do it again. . . . I'm a white man and he's a damn nigger."

Reality was Theron Lynd, the three-hundred-pound registrar of voters in Forrest County, Mississippi, who had never allowed a black to pass the literacy test, but who had registered almost two thousand whites who had never appeared at the courthouse. Or registrar John Wood in McComb, Mississippi, who pistol-whipped John Hardy, a young voting volunteer. Hardy staggered out of the courthouse and complained to the sheriff, who promptly arrested him for inciting to riot. Or registrar Sol Yeoman, in Lee County, Mississippi, who threatened voting rights worker James Crawford with murder. That night, after Crawford returned home to the black farmhouse where he was staying, cars with armed whites assembled on the road. The blacks stoically loaded their own guns, but with tears in their eyes, asked Crawford to leave, and sneaked him out a rear entrance.

Reality was the deputies in Clarksdale, Mississippi, who dragged Bessie Turner out of a demonstration into the jail, stripped her naked, and beat her breasts and genitals with heavy straps. Or the thirteen machine gun bullets that ripped into a carload of SNCC workers in Greenwood, Mississippi, hitting Jimmy Travis in the head and neck. And the endless round of casual beatings, the official bullying, the ramming of a car on the highway, the near-miss by a speeding truck suddenly hurtling around a corner. Or the airless "hot boxes" in county jails, where young volunteers like Bob Zellner were confined for weeks on end and brutalized by sadistic inmates, who were egged on by grinning jailers.

Reality was the constant imminence of death—as when James Forman of SNCC stood on a mid-afternoon street in Monroe, North Carolina, with a shotgun barrel inches from his face, the shotgun held by a drunken white, who had been handed it by a sheriff, surrounded by a crowd screaming, "Kill the nigger! Kill the nigger!" It was the development of almost jungle reflexes among the hardened volunteers, the instinctive glance out the window at night, the special synapses that flashed warning signals, like the night in Greenwood when Bob Moses, during a SNCC meeting, noticed a car parked across the street without license plates. Immediately the meeting was quickly broken up, and as the volunteers made their escape out the back, more cars were assembling. The next morning they found their office burned down and their files printed in the local newspaper.

The guerrilla heroes of the Deep South, the movement's Viet Cong, were the SNCC workers, the "Snick kids," with their blue jeans, naive and driving idealism, incoherent organization, boundless courage, and absolute, icy disdain for the finely rationalized political inhibitions of the administration. SNCC was the brainchild of Ella Jo Baker, a fifty-five-year-old staff worker in Martin Luther King's Southern Christian Leadership Conference, who had been assigned to organize an SCLC youth division. The first wave of sit-ins throughout the South, largely manned by college students, had been immensely successful, particularly in more urbanized areas, as merchants, with almost visible relief, dropped the encrusted restrictions of two centuries. For a time, it appeared that progress might be dazzlingly fast, and the established civil rights organizations, already jockeying for position and credit, were anxious to harness the enormous energies of the college-age generation under their respective banners. Baker, a woman of great moral force, who inspired almost reverential affection in young people, decided that the college activists ought not to be entangled in the growing factionalism. She helped a core group of black college students from working-class backgrounds—John Lewis, Robert Moses, Julian Bond, Charles Sherrod, Lawrence Guyot, Diane Nash—form an independent organization— SNCC. Its founding statement, heavily influenced by the Gandhian philosophy of King's SCLC, said:

> Love is the central motif of nonviolence. . . . Such love goes to the extreme; it remains loving and forgiving even in the midst of hostility. . . . By appealing to conscience and standing on the moral nature of human existence, nonviolence nurtures the atmosphere in which reconciliation and justice become actual possibilities.

The idealistic young people fanning out through the South to challenge the official apartheid put enormous pressures on the administration. The pressures increased as the movement began to recruit white middle-class students from the North—seven hundred for the "Mississippi Summer" project in 1964. Middle-class parents, some of them in high positions in official Washington, sensed the danger in which their sons and daughters had placed themselves and demanded action and protection from the federal government.

It was not a demand that the Kennedys could easily respond to. Robert Kennedy and his top civil rights aides, Burke Marshall and John Doar, doggedly clung to their litigating strategy. They were frightened by the implications of a national policing responsibility and, in any case, exercised only the most fragile control over the FBI, the one police instrument at their disposal. J. Edgar Hoover, a monumental presence as FBI director, was probably a racist himself. He hated Martin Luther King, and was more interested in chasing Communists than in enforcing civil rights. The convoluted corridors of Hoover's mind were developed during the 1950s Communist scare, and he suspected that the entire civil rights movement was a Communist trick to make the United States look bad. Under direct pressure from Kennedy, the FBI assisted in gathering facts for civil rights investigations, but would do no more.

The unwillingness or the inability of the Justice Department to intervene aggressively against the flagrant outlawry of the recalcitrant South was a source of steadily increasing friction between the administration and the civil rights organizations and the growing band of pro-civil-rights liberals. Marshall and Doar, and their understaffed civil rights division, did yeoman, often heroic, work—painstakingly collecting evidence to prove intentional voter discrimination, mediating disputes, flying from rural town to rural town, getting volunteers out of jail, exerting behind-the-scenes pressure on Southern officials and businessmen to accept change—and frequently displayed great personal courage in doing so. John Doar, for example, single-handedly squelched an incipient riot one night in Jackson, Mississippi, in 1963 after the funeral of Medgar Evers, the murdered civil rights leader. Between a gathering force of policemen bristling with arms and an angry black mob throwing bottles and bricks, Doar strode by himself down the middle of the street and dispersed the rioters—a tribute to both his personal forcefulness and his reputation in the black community as a fair and honest white man. In the same year, both whites and blacks gave Burke Marshall credit for equally effective, if less spectacular, mediation in Birmingham. Marshall's round-the-clock efforts rescued a situation that was careening toward all-out, bloody, and catastrophic warfare.

But to the front-line activists, the face of the administration was more often one of passive indifference, and its voice one of legalistic logic-chopping. When John Siegenthaler, Robert Kennedy's own aide, was beaten bloody and unconscious in a Birmingham bus station, FBI agents stood and watched, calmly taking notes, making no move to intervene. No federal crime was being committed. The night the mob surrounded the SNCC headquarters in Greenwood, hours before Jimmy Travis was machine-gunned almost to death, Bob Moses made a furtive call to the Justice Department to ask for protection. Sorry, was the reply, call us after a federal crime has been committed. Robert Kennedy, at least until 1963, made it clear that domestic tranquillity was higher on his priority list than civil rights, and he congratulated Sheriff Laurie Pritchett for maintaining calm in Albany, Georgia, during a drive to desegregate the bus terminal. Pritchett's trick was simply to arrest—quickly and quietly to be sure, but quite illegally—any demonstrator who approached the terminal or any black who tried to integrate the white waiting room. At one point he had literally thousands of civil rights demonstrators in jails throughout the county—and Kennedy was congratulating him. Whose side, SNCC's John Lewis persisted in demanding, was the federal government *on?*

It was not a rhetorical question. The FBI in the South was staffed by Southerners who had close ties to local law enforcement officials, and the SNCC kids soon learned not to trust them. In McComb, for instance, a white legislator, E. H. Hurst, killed a black farmer who had been involved in voting registration activities. Hurst was immediately tried and acquitted by a white jury. A black witness, Lewis Allen, supported Hurst's story of self-defense. Allen later confided to SNCC workers that he had lied under duress, and the SNCC workers passed the information on to the FBI. The next day, the local sheriff told Allen that he knew what the SNCC workers had been told. Later, Allen was found murdered.

The one investigation where the FBI *did* show energy was the 1961 prosecution of nine civil rights workers for picketing a white grocery store in Americus, Georgia, after a particularly brutal series of confrontations between rights demonstrators and local police. The civil rights workers claimed they were protesting the store's segregated employment practices. The FBI charged they were protesting the owner's role in acquitting a white of murdering Charlie Ware, a local black. Intimidating a juror *was* a federal crime. The FBI pursued the case aggressively and made it stick; it was 1966 before the verdict was reversed.

A classic confrontation occurred in Selma, Alabama, on "Freedom Day" in the summer of 1963. SNCC workers organized several hundred local blacks to come to the courthouse and register to vote. About five hundred local police and special deputies lined up along the county courthouse, led by Sheriff Jim Clark—six feet tall, big stomach, green uniform with a gold star, open collar, gold epaulets, green helmet with a gold eagle, a big gun strapped to his waist, and a long black riot club. The local police were reinforced by several hundred troopers from the special riot command of Al Lingo, the swaggering chief of the state police. The local blacks formed an orderly line outside the courthouse. In four hours, four of them were permitted inside, not to register, but to *apply* to register. FBI men and nervous Justice Department lawyers gathered on the federal building steps opposite the courthouse to watch as Clark's men cleared the sidewalks and kept the SNCC workers and other outsiders from congregating. Then Clark spotted two SNCC workers on the federal building steps and ordered them to move on. They refused. Clark's men charged the steps, past the FBI agents, past the federal lawyers, clubbed the organizers, dragged them down the steps, and threw them into a police van. Howard Zinn, a white history professor, was screaming at the agents, "This is a *federal* building! Is this a *federal* building?!"

At noon, the registrar announced a two-hour lunch break, and the courthouse was closed as the blacks stood stoically in the hot sun. Clark announced that anyone who left the line would not be allowed to return. SNCC workers brought sandwiches and bottles of water in a shopping cart. James Forman asked Clark if they could bring the registrants food and water. Clark refused. "You may not molest these people in any way." After a standoff of several hours, Chico Neblett, a SNCC worker, volunteered to cross the police line with the shopping cart. He started slowly across the street as the police line waited tensely. Then the trooper commander shouted "Get him!" and the line of troopers and police charged, clubbed him to the ground, kicked him unconscious, and jabbed him with cattle prods until his body jerked and writhed convulsively on the pavement. The Justice Department lawyers and agents looked on. No federal crime was being committed.

The Justice Department's narrow interpretation of its mandate was, in strict legal terms, wrong—and SNCC and its advisers knew it. A wave of civil rights legislation was passed immediately after the Civil War to ensure equal treatment for blacks, and remnants were still in force. Section 241 of the U.S. Code, for example, originally passed in 1870 and known as the "Ku Klux Klan Act," said:

> If two or more persons conspire to injure, oppress, threaten or intimidate any citizen in the free exercise or enjoyment of any right or privilege secured to him by the Constitution or laws of the United States . . . or . . . if two or more persons go in disguise on the highway . . . with intent to prevent or hinder his free exercise or enjoyment . . . they shall be fined not more than $10,000 or imprisoned not more than ten years, or both.

And section 242, originally passed in 1866, said:

> Whoever, under color of any law, statute, ordinance, regulation, or custom, willfully subjects any inhabitant of any State . . . to the deprivation of any rights, privileges, or immunities secured or protected by the Constitution or laws of the United States . . . by reason of his color or race . . . shall be fined not more than $1000 or imprisoned not more than one year, or both.

To the layman, at least, there was simply no question that Jim Clark was oppressing, threatening, or intimidating citizens in the free exercise of their constitutional rights. The Justice Department's bland refusal to act seemed shockingly supine at best and, at worst, racist.

There were, of course, practical arguments for the Justice Department's position. Over the years the courts had rather thoroughly emasculated the civil rights laws. In a 1945 case, for example, the Supreme Court had refused to sustain the conviction of a Georgia sheriff named Screws who had beaten a black man to death with a tire iron. The Court had no doubts of Screws's murderous intent, but the justices claimed to be uncertain about Screws's intention to deprive his victim of constitutional rights. The effect was to erect a highly artificial and difficult obstacle to winning cases of civil rights violations. Just as important, felony convictions under the civil rights laws required jury trials; and experience had shown that white juries in the South would not convict white men for mistreating blacks, even when Southern judges allowed the cases to come to trial.

But if it was true that the courts had narrowed the ambit of the civil rights laws, it was also true that the Supreme Court had new faces since

Screws, along with a newly activist judicial philosophy, and may have welcomed the opportunity to make new law. In any case, the Justice Department was in an awkward position when it took refuge behind the inadequacy of the law, for the administration had proclaimed that no further civil rights legislation was necessary. And the Southern judges who made civil rights enforcement such an exercise in casuistical futility were, as often as not, Kennedy's own appointees, approved and recommended by the selfsame Justice Department.

Ultimately, the Justice Department was forced to change its strategy. Litigation was simply too slow, and, despite the department's pleading, SNCC would not reduce the pressure. Doar explained: "As the curve [of violence] started up, Bob Moses and his guys decided the way to confront that curve was to bring a lot of white kids down and get some white kids hurt and the country would be up in arms." That's exactly what happened. In the spring of 1964, three young voting rights workers, James Chaney, Michael Schwerner, and Andrew Goodman, two of them white and from the North, were picked up in Neshoba, Mississippi, on a traffic violation. That night, they were taken out of the jail by eighteen men, including the sheriff and two deputies, taken out into the woods, and executed. Before they were shot they were beaten so badly that when their bodies were finally found, the coroner said they looked like victims of a high-speed crash. The steadily escalating violence—the Neshoba assassinations; the little girls murdered in a Birmingham church; the increasing resort to dogs, fire hoses, and cattle prods; the open sadism of local law enforcement officers—drove home to the country that the totalitarian South was alien territory. It was the brutal Southern repression of civil rights activity, more than any other factor, that finally convinced the country that meaningful civil rights legislation was a necessity. The result was the Civil Rights Act of 1964 and, even more important, the Voting Rights Act of 1965. The federal government simply took over voting registration in the recalcitrant South, as the civil rights organizations had been demanding all along.

The administration, in fact, had been slowly revising its view of civil rights well before the incident at Neshoba. The evidence is that Robert Kennedy was the first important official to press for more radical solutions. John Kennedy's change of attitude seems to have occurred in the spring of 1963, and by the time of the March on Washington, he had already resolved to move forward with a far-reaching legislative program. Sadly, there was still sufficient obstructionism in Congress that the legislation probably could not have passed without the emotional riptide that followed upon the young President's death and that was so skillfully exploited by Johnson to clear the legislative agenda.

Implicit in the administration's change of heart was the recognition that civil rights was a moral issue—its claim upon the government was transcendent. The Kennedys' pragmatic predilections were of some use in formulating tactics, but on the main issues they were irrelevant. The civil rights problem had to be faced and dealt with whole, whether it was politic to do so or not. The admission of moral quality as a criterion of government was a crucial shift in perspective, whether or not Kennedy and his advisers recognized it as such. It imposed new complexities on politics, for morality is more a personal than a public concept. The moral paradigm is absolutist, one not easily suited to the intricate tactical trade-offs of rights and wrongs that are the daily stuff of government. More important, to the pragmatist, government acquires legitimacy from its effectiveness; and it exacts cooperation and compliance because they are prerequisites to performance. But as the civil disobedience movement showed, when a government's legitimacy rests ultimately on its moral qualities, compliance and cooperation become a daily decision, based on the current assessment of its worthiness. The government's footing becomes more fragile, the forces acting upon it more centrifugal, and the allegiance of its citizens more personal and hence more fleeting.

Civil Disobedience

The assignment of primacy to the moral over the political resonates comfortably within the American tradition, however revolutionary its implications. The radical Black Panthers, with a wry sense of nuance, adopted the Declaration of Independence as their official platform. ("It is the Right of the People . . . it is their duty, to throw off such Government.") The higher claim of the civil rights movement over legal authority was formally stated by Martin Luther King in his famous "Letter from a Birmingham Jail" of 1963. The letter was a response to a group of Southern white clergymen who had criticized King for breaking local laws during a series of demonstrations. It is notable not only for its claim that civil disobedience is a legitimate technique to advance the cause of equal rights, but for its attempt to lay down a formal set of rules for its application and practice.

King argued that his violation of the law in Birmingham qualified as "legitimate" civil disobedience, as the concept was developed in the teachings and writings of Gandhi. In King's view, the pressing reality of social injustice in the South made action imperative. The lawbreaking was not casual, for King had carefully ascertained the facts of the law beforehand. He had negotiated fruitlessly and at great length with local officials. He had "purified" himself with prayer and meditation before his action. He had taken care that he would break the law nonviolently. The laws violated were either unjust laws—they applied only to a minority or they were undemocratically passed—or proper laws being applied unjustly. Finally, the violation was "open and loving," and King was willing to accept whatever penalty was imposed.

Civil disobedience became something of an intellectual industry in the mid-1960s. It was not a new idea, of course. Aside from Gandhi and Sam Adams, there was Henry David Thoreau, who had refused to pay taxes in 1848 to protest against the Mexican War; there were the Boston abolitionists who had forcibly prevented the return of fugitive slaves, and, if one cared to stretch the gospels a bit, there was even Jesus. The underlying assumption was that there was a higher law that took precedence over political codes. The problem for philosophers and moralists was to define that higher law and to establish the circumstances that made civil disobedience permissible. Some of the attempts were ingenious; in my view, none of them was wholly successful. One fairly typical formulation, that of John Rawls, defined civil disobedience as a "public, nonviolent, conscientious yet political act contrary to law usually done with the aim of bringing about a change in the law or policies of the government." The public character of the act was necessary if it was to result in the desired changes. The "conscientious" requirement meant that the lawbreaking was reasoned and principled—that the lawbreakers, in effect, could point to the higher law they were obeying, could demonstrate why it imposed a superior obligation, and could show that there was no available recourse within the current legal framework.

It was more difficult to demonstrate why civil disobedience had to be nonviolent. Most theorists, in company with King's Birmingham letter, argued that nonviolence advertised the lawbreakers' continued respect for the law and increased the effectiveness of the protest. But that rings more of tactical advice than of moral canon. By 1963, in fact, an important element in SNCC—oxymoronically but understandably—had rejected nonviolence and were carrying guns. Howard Zinn, who had become a sort of quasi-official SNCC theorist, insisted that change may *require* violence, citing sources as diverse as Albert Camus, Frederick Douglass, Ralph Waldo Emerson, and Reinhold Niebuhr. While scholars like Rawls, Ronald Dworkin, and Morris Cohen were constructing high-minded hypotheses drawn from civil rights or anti-Vietnam protests, Zinn was calling for takeovers of university buildings, "smashing a hospital gate" to keep the hospital from closing, "occupying a skyscraper and living in it," "running up bills and sending them to the federal government," forcibly keeping the police out of the ghettos, and other fevered products of a rich academic imagination. Violence, as H. Rap Brown, a later SNCC chairman, jeered, was "as American as cherry pie."

It may not be possible to construct a truly consistent theory of "legitimate" or "permissible" civil disobedience. Locke and Hume argued that selective disobedience entails rejection of the entire government. If individuals are the final arbiters of the law, the entire structure of authority must eventually collapse. Rawls and Zinn struggle to avoid that logic; but the arguments of both, if they have little else in common, are circular—each selects specific incidents of civil disobedience he approves of and then searches for principles to fit them. Nor is historical precedent of much help. Thoreau was more quirky than principled, and admitted that he enjoyed picking and choosing which laws to obey. Emerson made a hero and martyr of John Brown, who was probably a psychopath. Gandhi, at least in his Indian phase, and Sam Adams were forthright revolutionaries, not reformists; their civil disobedience was merely a tactic in the larger treason.

It is easy to conceive of instances where the law should be disobeyed. The logic of Nuremberg, after all, rested on the principle of a higher duty. But when the most extreme cases have been allowed for, the argument quickly collapses into mere subjectivity. Rawls maintains that "each person must decide for himself whether the circumstances justify civil disobedience," although he hastens to add that "it does not follow that one is to decide as one pleases." The distinction may be sufficient guide for a Harvard philosophy professor but is rather harder to employ as the platform of a mass movement. The early proclivity of the Kennedy administration to prefer tranquillity and ordered change over strict justice sprang from an instinctive Burkean reliance on settled institutions. As pragmatic liberals they were prepared to accept, even embrace, change. But their insistence that it proceed incrementally and at a pace that could be readily absorbed by the existing political structure seemed arid and unfeeling in the face of the pressing issues that were churning to the surface first in the South and later in Vietnam.

And, to an extent, their position *was* arid and unfeeling, and in the case of Vietnam, casually arrogant as well. But if pragmatism proved an inadequate guide as the country careened toward the confrontations of the late 1960s, it remained to be shown whether deduction from principles of individual morality could provide a more reliable compass.

Clash and Backlash

Most Northern liberals, I think, were taken by surprise when, in about 1962, the NAACP and CORE began to picket Northern construction sites to protest segregated trade unions. I was in college in Philadelphia then and, with some excitement, wrote a paper on the picketing. When I read the paper in class, most of the other students also seemed newly aware of the issue and were eager to talk about it. Until then we hadn't realized that the North had a civil rights problem, too. There was a profound shift of perception underway. In the first years of the 1960s, Northerners could savor their own horrified righteousness at the gross abuse of blacks in the South. But the more subtle discrimination in the North was just beginning to come into focus, at the same time that demographers were understanding in first faint outline the vast dimensions of the black *Völkerwanderung* moving from Southern farms to the urban North.

Blacks had always moved North whenever they had the opportunity, but before World War I the migration was a relative trickle. From 1900 to 1930, about 1.6 million blacks resettled in the North, most of them pulled by the expansion of armaments manufacture during the war years. The migration came to a virtual halt during the Depression, but accelerated again with the rearming for World War II and continued through the 1960s. In net figures, 1.7 million blacks moved North during the 1940s, 1.5 million in the 1950s, and 1.4 million in the 1960s. Blacks from Deep South states like Alabama, Louisiana, and Mississippi followed a well-defined migration trail up the Mississippi River to the Midwestern industrial cities—Chicago, Detroit, Gary. Eastern seaboard blacks from Florida, the Carolinas, Georgia, and Virginia gravitated toward Philadelphia and New York. The peak of the postwar migration coincided with a sharp upturn in the rate of birth among the entire American population, and the black birthrate was among the highest of all. The blacks moving North were disproportionately in their child-bearing years, and by the mid-1950s, the high birthrate was increasing the Northern black population even faster than immigration. For some cities the results were wrenching. In Newark, New Jersey, for instance, with about a half million people in 1960, the black proportion of the population grew from 17 percent in 1950 to 35 percent in 1960 and to 70 percent in 1970. The city experienced an almost total turnover of its population in just twenty years, with a sharp downward shift in average age, income, and skills. In the 1940s, the great majority of blacks lived in the South, overwhelmingly in rural areas. A generation later, most blacks lived in the North and the West, almost all of them in cities.

As the burgeoning black population in Northern cities spilled over from the traditional "colored" enclaves into white neighborhoods, working-class whites reacted with hatred and terror. Polarization in the blue-collar areas of the North coincided with the last cresting spasms of repressive violence in the South. The cadenced exhortations to "redemptive suffering" by Martin Luther King and his generation of black leaders rang with increasing irrelevance to the hardened veterans of the voting rights wars, who were turning their eyes now to the struggle in the North. In 1965, SNCC elected Stokely Carmichael chairman to succeed the mystic pacifist John Lewis and began openly to debate the failure of nonviolence and the necessity for black power. That same year, in Lowndes County, Alabama, SNCC workers, looking for a symbol to dramatize an unofficial slate of black candidates, hit upon the image of a springing black panther. In the North, James Baldwin chilled white readers of *The Fire Next Time* as he told with quiet eloquence of a new and distinctly nonpacifist sect called Black Muslims, who were preaching hatred of the "blue-eyed Satan." There was a new set of black heroes, hard men, far removed from the Baptist ministers of tradition. Eldridge Cleaver was a rapist. Malcolm X was a robber. In May 1967, lines of young blacks led by Huey Newton and Bobby Seale, wearing guerrilla berets and carrying shotguns and M-16 rifles, marched with military precision into the California state legislature. The rationalist descendants of John Dewey had placed their faith in achieving change by thought and experiment. A new generation was insisting on the methods of blood and fire.

A common characteristic of the new black leaders was that they were a generation younger than the leaders they supplanted. For the civil rights movement was drawing strength from, and was soon to be almost swallowed by, another revolution that was already gathering a juggernaut momentum of its own—that was the revolution of youth itself.

IV

❧

REVOLTS AND REVOLUTIONS

Youth

The Beatles came to America for the first time in 1964 and appeared on the "Ed Sullivan Show" the same evening my first son was born. The nurses in the hospital kept slipping away excitedly to a television down the hall from the waiting room. The Beatles used their long hair as a gimmick; during their songs they would shake their hair at the audience, and the female spectators—including the nurses that night—would all shriek with delight. It was funny and fun—and who would have guessed it was a cultural watershed. But, astonishingly, by the time Michael, my new son, was about two, most men I knew wore their hair like the Beatles; ears disappeared all across the country. Sargent Shriver went off as ambassador to France with a Beatles haircut. Baseball owners got into contract disputes trying to make their players keep their hair cut. Even policemen and construction workers had hair bushing out awkwardly from their caps and hardhats.

With hair sprouting throughout the land, America painted itself with psychedelic colors and filled its airwaves with rock music, as the youth culture virtually took over the country. Youth cultures have been a commonplace in most societies where the economy has permitted a modicum of leisure. Medieval university students were intensely conscious of their separate status and terrorized hapless town fathers. The "Lost Generation" and the flappers of the 1920s flaunted their drinking, jazz music, slumming, and sexual freedom. The trademark for my own

1950s generation of teenagers, at least for males, was greasy hair and leather jackets; our hero was James Dean in *Rebel Without a Cause;* and our music was rock and roll, of the simpleminded Bill Haley variety— perhaps we liked it because our parents thought it sounded awful. Our youth culture, such as it was, was a way of closing ranks against a large world that seemed to be moving along quite nicely without us. But we hardly thought of our status as "youths" as a badge of honor and certainly not as a permanent condition. By eighteen or nineteen most of my friends had settled into full-time employment, a number were married, and several were starting families. I went to college, but in 1957 I considered college an adult occupation, a first step in a career. In the last half of the 1960s, however, the "youth culture" began to dictate to society rather than the other way around, and quite serious observers thought they were seeing a fundamental shift in American life-styles and values.

The overwhelming impact of the youth culture in the 1960s is a good example of the powerful effects of sharp changes at the margin. Youths were only a small minority of the population throughout the 1960s, and university students a smaller minority still. Young people aged eighteen to twenty-four were only about 12 percent of the population in 1970, up from 11 percent in 1960. But the *number* of people aged eighteen to twenty-four increased from 16.5 million in 1960 to 24.7 million in 1970, and *that* was a 50 percent increase. The weight of young people in the total population did not change spectacularly; what was so jolting was the rate of change in their absolute numbers.

The sudden onslaught of young people resulted from the sharp increase in births in the twenty years after World War II. Women have always regulated births to comport with economic reality. During hard times in the 1930s, women either stayed single or married late; and if they did get married, as far as demographers can reconstruct, they vigilantly practiced traditional birth control methods or simply abstained from intercourse. More than a fifth of adult women remained single in the 1930s, a modern record; the average age at which women married rose to another record; and births dropped precipitately, to only 2.3 million in 1933, the modern low point—and this thirty years before the advent of the "pill."

The birthrate soared when good times returned in the 1950s, and total births hit a record 4.3 million in 1957. After the war, three different cohorts of women got married all at the same time—women in their thirties who had postponed their marriages; women in their twenties, the normal age of marriage; and women in their late teens, who accelerated their marriages in the emotional aftermath of the victory. With brighter economic prospects, families began having their first child sooner and relaxed their birth control vigilance. Interestingly, interview data shows that desired family size didn't change, but the chances of having accidental children increased sharply. Average family size began to creep up at the same time as family formation was breaking records. The result was the postwar "baby boom," one of the deep, driving forces in recent American history, with an impact all the more dramatic because of the abnormally low fecundity of the generation just preceding.

The generational experience of the baby boom children was strikingly different from that of their parents. In the first place, it was crowded. The upsurge in births came so rapidly and so unexpectedly that public facilities were simply not prepared to handle them. There was a rush to build hospitals as obstetrics wards overflowed and women in labor lined up in hospital hallways. Then there was a rush to build schools and playgrounds and a rush to train teachers when schools were forced into double and triple sessions. In the 1960s, the rush to build universities was even more frantic. Prior to the war, only a little more than a third of all young people actually were graduated from high school, and only about a third of them went on to college. In the 1960s, 75 percent of the baby boom generation were being graduated from high school and half of them, more than a million each year, were entering college. During the decade, higher-education enrollments doubled to almost ten million. In the scramble for the available places, students became as nerve-wracked and anxiety-ridden as the administrators who were scrambling to make more places available.

Despite the pressure of numbers, the baby boomers were raised with a daily conviction of their own importance. The rhythm of suburban life in the 1950s was almost totally centered around children. Mothers and fathers enjoyed indulging their children in ways their own Depression-scarred parents never could, and were encouraged to do so by the best child-rearing advice. The strenuous political and economic exertions just to build schools must have made some kind of subliminal impression on the children basking at the center of so much feverish activity. No generation had more money or leisure than the cohort of young people who came of age in the 1960s. They were the first to be identified as a target "market segment" by the powerful new advertising techniques developed in the postwar period, and they enjoyed immense influence over the disposable income of their parents—perhaps because their parents had never been accustomed to having much in the way of disposable income.

The market power of the young generation is attested by the absolute conquest of rock music. When Elvis Presley blended black rhythm and blues with the plaintive loneliness of American country music and added his own brand of sullenly mutinous sexuality, he created the perfect expression of the teenager's sense of rebellious otherness. The Beatles' fillip, and that of their progeny, like the Rolling Stones, was to add the wry truculence that is peculiarly the province of the English working classes to Presley's mixture. With teenage spending power solidly behind it, rock swept all other forms of popular music off the boards. The retail record industry took in more than a billion dollars for the first time in the early 1960s, virtually all of it from rock. Sales of expensive stereo components boomed, and local radio stations rode the rock wave to a financial comeback after being written off as dead in the competition with television. Established singing stars like Frank Sinatra and Doris Day stopped making records and had to forge new careers in the movies. Adults succumbed to teenage buying power, forgot how to foxtrot, and began to strain their sacroiliacs learning the Twist and the Mashed Potato. One rock critic wrote that the release of the Beatles' *Sergeant Pepper's* album was "the closest Western civilization had come to unity since the Congress of Vienna." If it was, it was unity on the baby boomers' terms; people who preferred Perry Como were out of luck.

The economist Richard Easterlin offers the provocative hypothesis that the relative size of a birth cohort compared to the generation just preceding will have profound effects at every level of life adjustment. When the low-birth cohort of the 1930s moved into young adulthood in the 1950s, they were a scarce and sought-after commodity, particularly those with the benefit of a college education. Easterlin's data show that young men in the 1950s had unusually high levels of earnings and low levels of unemployment compared to older men. Older men still earned more than younger men, but the employment and earnings gap was untypically narrow. It was the relative affluence of the young, Easterlin suggests, that made the nesting phenomenon of the 1950s possible. For the first time in decades, young husbands were earning enough by themselves to support a rising standard of living for growing families, with all the trappings of lawns, suburban mortgages, backyard barbecues, and wives devoted full-time to home and children.

In the 1960s and 1970s on the other hand, as hordes of unskilled youngsters came of labor market age, the competitive conditions documented by Easterlin were quite suddenly reversed. Not surprisingly, the earnings level of young men dropped sharply relative to their older coworkers and their rates of unemployment rose to staggering new highs. The reversal of fortune was all the more wrenching because the standard of comparison for economic success is not so much the standard achieved by one's peers as that achieved by one's parents—and that was a competition the baby boomers were foredoomed to lose. Easterlin suggests that when a young generation accustomed to affluence suddenly confronted economic uncertainty, it was only to be expected that women would reenter the labor force massively (how else to make ends meet?), marriages would be delayed, and birthrates would again drop precipitately, which, of course, is exactly what happened.

One consequence of the crowding phenomenon, according to Easterlin, is that the social stresses normally associated with a youthful population will be vastly exaggerated during a rapid upswing in cohort size and correspondingly dampened during a downswing. Most crime, for instance, is committed by young people; so with the relative decrease in the youthful population during the 1950s, a drop in crime rates was to be expected. In fact, the drop in crime rates was disproportionately sharp. By the mid-1950s, crime rates were at their lowest level since reliable records were kept, and were probably as low as at any other period in American history. Then as the youthful population burgeoned in the 1960s, crime rates shot up again; by the 1970s they had climbed back to the peak rates of the 1930s and continued to spiral upward to new records. In both periods, crime rates moved faster and further than the swings in the youthful population. Divorce rates illustrate the same effect. During the 1950s, divorce rates actually dropped for the first time in half a century, slipping far below the historical trend line. Then they soared far above the trend line in the 1960s and 1970s, almost exactly balancing out the drop in the 1950s. In sociological jargon, swings in the "age-specific" indicators of social stress were amplified by the sharpness of the swings in birth cohort size. And of course, the high rates of crime and divorce seemed all the more devastating by comparison with the golden 1950s.

Contemporary social observers seemed blissfully unaware of the building pressures. Clark Kerr, the president of California's sprawling university system, expressed the quiet satisfaction of most parents whose children had achieved college admission when he said in 1959: "Employers will love this generation. . . . They are going to be easy to handle. There aren't going to be any riots." Kerr's misjudgment was as spectacular as John Kennedy's a few years later when he announced the end of ideology. At the start of the 1964 academic year on California's Berkeley campus, the university authorities, faced with a litter of leaflets and card tables crowding the mall in front of Sproul Hall, announced a rule against collecting money for off-campus causes. Police told a student named Jack Weinberg that he would be arrested if he didn't stop soliciting for CORE. When Weinberg argued and a crowd gathered, police put him under arrest and began to drag him to a patrol car—and found they were no match for students who were civil rights veterans schooled in the "Mississippi Summer." The crowd lay around the patrol car and immobilized it for a day and a half. The university agreed to negotiate, Weinberg and the patrol car were released, and the Berkeley "Free Speech Movement," later the "Filthy Speech Movement," came into being, along with the first of the 1960s charismatic campus leaders, Mario Savio, and two months later, the first of the head-banging confrontations between campus activists and blue-helmeted police. Within months, to parental horror, there were student "insurrections" throughout the country—Yale, Maryland, Ohio State, Colorado, Columbia.

The campus rebellions seemed to flip values upside down. Parents found their little achievements and proud strivings of twenty years held up as objects of scorn. Instead of being credited with building a peaceful prosperity, they found themselves accused of creating a corrupt system of institutionalized racism and soulless technocracy, of immorality in the Third World and Vietnam, of exploitation of the world's poor.

Traditional youthful fractiousness explains some of the rejection of parental values in the 1960s; and the competitive pressures of a swollen generation explain some of the surging disorders. But they don't explain why professors and leading intellectuals flew to join on the students' side. Just as the pragmatic style was achieving its moment of most complete realization in the Kennedy-Johnson years, and seemed to have engaged the world with almost unalloyed success, its fundamental assumptions were coming under a withering intellectual enfilade. The pragmatic tradition was running out of creative energy, its lack of moral resonance was becoming all too apparent, and it was being shouldered aside in the search for more transcendent systems of thought.

Existentialism and the Revolt Against Pragmatism

In the mid-1950s, a new import from continental Europe called "existentialism" began to spread among American intellectuals and a decade later dominated campus intellectual life. Norman Mailer is a bellwether of the interests of the fashionable intelligentsia, and "existential" began to crop up in his writings almost as often as his favorite Anglo-Saxon expletives and was used almost as flexibly. From *The Armies of the Night*, for instance: " . . . with every phrase one was better or worse, close or less close to the existential promise of truth." Or: "He [Mailer himself, that is] would confess straight out that he was the one who wet the floor in the men's room, he alone! While the audience was recovering from the existential anxiety of encountering an orator . . . " When Jack Newfield of the *Village Voice* shed his distaste for Robert Kennedy shortly before Kennedy's death, he dubbed him an "existential hero." "Existential" became something of an all-purpose intensive: if a speaker at a campus sit-in spoke of an "existential truth," he meant, more or less, that it was *really* true.

Existentialism was never an internally consistent school of philosophy, but "more of a mood or an atmosphere," as one scholar put it, which in itself is tellingly characteristic of the intellectual style of the late 1960s. Although some existentialists, like the German Martin Heidegger, were professional philosophers who wrote tomes weighted down with all the clanking apparatus of Hegelian metaphysics, the leading ideas were as often articulated by theologians, like Paul Tillich and Martin Buber, or by novelists and playwrights, like Albert Camus, Simone de Beauvoir, Jean-Paul Sartre, and Samuel Beckett. Existentialism had room enough for Marxist atheists like Sartre, conservative Catholics like Gabriel Marcel, German moralists like Karl Jaspers, and even radical psychiatrists like R. D. Laing. What bound them together was a deep sense of the individual man's loneliness, of the marmoreal unreachability of God, and of blank terror before the vast emptiness of space and time. Existentialism's central image is that of a man shivering alone on a dark plain, engulfed by an icy wind blowing from a random future, shouting into the void—his cries go unanswered, for they have no meaning, and there is no one to hear.

The roots of existentialism stretch back into the nineteenth century, most directly to the writings of the Danish Christian philosopher Søren Kierkegaard, and collaterally to the manic irrationalism of Friedrich Nietzsche and the post-Hegelian "phenomenology" of Edmund Husserl. Kierkegaard attempted to strip away the pomposities of institutionalized Christianity and mocked the busy solemnities of North European burghers in a universe that was fundamentally contingent and absurd. The path to a genuine Christianity, he argued, was to abandon the bourgeois conception of God, accept the meaninglessness of the world, and by a supreme act of belief make the existential leap into darkness, bereft of even the slightest reassuring gesture from a wholly ineffable deity. From more or less the same starting point, Nietzsche's *Thus Spake Zarathustra,* some fifty years later, arrived at the conclusion that "God is dead." Man is his own creation: through the Will to Power, he can become Superman. Sartre expressed the same thought in the twentieth century.

> To begin with, [man] is nothing. He will not be anything until later, and then he will be what he makes of himself. Thus there is no human nature, because there is no God to have a conception of it. Man simply is. Not that he is simply what he conceives himself to be, but he is what he wills . . . after that leap towards existence. Man is nothing else but what he makes of himself. That is the first principle of existentialism.

European intellectuals were generally men of the left. When their world-socialist illusions were destroyed by Stalin's cynical treaty with Hitler, by the cold mendacity of his purge trials, and by the murder of romantic figures like Bukharin and Trotsky, they were left, they felt, only with a choice between nihilistic despair or bold confrontation with the absurd. Camus argues the nobility of existential self-reliance in *The Myth of Sisyphus.*

> The gods had condemned Sisyphus to ceaselessly rolling a rock to the top of a mountain, whence the stone would fall back of its own weight. They had thought with some reason that there is no more dreadful punishment than futile and hopeless labor. . . . You have already grasped that Sisyphus is the absurd hero. He *is,* as much through his passions as through his tortures. . . . Sisyphus, proletarian of the gods, knows the whole extent of his wretched

condition: it is what he thinks of during his descent. The lucidity that was to constitute his torture at the same time crowns his victory. There is no fate that cannot be surmounted by scorn. . . . His fate belongs to him. His rock is his thing. . . . The universe henceforth without a master seems to him neither sterile nor futile. Each atom of that stone, each mineral flake of the night-filled mountain, in itself forms a world. The struggle toward the heights is enough to fill a man's heart. One must imagine Sisyphus happy.

Existentialism's triple themes of anguish, abandonment, and despair recur frequently in Western thought—in the bleak meditations of Spinoza, the outcast Jew, for example. But they had particular appeal to a generation of youth, for existentialist anxiety, the search for identity and roots, the sense of rudderless drift, of being acted upon, is quintessentially the adolescent experience, and one hardly mitigated by comparative affluence. If anything, the release from the struggle for daily bread made the feeling of pointlessness more pervasive.

The sudden vogue of existentialism among American intellectuals was, in an important respect, simply another example of the market power of youth, like rock music or Beatles haircuts. Adults wore their children's ideas like their clothes and their colors. The rapid waning of existentialism's influence just a few years later attests to the faddish nature of its conquest. But shallow fashion is not the whole explanation. The deeper meaning of the turn toward irrationalism was a growing distaste, even disgust, for the aridly reductionist bias in American pragmatism and for its apparent willingness to submerge principles and ideals in the cold search for method and efficiency—a charge that gained sting from the policy overreachings of the Kennedy and Johnson administrations in Vietnam and from their initially torpid response to the moral imperatives of the civil rights movement.

The unpleasant reductionist strain in pragmatism traced back to British roots. British thought, in contrast to the romantic effusions of continental philosophy, has characteristically taken a sober, common-sense view of the world. Well before the empiricism of Locke and Hume, William of Occam plied his famous razor to slice away at the superfluous abstractions of medieval thought. To the practical British mind, if one can sit only in particular chairs, then of what possible use is the Platonic Idea of the Perfect Chair? Dr. Johnson resolved the epistemological quandaries of Bishop Berkeley by kicking a rock—proof enough of its reality for him, he huffed. James displayed his empiricist heritage in essays like "Does 'Consciousness' Exist?" (1904). He says that "consciousness is the name of a nonentity and has no right to a place among first principles. Those who still cling to it are clinging to a mere echo, the faint rumor left behind by the disappearing 'soul' upon the air of philosophy."

By rigorously applying the principles of mathematical logic, Bertrand Russell demonstrated, at least to his own satisfaction, that most of the supposed great questions of philosophy were simply the product of syntactical muddle. Ever since Plato, he smiled, philosophers had confused the use of the word "is" as a copula—John *is* tall—with "is" as an expression for existence—there *is* a British queen. Since any noun can take a copula, philosophers assumed that *existence* must be a universal attribute, independent of particular entities, thus *being* in itself. When Hegel stripped this supposed universal abstract down to Pure Being and named it God, Russell and other good Englishmen threw up their hands.

British thought between the wars was dominated by Ludwig Wittgenstein's language philosophy and A. J. Ayer's radical positivism. Most of Wittgenstein's writings are in the form of gnomic epigrams that relentlessly analyze the language of common sentences, squeezing out any shred of obscurity or ambiguity—and, in the course of doing so, manage to reduce to meaninglessness all the issues philosophers have sweated over for centuries. Wittgenstein freely admitted that his analysis "destroyed everything interesting," and concluded that philosophy could neither supply any useful answers nor even ask any important questions. Ayer and the positivists (building on the work of the American Charles Peirce, who was virtually ignored in this country except by James) reduced the question of meaning to one of verifiability. A proposition that could not be proved true or false by external criteria was meaningless. With a wave of the hand, in effect, the positivists dismissed all the questions of morals and ethics that were being raised so insistently in the 1960s.

The achievements of Anglo-American pragmatism and positivism are undeniable. The clarity introduced into philosophic discussion was of immense importance at a time when physics was reshaping man's worldview. And, surely, some corrective was needed for the orgiastic mentation of a Hegel, a Schopenhauer, or a Nietzsche. One can already hear the drumbeats of Hitler's goose-stepping Brownshirts in Hegel's

thudding pages on "The State." But positivism could become insuffera-
bly arid and arrogant. In the hands of Gilbert Ryle at Oxford, for
instance, it slipped into a smugly self-assured behaviorism. A concept
like "love," to Ryle, meant nothing more than a set of "conversational
avowals, interjections, tones of voice, gestures, and facial expressions."
And here is Ryle on the development of concepts:

> How can a person who starts with mere sensations reach the stage
> of finding out that there are physical objects? But this is a queer sort
> of how-question . . . since we all know the answer perfectly well.
> . . . There is no more of an epistemological puzzle in describing how
> infants learn perception recipes than there is in describing how boys
> learn to bicycle. They learn by practice, and we can specify the sorts
> of practice that expedite this learning.

Modern researchers in cognition think the problem is very much more
complicated than that. Similarly, the spate of writing in the 1950s and
1960s on artificial intelligence was dogmatically positivist, and its facile
assumption that the human mind is merely a compact model of a digital
computer has turned out to be quite wrong.

American education was heavily influenced by Dewey's version of
pragmatism. For all the humaneness of his intentions, he had the same
dry, mechanistic view of human nature as Ryle and Ayer. How much
could be achieved, he wrote,

> if our schools were actually managed on a psychological basis like
> great factories are run on the basis of the physical and chemical
> sciences.

And he looked confidently forward to "increasing control in the ethical
field" and in "the formation of aims" so human effort could be properly
channeled to socially useful ends. Predictably, Dewey was mightily
impressed by a visit to the Soviet Union in 1928, and rhapsodized that

> the system compels teachers to be cognizant of the *Gosplan* [the
> Soviet five-year industrial plan]. . . . An educator from a bourgeois
> country might well envy the added dignity that comes to the func-
> tion of a teacher when he is taken into partnership in plans for the
> social development of his country.

Dewey's infatuation with factories and five-year plans was carried to
its logical extremes by B. F. Skinner in the 1950s. In *Beyond Freedom
and Dignity,* Skinner writes:

The intentional design of a culture and the control of human behavior that it implies are essential if the human species is to develop. . . . What is needed is more intentional control, not less, and this is an important engineering problem.

And in *Walden Two:*

We try to design a world for those who cannot solve the problem of punishment for themselves, such as babies, retardates, or psychotics, and if it could be done for everyone, much time and energy could be saved.

When college students insisted that administrations wanted to "fold, spindle, and mutilate" them, in other words, they weren't entirely imagining things. And their suspicion that somebody out there wanted to dehumanize and program them carried more than a germ of truth. The movies of Fritz Lang enjoyed a campus renaissance in the 1960s because his sterile insect landscapes struck a scary chord.

Liberation

Irrationalism, existentialist anxiety, the sheer numbers of adolescents with not much to do, all led to the blooming of the "counterculture" in 1967, the summer of the big Be-In in San Francisco's Haight-Ashbury and New York's East Village, of Ken Kesey's Pranksters rollicking through the West in a psychedelic bus, of flower children and sweetly gentle "Diggers," of dropping acid and freaking on speed, of rock and communes and "relating" and sharing and Love. By the fall, most major campuses had developed colonies of hangers-on, the "skuzzies," the "groddies," and the "heads," who panhandled, sold their beads and leather crafts, rapped about Siddhartha and Steppenwolf, and squatted in the dormitories. "Alternative" universities flourished. A sample course design:

A free-wheeling succession of open-ended situations. Ongoing vibrations highly relevant. Exploration of Inner Space, deconditioning of the human robot, significance of psycho-chemicals, and the transformation of West European Man. Source material: Artaud, Zimmer, Gurdjieff, Wilhelm Reich, Karl Marx, Gnostic, Sufi, and Tantric texts, autobiographical accounts of madness and ecstatic states of consciousness, Pop Art and twentieth century prose.

The counterculture was a media event. There were cover stories in *Time, Newsweek,* and the *New York Times Magazine;* CBS's Harry Reasoner did a special broadcast and soberly analyzed the implications for America. There was a spirit of liberation in the air, not only of blacks, but of homosexuals, of women, of students themselves, the whole group whom the psychiatrist and historian Erik Erikson called "the other." Erikson asked: "But what if, as seems to be happening to America, a whole new civilization is conscious of creating itself?" Theodore Roszak said: "We may well be in the presence not of just the latest wrinkle in youthful rebellion, but of an emergent social movement." The historian James Silver announced "the first authentic American social revolution." The critic Leslie Fiedler called the campus fringe groups "the spearhead of a revolution." The pollster Daniel Yankelovich dubbed them "The Forerunners." Academic sociologists rushed to their Durkheim and Weber, cleared their throats, and harrumphed out sentences like:

> What I would like to suggest here is that there is, as Max Weber would have put it, an elective affinity between prominent styles and themes in the hippie subculture and certain incipient problems of identity, work, and leisure, that loom ominously as Western industrial society moves into an epoch of accelerated cybernation, staggering material abundance. . . .

And so on.

The heads of otherwise serious people were quite completely turned. Charles Reich, turning forty, wrote *The Greening of America,* the silliest book ever penned by a Yale law professor caught in the grip of mid-life crisis. Silly it may have been, but it was a runaway best-seller, was serialized in the *New Yorker,* and was soberly discussed in respectable intellectual circles. The "Corporate State," Reich wrote, "has added depersonalization, meaninglessness, and repression, until it has threatened to destroy all meaning and all life." In response, the youth of America was in the process of evolving a "new consciousness" which Reich dubbed "Consciousness III." The new consciousness would make possible "a culture that is nonartificial, and nonalienated, a form of community in which love, respect, and a mutual search for wisdom replace the competition and separation of the past, and a liberation of each individual in which he is enabled to grow toward the highest possibilities of the human spirit." Reich's book is really a threnody to his own lost youth, spent grinding away in dusty law libraries.

> What have we all lost? What aspects of human experience are either missing altogether from our lives or present only in feeble imitation of their real quality? Let us take our list off the yellow pad where it was jotted down one fine morning in early summer.

> *Adventure, Travel* The Yukon, the Hebrides, a blizzard, fog on the Grand Banks, the lost cities of Crete, climbing a mountain on rock and ice in elemental cold and wind.

> *Sex* Experiences with many different people, in different times, circumstances, and localities, in moments of happiness, sorrow, need, and comfortable familiarity, in youth and in age.

And on the list goes, through Bravery, Worship, Fear, Dread, Awareness of Death, Spontaneity, Romance, Dance, Ceremony and Ritual, Harmony, and Inner Life. Reich does not explore the logistics of hauling most of America over to Crete to poke around for lost cities, but he does tell us how to engineer the deeper revolution:

> Now all we have to do is close our eyes and imagine that everyone has become a Consciousness III: the Corporate State vanishes.

It seems worthwhile to ask how such intelligent people could have been so misled by the sound of their own voices. I think there are several reasons. For one thing, journalists, intellectuals, and other social commentators have an almost infinite capacity to read long-term trends into current events. When the economy failed to bounce back immediately during the Depression, for instance, economists formulated the theory of "secular stagnation" and demonstrated that the depression would be permanent. When political passions faded in the 1950s, social theorists proclaimed the end of ideology. When the economy performed well during the first half of the 1960s, economists announced that the problems of growth had been solved and began to worry about leisure. And since it usually takes a few years to perceive an underlying cohesion in events, the trend-spotters more often make their pronouncements just in time to be proved completely wrong. By the time the demographers were sure they were seeing a "secular drop in the birthrate" in the early 1950s, the baby boom was already under way. Suburban school construction didn't really get into full swing until the real need for vast new capacity had passed by. It is hardly surprising, therefore, that the counterculture was not immediately perceived to be a phenomenon as transient as youth itself; and in the particular instance, since a significant proportion of intellectuals seemed to have felt that a counterculture was both desirable and necessary, they were the more disposed to see events confirming their hopes.

The 1960s were also the first time that America had a sizeable university community—students greatly outnumbered farmers, for instance—and radicalism has always flourished in the universities. Personal trauma is intellectualized and universalized; daily contemplation of the ideal inevitably leads to reflections on its achievability. The student movement in *fin de siècle* Austria, for example, *Die Jungen,* intoxicated with the atavism of Wagner and Nietzsche, was the spearhead of pan-German nationalism, to the despair of an older generation of bourgeois liberals. In American universities, old-fashioned and usually vaguely Marxist radicals like Herbert Marcuse and Paul Goodman found that their long-standing critique of the Corporate State suddenly had an audience. The civil rights movement had attuned students to issues of injustice and inequality, while "the establishment"—the Kennedy Justice Department, Big Business, the Southern power structure—seemed either oblivious to the worst outrages or actually in complicity. At the same time, two decades of economic growth had made the price of progress painfully clear—septic rivers, noxious air, and littered landscapes. And if civil rights and environmentalism weren't enough, there was Vietnam, an international adventure of questionable wisdom and dubious morality, with the threat of the draft and sudden death in the jungle for good measure.

The elitist exclusivity of radicalism was also part of its appeal. For all the cant about "participatory democracy," Reich, Goodman, and other aging spokesmen for radical youth, like Edgar Z. Friedenberg, were disdainful of the tastes and values of the average man. Scorn was a good defense for students who were drifting amid uncertainty—not sure why they were in college, not sure what they would do when college was over, not sure if society would even have room for them. Here is Friedenberg:

> For, of course, Spiro T. Agnew is right about this: young militants are indeed "effete snobs," more privileged than their fellows, not only convinced of their moral superiority but arrogant in daring to

raise, in this technology-mad land, a moral question at all. . . . The flower children are indeed the enemies of mass, industrial society. . . . The "anti-American" generation, like its French and other counterparts, might do well to abandon its heartbreaking efforts to make common cause with a working class that applauds the police who beat the shit out of it, and wear its "effete snob" buttons more proudly. . . . For the United States, like those of its neighbors with a comparable level of development, has become, in terms of culture, triumphantly and often vindictively, an affluent poor-white-trash nation.

Reich's vision of the middle class is almost paranoid. America, to Reich, is "one vast, terrifying anti-community," and he writes of walking down a suburban street "where people follow you with narrow, watchful eyes."

And Paul Goodman in *Growing Up Absurd:*

The organized system is very powerful and in the full tide of success, apparently sweeping everything before it in science, education, community planning, labor, the arts, not to speak of business and politics where it is indigenous. Let me say that we of the previous generation who have been sickened and enraged to see earnest and honest effort and human culture swamped by this muck, are heartened by the crazy young allies, and we think that the future may perhaps make more sense than we dared hope.

The relationship ran both ways: for the older radicals, the revolutionary students' easy acceptance of drugs and sex was an object of envy. Most college faculty, after all, were not much older than the students —or at that awkward age where, as one magazine put it, they were "Too Old To *DO IT,* But Too Young Not To Want To Try." James Silver, for example, was a Mississippi history professor who had shown considerable courage exposing the apartheid of his home state, but his remarks to a group of student activists captures just the note of wistfulness and guilt.

I have no business being on your program tonight because I am not an authentic revolutionist. I am not even an activist. I have not been in jail, I have not been involved in demonstrations, and I guess all I can say is that I'm sorry.

A common characteristic of both students and professors, and one of the great ironies of the radical movement, was that they accepted at face value all the claims of the pragmatic technocrats and exaggerated them even more outlandishly than the technocrats themselves. All the hopes of the radicals for liberation, for "self-actualization," for Consciousness III, were based on the confident assumption that the technocrats were right when they preened themselves for having solved once and for all the problem of production. Most of the radical themes, in fact, were first sounded by the technocrats themselves. Here is David Riesman, for example, a thoroughly establishment scholar, writing in the late 1950s:

> The traditional American ideology which is concerned only with equality of political and economic opportunity and freedom from control—in other words, with the major problem of scarcity alone —must readjust to face the problems that have suddenly become visible because of abundance: lack of participation in life and lack of opportunity and education for self-expression.

The radicals were not nearly as judicious. Reich's confidence in the technocrats he so enjoyed excoriating was altogether starry-eyed.

> Technology . . . promises a life that is more liberated and more beautiful than any man has known. . . . We know what causes crime and social disorder, and what can be done to eliminate these causes. We know the steps that can be taken to create greater economic equality. We are in possession of techniques to fashion and preserve more livable cities and environments. Our problems are vast, but so is our store of techniques; it is simply not being put to use.

Marcuse similarly had no doubts that the "technological processes of mechanization and standardization" would "alter the very structure of human existence" so that "the individual would be liberated from the work world's imposing on him alien needs and alien possibilities." Goodman went even further. If we only applied "the techniques of industry" to the problem of equitable production and distribution of subsistence, he had no doubts that abundance could be achieved with only a fraction of the labor presently employed. He wrestled with the problem of assuring that subsistence work would be fairly distributed and decided that the best answer would be "direct state production of subsistence by universally conscripted labor." The fact that his plan might be coercive gave him momentary pause, but he concluded that "in fact, if not in law" it "was less coercive than the situation most people are used to" and the net effect of his entire scheme would be "liberating."

On the basis of their own statements, it is tempting to dismiss the radicals as being totally out of touch with reality; and to a large extent they were. There were never more than a few thousand flower children even in the palmiest days of the movement, and the revolutionary posturing was more pathetic than threatening. Only a small proportion of college students was actively involved in campus disruptions. A poll of Berkeley students at the start of the Free Speech Movement in 1964, for example, showed that more than 80 percent thought they were getting a good education and were satisfied with the administration. The clamorous attention the radical students and their mentors received in the media attests more to the self-preoccupation of intellectuals and professional communicators than to the significance of "the movement." For all his sour Know-Nothingism, Spiro Agnew had the firmer grip on reality when he dismissed the supposed social transformation as the pipe dream of an "Eastern media establishment."

The cultural arrogance of radical intellectuals was particularly unattractive. Many of the early leaders of the women's movement—Betty Friedan was an exception—seemed to be addressing a sisterhood limited to women with advanced degrees, elegant tastes, and live-in (female) help. Their message was of limited relevance to the millions of lower-middle-class women who were reluctantly entering the labor force just to make ends meet. The disdain for suburban life—the "sterile suburbs of loneliness and alienation"—was another case of narrow-minded cultural xenophobia. Herbert Gans's studies of the "Levittowners" showed, in fact, that lower-middle-class suburbanites were quite satisfied with their new homes and delighted to have escaped the cramped housing, the dirt and noise, and the raw edge of city life. My own family made the trek from city to suburb when I was in grade school, and it was an entirely prideful and pleasurable experience. The small lawn gave a sense of peace and proprietorship, and was "liberating" in a real sense. Whenever I took the bus back to Philadelphia to visit relatives, I got a headache.

But if it was true that there was considerably less going on in the 1960s than met the eye, it would be equally erroneous to assume that nothing important was happening, and the youth bulge was only part of the story. The burst of irrationalism and intellectual experimentalism stemmed from the fact that the creative period of pragmatism and empiricism had, at least temporarily, run its course. The civil rights movement, above all else, had thrown questions of morality and values into sharp relief, questions that the incremental style of the technocrats was particularly ill-equipped to deal with. And the very skepticism that the empirical tradition fostered was being thrown back upon itself. It had by now become so much a part of the cultural ambience, and so ingrained in the younger population, that long-standing conceptions of role and authority—especially with respect to women and minorities— were coming under sharp challenge. The anti-ideological bias that had been so conducive to rapid technological progress was now undercutting the consensus that the technocratic state needed to function smoothly. And if the radicals displayed an overweening arrogance, it was matched by the hubris of the technocrats. Marcuse's vision of a pervasive and totalitarian technologic state, absorbing all human creativity to its cause and subjecting the human spirit to its service, was certainly an exaggeration, but it was not altogether implausible. B. F. Skinner's psychological writings provided a text, and the adventure in Vietnam a living example. There was a large element of juvenile self-pity in the student grievances, but there is no reason to suppose that they couldn't sense the explicit, if subtly disguised, coerciveness in Dewey's mechanistic theories of education. It was the failures and overreachings of the pragmatists, in short, that gave force to the radical critique of society; and by the late 1960s, the inadequacies of the pragmatist, rationalist vision were becoming so apparent that they were exposed for all to see.

V

TWO WARS

The War at Home

When the opportunity came to help start the local Community Action Program in Trenton, New Jersey, in 1965, I jumped at it. Community Action, or CAP, was the local operating arm of President Johnson's War on Poverty, and for me it was an exhilarating chance to be on the cutting edge of social reform. The War on Poverty was a new kind of enterprise in American politics: its grandiose objective was nothing less than the total elimination of poverty in the United States within ten years. Making due allowance for the expansive idiom of the Johnson White House, I think that total victory was seriously and sincerely intended. It was one more example of the heady new confidence that the country really was "moving again." The fact that Johnson was able to announce an unprecedented social undertaking almost simultaneously with major new tax cuts reinforced the confidence. Social conscience was no longer a luxury; it was free.

Poverty was not high on John Kennedy's agenda when he took office, particularly when compared to national defense and international relations. His advisers, for the most part, did not consider poverty to be an independent problem at all, but one that would take care of itself once the economy was back on track—with the possible exception of local pockets of technological displacement in places like Appalachia. It was the civil rights movement that made poverty, particularly black poverty, an issue of foremost concern. It was well known that blacks were disproportionately poor, and a major premise of the civil rights movement was that black poverty reflected disproportionate lack of opportunity. There was a correlative, if largely implicit, assumption that once blacks had equal access to housing, jobs, and health services, their economic position would be quickly equalized. Even as Lyndon Johnson was ramming major civil rights legislation through the Congress, it was becoming clear that nothing of the kind was going to happen. The squalid black slums were growing, not shrinking. Particularly in Northern cities, drug addiction, family disintegration, and unemployment were metastasizing faster than ever.

The social disorder in the black slums created a crisis of morale in the civil rights movement. For black leaders, after the long and tearful struggle to achieve their dream of equality, the ghetto reality was a bitter cup of myrrh and gall. Sensitive to the sneers of their enemies, they reacted almost paranoiacally to any suggestion that the problem lay with blacks themselves. There was a storm of outraged protest, for example, when Daniel Moynihan wrote a report pointing to the facts of black family breakdown, even though Moynihan had intended only to build support for job training and housing programs for blacks. The issue was lethally divisive, polarizing racial issues along radical and conservative lines. To activists in the movement, the persistent black problems were simply evidence that discrimination was more pervasive and insidiously repressive than they had ever suspected, justifying the most extreme measures. The mass of white voters, on the other hand, was already showing signs of restlessness. It was one thing to support the voting rights drive in the South. But for the urban blue-collar worker, living on the fringe of the Northern black expansion, fearful for the value of his home, fearful of black crime, resentful of rising welfare rolls, it was infuriating to be told that *his* attitudes were the heart of the problem. Massive intervention by the federal government to ensure that blacks' new legal opportunity was converted into economic reality was the only way, it seemed, to prevent a dangerous split in the national polity.

When the decision was taken to eliminate poverty, Johnson's top officials—mostly holdover Kennedy technocrats, including a number of recruits from McNamara's Pentagon—set about the task with the brisk, no-nonsense, sleeves-rolled-up, let's-get-it-over-with, grim good humor that fit the cherished legend of their fallen hero. Lights burned late at brainstorming sessions all over Washington. In other times, the scale and complexity of the problem might have been daunting, but the new poverty warriors had the confidence of professional problem solvers. As John Kenneth Galbraith expressed it:

The question [of the elimination of poverty] is less one of feasibility than of will. . . . Educational deficiencies can be overcome. Mental deficiencies can be treated. Physical handicaps can be remedied. The limiting factor is not what can be done. Overwhelmingly, it is our failure to invest in people.

The robust optimism concealed a wide variety of approaches to the problem. Civil rights and union activists wanted grass-roots organization of the poor to subvert repressive power structures. Robert Kennedy and his assistants at the Justice Department pressed the expansion of their programs to organize delinquent youths, on the theory that young people needed a sense of power over their lives. The social work professionals at Health, Education, and Welfare argued for better health care, more children's services, and higher welfare payments. The Labor Department thought the key was job training and employment programs. The Ford Foundation pointed to its experiments to attack poverty by coordinating the social services that were already in place.

The tactical disputes ground down to a stalemate in early 1964, and Johnson called in Sargent Shriver, the director of the Peace Corps, to cobble together a legislative package. Shriver's compromise was a bureaucratic and diplomatic tour de force, but conceptually something of a mess; basically, it was a pastiche of all the various recommendations, ranked roughly according to the influence of their advocates. But there was a common theme: that social science had progressed to the point where it was possible to engineer a series of precisely measured modifications in the physical and psychological environment of the poor that, essentially, would cause them to act as if they were middle-class.

To the technocrats, overcoming poverty was just another systems problem like managing the economy or winning the race to the moon. Economics and space-program jargon dominated poverty task force discussions. Complicated flowcharts showed how the poor would be processed smoothly through various stages of life-skills education, literacy training, and job preparation into permanent employment. Space-age companies like Litton Industries received major contracts to train dropout youths. Community organization was discussed as a subtle form of input-output analysis, a somewhat complicated question of Skinnerian stimulus and response—adroit dollops of social pressure here would produce just the desired outcomes over there. McNamara-style program budgeting would bring entire arrays of social services to bear on each poor family—health care, treatment for drug addiction and alcoholism, marriage counseling, mental health services, whatever—to support the communal march forward to social respectability and economic independence.

The programs were supposed to produce results quickly. Shriver's main criterion for including proposals in the final package was that they had to promise visible progress before the 1966 midterm congressional elections. He courted conservative congressmen assiduously with detailed estimates of the cash savings that would accrue to the nation from reduced welfare, reduced crime, increased tax payments, public savings of all kinds, if only the programs were enacted, and there is no reason to doubt his sincerity—as director of the program he intended to be answerable for its results. Shriver also went on a campaign to induce states to raise welfare payments out of the savings from the poverty programs; since welfare rolls could be expected to drop rapidly, the nation could afford a decent payment standard for the unfortunate few who could never become self-supporting. His enthusiasm was widely shared. For example, when Nelson Rockefeller proposed the New York State Medicaid program in 1966—a comprehensive medical insurance program for the poor that was originally designed to cover almost half the state's population—he quite seriously argued, and seemed to believe, that improved medical care would cut welfare dependency so rapidly that the state would save money.

Such a massive conspiracy of self-delusion is altogether astounding. There was virtually no evidence to support almost any of the claims that were being made. Even the basic analysis of the problem was confused. Criminal black teenagers may have been an important social problem, for instance, but they accounted for only the tiniest minority of the poor. The largest single group of poor people in the country, in fact, was older white women, whose problems received hardly any attention at all. And while it was true that slum families tended to be socially disorganized and experienced high levels of drug addiction, alcoholism, and illegitimacy, there was no reason to believe that these were treatable conditions, like the mumps. All of the planning suffered from a kind of nominalist hallucination—if juvenile delinquency was a problem, the creation of something, anything, called a "juvenile delinquency program" would fix it. It was rationalism run amok. The slightest scraps of data and the broadest sociological associations—as that between education and income, for instance—were used to underpin huge, wobbly towers of interventionist hypothesis. Unfortunately, the fact that upper-income people tended to have good educations did not mean that literacy training in the slums would raise people out of poverty. There has been exhaustive analysis and reanalysis of the educational data since the 1960s, and it is still not clear whether income follows education or vice versa. It was the sheerest wishful thinking, however, to assume that programs which, under the best of circumstances, might increase a semiliterate adult's reading skills by a grade level or so would have any measurable general effect on income levels. But if there were lingering doubts, they were quickly dispelled by the ideological crisis in the civil rights movement. Massive intervention was not only logically elegant and fiscally sound, it was morally right. Rationalist conviction wedded to moralist fervor was a formidable combination that swept away doubts and inconsistencies.

I was not among the doubters when I arrived in Trenton, an aging blue-collar city of 100,000 people trapped in crepuscular anonymity between the shadows of New York and Philadelphia. There were five of us on the core staff of the new antipoverty program headed by a bright and affable ex-reporter, Greg Farrell, who had been chosen for the job because he had written a newspaper series about the War on Poverty, and therefore knew more about it than anyone else available. The others included a social worker and community organizer, the only black; an ex-union organizer, with some experience on manpower training programs; an ex-student radical, who had decided to "work within the system"; and myself—I had been a reading teacher and a fledgling corporate executive. The oldest of us was thirty-two, the rest in our twenties.

Even collectively, we knew very little about starting an assault on poverty, and we eagerly devoured the flood of written material that was flowing out of Washington—quite explicit how-to documents, not unlike instructions for building a boat in the basement. I remember reading several books on program budgeting, or PPBS, which was being touted as the philosopher's stone of social programming, and wondering why I was missing the point. The principle of planning on the basis of expected outcomes seemed obvious enough, but I was sure there was more to it than that—otherwise why such an enormous flap of interest in the technique? On the other hand, when I spoke to local school board officials about the use of program budgeting, I made it sound profound —doing my part to maintain the pecking order of mystification. It didn't occur to me that the people in Washington were winging it the same way.

In those first days of the antipoverty program, the emphasis was on getting funded—designing programs and sending off grant applications to Washington. When we began to organize the Trenton program, we had only about two months to get our grant applications into the national office before spending authority dried up at the close of the federal fiscal year. All of us could write, and we started grinding out program applications—everything we could conceive of. We assumed hundreds of other cities around the country were doing the same thing, and we would be lucky to get even a few programs funded. In fact, most cities were paralyzed by start-up politics, and the grant programs turned out to be undersubscribed. In the space of about two weeks in June, at first to our delight and then with something more akin to horror, we received a string of telegrams informing us that essentially everything we'd asked for would be funded—prekindergarten programs, literacy training, summer jobs for youth, manpower training and employment services for adults, recreational programs, social workers, homemaking instructors, tens of millions of dollars' worth—on a per capita basis, someone calculated, more than any other city in the country.

Trenton got more than its fair share, but federal officials were anxious to spend their budgets—during that June, award telegrams went out across the entire country. The sudden availability of hundreds of millions of dollars with few strings attached had predictable consequences. In New York City, for example, battle was immediately joined between City Hall, the state house, Adam Clayton Powell and the black political establishment, radical social agencies, the old-line settlement houses, the civil rights groups, local black ministers, and militant new Puerto Rican organizations, all of them sniffing the scent of power, money, and patronage. There were marches, sit-ins, pickets, and filibusters in the Congress, and vitriolic exchanges between City Hall and Albany. Black groups fought with Puerto Rican groups; community organizations wrecked each other's offices. The program results, according to one federal official, were "a lot of garbage." Across the river in Newark, the politics were less complicated, but no less chaotic. In order to ensure equitably distributed "community control," the antipoverty program was organized in the form of cascading tiers of governing boards, with almost a thousand members in total. Few of the people had any idea what they were supposed to do, or why they were sitting on the boards, and the programs quickly degenerated into internecine warfare among the poor. Harried Washington officials, who just a few months before had been confidently designing grand schemes of social uplift, hovered anxiously on the sidelines, trying to coax applications for pet programs out of the quarreling and confusion.

Politics in Trenton were blander than in New York or Newark. To his credit, the mayor, Arthur Holland, was compulsively honest, and the black community was still docile. So after some initial months of floundering, our programs became—purely in a relative sense—models of efficiency. There were functioning neighborhood centers, a full menu of programs, almost a hundred staff, several thousand people receiving some kind of service, and more or less adequate financial controls. Trenton began to enjoy a small reputation as a city where the antipoverty programs worked, and we began to be called upon to consult with other cities; rather to our surprise, we were experts. The reputation was flattering, but it provoked uneasiness. It didn't require an excess of intellectual honesty to realize that our programs were, at best, *running* rather than *working*. Viewed with bleak detachment, there was no reason to suppose that our programs, even if they got better and better, would eliminate poverty in Trenton. In ten years, there would still be welfare mothers and welfare children, there would still be slums, there would still be isolated old people, there would still be alcoholics, and drug addicts, and criminals and hustlers, there would still be dilapidated housing and neglected children.

The interesting question is why anyone would have expected otherwise. I think the answer rests with a kind of professional courtesy extended among experts in that era of expertise. Social workers never questioned that economists had plumbed all the mysteries of the economy; and the economists who designed the antipoverty program never doubted the availability of a similarly encompassing social technology. The social work theory of the 1960s was heavily psychologized, which is why, I suspect, the antipoverty program was premised on the assumption that poverty existed primarily in the heads of the poor. The antipoverty program emphatically rejected the notion that the way to solve poverty was to give people more money; it aimed instead to change people's behavior. Poverty was not so much a lack of money, but a "condition of helplessness, hopelessness, and despair," as one official how-to guide put it. To an extent, of course, the focus was justified: delinquent teenagers and unemployed drug addicts need to straighten out their act if they are to cease to be a drain on public resources. But the disproportionately psychologized outlook of the programs had two consequences. For one, it caused a serious underestimate of the money that would be required really to make a dent in poverty. Since the largest number of the poor, like the older white women, were hardly in need of attitudinal reform, it would cost a lot of money, as we learned a decade later, to give them a decent income. Secondly, it fostered the illusion of the quick victory. If the problem was primarily one of attitude, and if a technology existed to deal with attitudes and outlooks, one had only to bring the technology to bear to solve the problem. The psychological emphasis is particularly characteristic of the 1960s and is worth some discussion in its own right.

Psychological Warfare

Americans, or at least upper-middle-class Americans, began to worry about their happiness in the 1950s. It was a disease of affluence; before that, such rarified concerns were crowded out by the more clamorous requirements of winning the war or having enough to eat. A change in mood was signaled by David Riesman's best-seller, *The Lonely Crowd,* published in 1950, which argued that the American pursuit of success was creating a nation of tensely rigid conformists. The book set the terms of cocktail party conversation for the next ten years and spawned a minor industry of self-criticism—John Keats's *The Crack in the Picture Window* and William H. Whyte's *The Organization Man* are typical examples. The country began officially to worry about worrying in 1957, when Congress established the Joint Commission on Mental Illness and Health to find out, among other things:

> How well or badly adjusted do [Americans] . . . consider themselves to be? Are they happy or unhappy, worried or unworried, optimistic or pessimistic in their outlook? Do they feel strong or weak; adequate or inadequate? What troubles Americans, as they see themselves? And what do people do about their troubles?

The original impetus for the creation of the commission was the pressing need for reform in state mental hospitals. By the mid-1950s, mental hospital beds were the fastest growing medical sector in the country, and patients in most large state "insane asylums" lived in conditions of bestial degradation. The glimmer of hope was that new families of psychoactive drugs could bring schizophrenic hallucinations under temporary control and mitigate the necessity for close confinement.

The commission recommended the creation of a system of community mental health centers on the theory that drug therapy would make treatment at home a practical and inexpensive alternative—and a much more humane one—for most patients in the insane asylums. The logic was admirable, but as so often happens with social reform in America, the process of building the constituency necessary to pass a program required that reasonable goals and sensible objectives become vastly inflated. By the time its recommendations were embodied in the Community Mental Health Act of 1962, the commission had cast its net far beyond the relatively straightforward problem of the mental hospitals, and mental health had taken on the aspect of an evangelical movement, the kind of fashionable cause Jacqueline Kennedy and her friends lobbied for. The final legislation contained a long list of mandatory services aimed at solving almost any problem of unhappiness or maladjustment —marital counseling, delinquency services, programs for unwed mothers, alcoholism treatment—most of which had little to do with the chronic schizophrenics languishing in the state hospitals. In fact, to make funds available for the new services, large numbers of state patients, many of them seriously ill, were simply discharged, with no follow-up services, to make their way as best they could.

The mental health legislation marked the emergence of the social work profession as a powerful interest group in its own right. Women entered college in large numbers for the first time following World War II, and social work was one of the few professions open to the career-oriented among them. It was also a next-best answer for Jewish men— a way to satisfy their strong professional orientation short of attending law school or medical school. As the graduate schools of social work assumed greater importance in the universities, there was an urge to acquire a respectable professional apparatus—theoretical models of social deviance and officially sanctioned modes of professional intervention, most often a bastardized form of Freudian psychotherapy, but including an eclectic admixture of whatever social and psychological theories were from time to time in fashion. Social work acquired a heavily psychologized jargon and a patina of professional expertise. Welfare investigators talked of "exploring family psychodynamics" and "providing treatment" to their cases. Residential programs for delinquent teenagers became "milieu therapy." A misbehaving youngster was "acting out his conflicts." Busy work for mental patients became "occupational therapy." The prison workshop, where the inmates made license plates or did laundry, became, with a straight face, "the skills development component of the correctional treatment program."

The new social work profession, or pseudo profession, organized much of its theoretical material around juvenile delinquency—there were psychodynamic theories, functional theories, "labeling" theories, theories of class conflict. The creation of the family court was premised on the assumption that every criminal youngster was somehow psychologically or socially disabled and in need of a "treatment" that would cure his criminal proclivities. Superficially, at least, many of the treatment programs achieved quite positive results, for the simple reason that a very large proportion of teenagers commit criminal offenses, and almost all of them become law-abiding as they get older, whether they are "treated" or not. Juvenile delinquency was the hot item in social work therapy, and it exercised a disproportionate influence on the War on Poverty. Robert Kennedy's staff at the Justice Department added weight to the emphasis on youth; they had been working on antidelinquency programs for some years and saw the new effort as a major opportunity to expand their programs. And finally, unruly black teenagers were one of the visible signs of urban problems, particularly during the "long, hot summers"—the swordbearers, some feared and others hoped, of an underclass revolution.

The upsurge of interest in mental health, the existence of a large and psychologically oriented social work profession, the focus on juvenile delinquency, where the "treatment" ethic already prevailed—all predisposed toward the assumption that the War on Poverty would be fought for the heads, if not actually the hearts and minds, of the poor. It was the classic rationalist error. The simplest models of reality were developed from the most partial data. Simplified problem analysis led to neatly symmetrical solutions, with elegance preferred over relevance.

The War on Poverty was, unfortunately, not the only example of rationalist misconceptions and overreaching. At about the same time as the antipoverty initiatives were collapsing into unseemly struggles for power and patronage, the administration's war in Southeast Asia was lurching to a bloody stalemate, and the developing tragedy bore, grossly speaking, the same hallmarks as the misadventures at home.

The War Abroad

There was a fateful symmetry between Lyndon Johnson's War on Poverty and his War in Vietnam, besides the obloquy heaped upon both ventures by his successors. As with the War on Poverty, the American objectives in Vietnam were expressed psychologically. The intent was never to win a classic military victory, but to "win the hearts and minds" of the South Vietnamese for democracy, or to "convince the North Vietnamese that they could not win," or to "demonstrate to our allies that we stand by our commitments," or to "persuade the Communists to give up their attempts of force and subversion." And, again as in the War on Poverty, there were the same complicated rationalist chains of reasoning: if the United States does *x*, then the South Vietnamese will do *y*, which will cause the North Vietnamese to do *z*, and so on.

The Flaming Dart and Rolling Thunder bombing programs against North Vietnam and the Ho Chi Minh supply trail illustrate the rationalist, incrementalist style of strategic thinking. The original decision to bomb the North was taken after a Viet Cong attack on the American adviser barracks at Pleiku. The assumption was that punishing the North would force Ho to exercise greater control over the Viet Cong and eventually to see that his self-interest lay in a negotiated settlement. The defense intellectuals called it the "compellence" theory of bombing. It was important, therefore, that the bombing be surgically directed and that the pressure be increased only gradually, much to the chagrin of the military, who wanted massive attacks to destroy the North's fighting ability once and for all. Ambassador Lodge expressed the twisting logic of the theory this way:

> If you lay the whole country waste, it is quite likely you will introduce a mood of fatalism in the Viet Cong. Also, there will be nobody left in North Viet Nam on whom to put pressure. . . . What we are interested in here is not destroying Ho Chi Minh (as his successor will probably be worse than he is), but getting him to change his behavior.

The theory was grounded on a landfill of false premises. In the first place, it was not at all clear that Ho actually could control the Viet Cong (or, as later diplomatic failures demonstrated, that the Russians or Chinese could control Ho). Secondly, the notion that bombing could be applied "surgically" and that its diplomatic and military effects could be measured with precision was an intellectual's illusion. The bombing results were never clear-cut, and their interpretation occasioned bitter intrabureaucratic squabbles between the Air Force generals and the CIA and civilian Pentagon analysts, particularly after Ho dispersed his limited industrial capacity throughout the countryside. Moreover, the diplomatic semaphores between Ho and the United States were inherently ambiguous, like sending "smoke signals in a high wind," as one Pentagon official put it. Several times, when Johnson ordered bombing pauses to encourage negotiations, Ho overtly stepped up the pace of supplies to the South and then, maddeningly, just after the bombing resumed again, sent a signal—always a clouded one—that he was interested in talking. Conversely, the one or two times Ho seemed to respond positively to a negotiating initiative, as in the Operation Marigold diplomatic assault of 1966, the opportunity was aborted by untimely bombing, either because of military bloody-mindedness, or, more likely, because the administration was unable to impose sufficiently fine coordination upon its military and diplomatic apparatus. By 1967, trapped in a labyrinthine logic of his own making, Johnson was resisting bombing pauses out of fear that Ho's failure to respond would strengthen the right-wing voices demanding a massive increase in the scale of the bombing.

Most importantly, the Rolling Thunder strategy failed because, in all likelihood, Ho and his politburo never saw any persuasive reason to stake the outcome on negotiations. Civil wars are almost never settled by compromise. The American, the Russian, the Spanish, and, ultimately, the Vietnamese civil wars all ground on until one side or the other was totally defeated. Ho viewed the fighting through a wholly different set of lenses than that of the defense intellectuals. As Paul Warnke said upon leaving the Pentagon in 1969, "The trouble with our policy in Vietnam is that we anticipated that the North Vietnamese would behave like reasonable people." By 1967, the administration was straining every diplomatic channel to convince Hanoi, almost plaintively, that the United States wanted only a face-saving solution. All of the pragmatic optimization scenarios showed that Ho's best strategy was to allow the United States to leave with "honor," then take over the country at his leisure. But Ho didn't frame the problem the same way. He had devoted his life to his cause, and the prize had too often been snatched from his grasp, almost at the moment of triumph. Game theory, "minimax" concepts, and microeconomic maximization principles were simply irrelevant; he was interested in winning, and was willing to stay the course and pay the price.

Ho's unwillingness to come to the bargaining table has been conveniently forgotten by liberals in their latter-day rush to distance themselves from Johnson's Vietnam policies. But almost to a man, the same liberals insisted on negotiations as a prerequisite to a settlement. Until well into 1966 and 1967, and even considerably beyond, there was virtually no one, inside or outside of the administration, advising unilateral withdrawal, or withdrawal without some significant North Vietnamese or Viet Cong concessions. Political critics from the left, like Eugene McCarthy and Robert Kennedy, and later even George McGovern, never proposed that the United States simply leave; they always proposed that the United States *negotiate*. The strongest attacks from the press, like those of Walter Lippmann, Neil Sheehan, and David Halberstam, always presupposed that Ho would negotiate if only Johnson asked him to. Even George Ball, the earliest and the strongest dissenter within the administration, always stopped short of recommending just pulling out and leaving the South to its fate. Only Wayne Morse and Ernest Gruening in the Senate, and one or two middle-level State Department officials, like Paul Kattenburg, were prepared to face the consequences of total and unconditional withdrawal without negotiations, and they were almost totally without influence. Morse and Gruening, in particular, were viewed as a kind of radical fringe by the liberal establishment, including the professional "doves" on the Foreign Relations Committee, like William Fulbright, Frank Church, and Joseph Clark. When Johnson argued with Lippmann in 1965 about negotiations, he asked if Lippmann was proposing "the Wayne Morse way, which amounts to turning the place over to the communists." Lippmann wasn't. The assumption by liberals that the North wanted to bargain later infuriated Henry Kissinger, who argued, with some justice, that in his secret talks he had offered every incentive that any dove had ever proposed but to no avail. Ho was satisfied to win the war his own way.

Liberals also like to forget that, until rather late in the day, they generally supported the war. The Washington *Post* and the *New York Times,* for instance, supported the war policy at least through 1966, and even the *New Republic* was still backing the administration in 1965. In fact, almost right up to the Tet offensive in 1968, American support for the war was overwhelming. After Johnson's decisive escalation in 1965, his polls showed that 10 percent of the public wanted "to go hotheaded —Goldwater types," as Johnson put it—20 percent wanted more bombing, and the rest thought the administration's policies about right. Both Kennedy and Johnson felt they had more to fear from the right if Vietnam was lost than from the left if they pursued the war. It was fear of right-wing reaction if Vietnam was lost that caused Kennedy to acquiesce in the coup against Diem in 1963 and then endure a comic-opera succession of military dictatorships in order to keep the war alive. The men in charge of the government, the editorial writers and political commentators, the congressmen who voted for the Tonkin Gulf Resolution, it will be recalled, had seen within their professional careers the loss of China to the Communists, the Soviet conquest of Eastern Europe, and the Korean War. To these men, to whom Munich had been a formative experience, the necessity of containment, the logic of the domino theory, and the danger to India from aggressive Asian Communism did not seem such idle concerns, regardless of the opinions of the youthful protesters who were beginning to stir on the campuses. Most voters seemed to agree. The majority of the country wanted out of Vietnam, but only with a victory. Significantly, three-fifths of the people who voted for *McCarthy* in the 1968 New Hampshire primary thought that Johnson was insufficiently aggressive in pursuing a military victory.

By the mid-1970s, it was difficult to find anyone who would admit to having been a war supporter, or who, if he admitted it, would not protest at having been somehow gulled. Indeed, I suspect that much of the antigovernment spirit of the 1970s—the "post-Watergate morality," the elaborate safeguards against executive action, the curbing of executive secrecy—stem in good part from liberals' attempt to exonerate themselves from complicity in the war. It was easier to claim deception by a renegade President or Presidents than to concede collective responsibility. As Ian Maitland, Henry Fairlie, and Leslie Gelb have separately pointed out, however, anyone at all attentive to foreign policy knew, or should have known, where the war was going. This is not to say that there was no duplicity. The military, for example, consistently emphasized the positive when reporting, and the Air Force always disseminated the most insupportably optimistic reports on bombing runs. But the professional soldiers were quite forthright from the early 1960s on what was required to win militarily in Vietnam—up to a million men and five to seven years. The Tonkin Gulf incident that Johnson used to justify the initial bombing of the North may never, in fact, have actually happened. But jittery crewmen *thought* it did, which is quite different from staging a provocation. In any case, the Congress was quite aware of what it was so enthusiastically voting for when the Tonkin Gulf Resolution was passed. Senator Fulbright, the bill's floor manager, stated on the floor that the resolution gave the President power to expand the war and carry it to the enemy virtually wherever and when-

ever and as much as he pleased. If the rationalist defense analysts
expected far too much from the limited bombing campaign, it was not
because the military deceived them. Despite its own press releases, the
Air Force was privately steadfast in its insistence that limited bombing
was of little value. If large numbers of policymakers, journalists, congressmen, and liberal intellectuals chose to delude themselves about the
war, or their ability to wage it at low cost, or its ultimate outcome, it
was their own delusion, and one virtually endemic among the liberal
establishment of the day.

Ironically, North Vietnam's delusions may have been of the same
scale as America's. Despite the American preoccupation with guerrilla
warfare, the North repeatedly resorted to pitched-battle tactics, almost
always with disastrous results. In almost a mirror image of the American miscalculations, Ho seemed to believe that each new escalation
would be enough finally to turn the tide. After Kennedy introduced
American advisers on a large scale, Ho responded by sending in Northern regulars, and then sharply escalated the scale of the fighting during
the Buddhist crisis and the Saigon student riots in 1963. He escalated
again in 1964, when the post-Diem military regime seemed about to
topple. The direct attacks on American bases in 1964, and the willingness of the Northern troops to engage in full-scale conventional firefights
in 1965, seem part of a strategy to drive the Americans from the country, perhaps banking on Johnson's declaration that American troops
would not carry the burden of the fighting directly.

In his own comments on the war, Vo Nguyen Giap, the North's chief
strategist, stresses that victory was won with "large-scale combined
attacks with many large strategic army columns equipped with modern
weapons and having high mobility." Giap seems to have been mesmer-
ized by his great victory against the French at Dien Bien Phu. His
stand-and-fight tactics were wholly inappropriate against the Americans, however, who had such an immense advantage in firepower and
mechanized mobility. When Giap attempted to invest the Marine outpost at Khe Sanh, in 1967, for instance, his troops suffered appalling
casualties before they withdrew. Khe Sanh may have been a diversion
to set the stage for Giap's great Tet holiday offensive in 1968, and if so,
it was a bold tactic, but one pursued at prodigal cost.

Tet was the turning point of the war, and an immense psychological
victory for the North. The mere fact that Ho and Giap could mount
such well-coordinated and sustained conventional attacks throughout

the country called the entire American and South Vietnamese war effort into question and put the lie to all the roseate statistics that had been emanating from Saigon. But large segments of Ho's army were annihilated in the counterattacks that followed—in the bitter struggle for Hué, for example. The Communist military infrastructure in the South was so badly chewed up by the post-Tet American counteroffensive that it took Ho and Giap more than two years to rebuild it; in strictly conventional terms, once the initial surprise was over, they absorbed a fearful beating. And the Tet offensive might not even have led to an "agonizing reappraisal" on the part of the Americans, if the Joint Chiefs had not seized upon it as a politically opportune moment to ask for major new call-ups of troops to rebuild their strategic reserve. William Westmoreland, the general on the spot, was surprised when he was told to ask for more soldiers. He thought he had come out on top in Tet and needed only minor reinforcements. But Westmoreland dutifully prepared the request—for 206,000 men on top of the 600,000 already committed—and when it got to the White House, Johnson interpreted it as a confirmation of a major defeat and called for the complete review of policy that culminated in his resignation. Perhaps Ho and Giap were shrewd enough to divine how events would unfold; but that seems implausible. More likely, they squandered their military strength in a misconceived attempt to replicate their great victory against the French, but were spared the consequences of their own miscalculations by the compounded miscalculations of the Americans. History—and lucrative book contracts—await the faceless functionary who will supply us with North Vietnam's version of the Pentagon Papers.

Failure

Lyndon Johnson's decision not to run for a second term sounded the knell for the rationalist era that had been ushered in just eight years before. All of his and John Kennedy's proud new policy initiatives lay in shattered wreckage. In Vietnam, it was clear that American firepower and troops could prevent a Communist takeover indefinitely, but only if the country was prepared to endure a continued high rate of casualties, provide open-ended subsidies to the repressive military dictatorship in the South, and risk an irretrievable loss of national comity. A "victory," in the sense of winning the country for democracy, was by then a cynic's sour joke. More devastatingly, America had lost its postwar illusion of omnipotence. John Kennedy had suggested that America lacked merely the will to achieve global greatness. The expenditure of $100 billion in Vietnam and the loss of 50,000 American lives, if nothing else, demonstrated resolve. But the enterprise was a failure; the result was only corrosive doubt and disillusionment. Kennedy and Johnson had told the country that it did not know the limits of its greatness. Now it did, and they were crushingly small, and it had still to plumb the depths of its weakness.

At home, Johnson's dreams of a Great Society were dashed; his "beautiful woman," as he liked to call his antipoverty programs, had become a bedizened old whore. Appalled by the confusion and disorder in local programs, and reinforced by the rising tide of urban violence, conservatives in Congress moved to standardize programs and restrict local flexibility. The result, inevitably, was a progressive bureaucratization, a takeover by social work professionals, and a stifling of any unorthodox initiatives, no matter how promising. To the profound disappointment of community organization activists, the local antipoverty agencies were rapidly transmuting into tired civil service organizations, preoccupied with job grades and tenure, hardly the advance guard of a new age of social reform. The brave talk of curing poverty in ten years had become yet another sour joke.

Johnson's last spasmodic attempt to rescue his Great Society was the Model Cities program, launched in 1966. It was a sign of the times that the program's name was changed, after some embarrassment, from its original "Demonstration Cities," because the word "demonstration" had by this time acquired so many unpleasant associations. Johnson may have lacked the polished patina of Kennedy's Harvard technocrats, but he shared, and in many ways magnified, their rationalist assumptions. The original plan for Model Cities was to focus on just a handful of metropolises and bring all the resources of the federal government to bear in one massive effort to turn them around, to make them models of everything Johnson hoped to accomplish. It turned out to be impossible to keep the program sharply focused on just a few target cities, and for a politician of Johnson's astuteness, it was naive even to consider doing so. The price of getting the program through Congress was that it had to be expanded to include every city of any size in the country. And, of course, with the pressures of the war, the result was that the program's resources were so thinly distributed that it could not make a sizeable impression anywhere. Model Cities became just an adjunct of the antipoverty program, with slightly more emphasis on housing and physical development. Urban decay continued apace.

It is a common refrain that the Great Society programs failed because they were starved for funds by Johnson's war in Vietnam. My own view is that high levels of funding would merely have added to the chaos and would have made the ultimate task of dismantling ineffective bureaucracies that much more painful and disruptive. The reality was that the programs were, even at their very best, only tenuously related to whatever it is that causes people to lead disorganized lives, to stay on welfare, or to compete ineffectively for jobs. The whole effort was founded on the misconception that there was a technology available for purchase that would solve a kaleidoscope of subtly varied problems. There was no such technology. Most programs helped some people, and a few programs, usually small ones, run by charismatic individuals, were quite successful. But there were no programs which were capable, on a mass scale, of moving people out of poverty by mobilization of their own resources and keeping them out. It just wasn't so.

Like the war in Vietnam, the illusions of the antipoverty program persisted because so many people—and not just Kennedy technocrats —were so anxious to be gulled. In 1968, for example, the top executives of the country's major businesses decided to take the manpower problem in hand and began to claim significant success in Detroit. I was working in the New Jersey governor's office at the time, and at his request, I went out to see what the secret was. Employment offices had been set up throughout the poor neighborhoods, and thousands of men had been hired into the automobile and related industries. Top executives were manning the neighborhood offices or, from their own desks, were tracking individual cases through the system. (I sat in several soccer-field-sized offices myself and saw it happen. The commitment was most impressive.) Probing more deeply, I found what I had already become jaded enough to expect. All of those industries normally hired large numbers of seasonal laborers on an hourly basis. The pay was good, but the jobs were uncertain, and the workers were overwhelmingly black, most of them from Detroit's poorer neighborhoods. The massive employment effort was merely filling those same jobs—no more, no less— but through a different set of employment offices and with a lot more management ceremony. For the most part, the same men were probably being hired; or perhaps unemployment was being shifted slightly, if that was of any value. The program was a fake, although not intentionally so. Hardheaded business executives were as capable of self-delusion as anyone else.

Perhaps most disappointing to the original advocates of the antipoverty program was the sharp nationwide rise in welfare dependency. The basic welfare caseload—Aid to Families of Dependent Children, or AFDC—*quintupled* between 1960 and 1975, with most of the growth concentrated between 1965 and 1970, that is, roughly coincident with the launching of the Great Society programs. Spending increased even faster than the caseload because average grants were being increased at the same time. The cost of Medicaid, the welfare medicine program that Governor Rockefeller, it will be recalled, hoped would reduce welfare in New York, soared from zero in 1965 to $12 billion ten years later. Far from reducing welfare, the antipoverty programs contributed to its increase. One of the first priorities of the activist organizers in most community action programs was getting better treatment from welfare centers, particularly for blacks, who were systematically excluded from welfare benefits in many parts of the country. Civil rights lawyers won a series of signal Supreme Court decisions that protected the privacy of recipients against welfare investigators and extended the "equal protection" clause of the Constitution to the administration of benefit programs. Charles Reich wrote an influential law journal article on the "New Property," listing welfare as a basic, constitutionally protected right. Welfare rights organizations formed throughout the country and demonstrated, and occasionally rioted, for faster case processing and better grants. The net result was that in the poor community the stigma of receiving welfare was effectively removed. In New York City, for example, only about a third of people who were eligible for welfare in the early 1960s actually received it; it was considered disgraceful to apply. By 1975, some two-thirds of the eligible black families and three-quarters of the eligible Hispanic families were on the rolls. With a clarity of logic that had somehow eluded the antipoverty program designers, poor people readily appreciated that bigger welfare checks were a more direct and certain way to increase their incomes than the confusing personal-improvement schemes hawked by Washington. The administration had hoped to eliminate both poverty and dependence at low cost. By 1970, it was making a small dent in the poverty problem, but only by spending vastly greater amounts on income support programs and by enormously increasing dependency. We can only speculate about the long-term effects on the ability of the poor to achieve economic self-sufficiency, but they are troublesome.

The last proud pillar of Kennedy's technocratic policy platform was his economic program. But the cost of waging and losing wars on both the domestic and the international fronts was too much of a strain. With the pusillanimous concurrence of his Council of Economic Advisers (proving that economists were politicians as much as they were scientists), Johnson refused to ask for a tax increase to finance the escalation in Vietnam in 1966 because he was afraid that Congress would respond by cutting his domestic spending programs. Strict Keynesian policy called for a major tax increase to finance the war. The economy had been running flat out for five years and was already showing signs of a classic late-boom inflation, when production bottlenecks and labor shortages start to put upward pressure on prices. The sudden stimulus of new military spending stripped the economic gears, and by 1968, when Johnson finally asked for his war tax, the inflation rate was passing the 6 percent mark. As of 1982, the economy had still not worked its way out of its inflationary problems, although it is not fair to blame, as some commentators are wont to do, the entire fifteen-year inflationary run on Johnson's Vietnam policies. Other factors, like the energy crisis, played a major role; by the early 1970s, the lingering impact of the Vietnam fiscal policies was too small even to calculate. But if Johnson's economic errors were not as cataclysmic as his detractors would urge, still he strayed indefensibly far from sound principles and precipitated an era of economic uncertainty as debilitating as any since the Great Depression itself.

The entire rationalist policy structure had collapsed. The economy was heating up beyond control, the Great Society programs were a failure, and a third-rate Communist power had beaten America in a war of America's choosing. There was really nothing left of the policies that Kennedy had initiated with such glorious panache and blazing enthusiasm only eight years before. Pervasive failure called basic principles into question. There was a moral and intellectual vacuum which irrationalisms of every kind rushed to fill. Moral debate was supplanted by mere stridency, reason by romantic effusion, and political dialogue, in the cities and on the campuses, was transmuted into incendiary violence.

VI

VIOLENCE

The 1960s violence started with the reaction of Southern police to civil rights activists. The most sustained violent confrontation of the movement took place throughout the spring of 1965, in and around Selma, Alabama. A nationwide television audience saw police use dogs, horses, clubs, tear gas, fire hoses, and cattle prods against defenseless marchers. A clergyman and a housewife, both white civil rights sympathizers from the North, were murdered.

Early in 1965, the Students for a Democratic Society (SDS) announced plans for a march in Washington to protest the war in Vietnam. The students' liberal supporters, particularly those from the civil rights movement, were mostly opposed to the idea, because it would distract attention from civil rights and alienate the President. Then the administration began the Rolling Thunder bombing of the North, and to SDS surprise, twenty thousand people showed up for the march, most of them students, from more than fifty campuses, but also including representatives from all the major liberal and radical organizations. The same week, faculty at the University of Michigan decided to suspend classes to protest the bombings and held an all-day and all-night "teach-in" on the war. The idea was quickly picked up at other universities around the country, and on May 15, a national teach-in, with telephone hook-up to 122 colleges and universities, was held in Washington. The first teach-ins attempted to debate both sides of the Vietnam issue; but at Berkeley later in May a teach-in attended by twelve thousand students turned into an antiwar rally, and set the pattern for the massive campus antiwar demonstrations that marked the rest of the decade.

Three months later, in August, in the Watts section of Los Angeles, a California state patrolman attempted to arrest a drunken driver, Marquette Frye. The arrest was apparently proper, and Frye's mother, who was on the scene, pleaded with him to go quietly. Frye resisted and was handled roughly. Frye's mother and brother intervened and were arrested. A crowd gathered, and there were grumbles that it was "just like Selma." A woman spit on the police, and they shoved a path through the crowd to arrest her. Police reinforcements arrived to hustle away the arrestees, and the crowd began to throw bottles and rocks. More police arrived and were met with a hail of missiles. Some fires were set. By early morning the police had dispersed the crowds with minor injuries on both sides and a small number of arrests. A tense day followed—and then Watts suddenly erupted in a spectacular orgy of burning and looting. The National Guard was called in, and the riot was eventually put down with a heavy use of firepower. Thirty-four people were killed, hundreds were injured, four thousand were arrested. Property damage was estimated at $35 million. The slogan "Burn, baby, burn!" swept through the nation's black ghettos.

The year 1965 closed with antiwar demonstrations in more than sixty cities, many of them accompanied by marginal violence. Fifteen thousand people marched on an armory in Oakland and were beaten back by police. There was the first public draft card burning in New York. There was another massive march on Washington. In separate incidents, two men, emulating the Buddhist bonzes of 1963, publicly burnt themselves to death to protest the war.

There was scattered ghetto violence in most major cities in 1966. In Chicago, three days of rock throwing, firebombing, and random gunfire followed a police attempt to turn off fire hydrants in black neighborhoods during a heat wave. It took four thousand guardsmen to restore order; three blacks were killed by stray bullets, including a thirteen-year-old boy and a fourteen-year-old pregnant girl. Four blacks were killed in Cleveland amid reports that extremists were trying to precipitate paramilitary action against the police.

Stokely Carmichael took control of SNCC, and whites were officially disinvited from participating in its organizing activities. The SNCC voting drive in Lowndes County, Alabama, unfurled the Black Panther banner. SNCC made contact with revolutionary regimes in Cuba and

Africa, and when a black SNCC worker was murdered for using a whites-only rest room in Alabama, a SNCC statement linked the killing with the war in Vietnam—part of the white colonial drive to "squash liberation movements" of people of color throughout the world. Later in the summer, Carmichael leaped to the platform at a rally in Greenwood, Mississippi, cut short the crowd's incantation of the familiar civil rights refrain, "Freedom now!" and shouted out the new slogan: "Black Power!"

Early in 1966, faced with the need for increased call-ups to supply ground troops in Vietnam, Johnson ended the automatic draft deferment for graduate students. The *Harvard Crimson* called the move "certainly unfair" to students—the war, presumably, should have been fought by working-class hoplites. There were demonstrations on most major campuses to protest military recruitment and the transmission of grade information to draft boards. By fall, there were two hundred SDS chapters throughout the country, virtually all of them dedicated to organizing protests and demonstrations against the war—draft card burnings, teach-ins, disruption of ROTC activities, mass marches, torchlight parades, strikes against classes.

By 1967, the civil rights movement was moribund, its moral claims drowned out by the rising demand for black separatism, and its moderate field leaders distracted by well-paid opportunities in the antipoverty program. Lingering rights intransigence in the South was eclipsed by explosive violence in the North. A white policeman was stomped to death in Plainfield, New Jersey, after shooting a black man. Twenty-six people—twenty-four of them black—were killed in a wild week of burning, looting, and gunfire in Newark. Forty-three people—ten of them white—were killed, and hundreds burned out of their homes, in an even wilder outbreak in Detroit. The property damage in the Detroit riot was estimated at $45 million, the worst in American history. There were serious disturbances in fourteen other New Jersey cities that summer, as well as in Tampa, Cincinnati, and Atlanta. Every black slum in the country reverberated with the rumblings of imminent violence.

In February 1967, the National Black Power Conference voted to oppose the draft as a conspiracy against black youth. And in April, the Spring Mobilization against the war drew hundreds of thousands of people to New York's Central Park, where there was a mass draft card burning, and where Martin Luther King made a major address against the war, breaking ranks with the moderate civil rights leadership. The Reverend William Sloane Coffin organized draft card burnings in Boston and Washington, and was arrested for dumping a case of rejected draft cards in the offices of the Pentagon. In the fall, there were street battles between police and students in San Francisco and Oakland, as Berkeley students announced new "mobile strike" tactics. Fifty thousand people marched on the Pentagon; flying squads attempted to breach military police lines and raid the offices. Jerry Rubin and Abbie Hoffman, founders of the Youth International Party—Y.I.P., or "Yippies"—announced they would levitate the Pentagon three hundred feet into the air and spray the crowd with LACE, a chemical that would cause everyone to be overcome with uncontrollable sexual urges. Allen Ginsberg sat on the sidelines and chanted a mantra. Norman Mailer got himself arrested and wrote a best-selling book, *Armies of the Night.*

The next year, 1968, opened with the Tet offensive, undercutting all the administration's claims to progress in Vietnam; the antiwar demonstrations intensified. On March 31, Lyndon Johnson announced that he was rejecting the military's demand for more troops, was ending the bombing, and would withdraw from the presidential race. On March 28, Martin Luther King addressed a crowd in Memphis during a garbage strike. To his despair, the rally degenerated into a riot, and a black youth was killed. On April 4, King was murdered, and savage looting and burning broke out in every major city in the country. Flames crackled within three blocks of the White House. Mayor Daley of Chicago ordered his police to "shoot to kill" looters. Two months later, Robert Kennedy was murdered, right after scoring a narrow victory in the California presidential primary. In August, ten thousand demonstrators, about half antiwar students, half political radicals and Yippies, and almost all white, descended upon Chicago to disrupt the Democratic Convention. There were running battles with the police the entire week, culminating in a wild melee on the last night of the convention. Police and demonstrators threw tactics to the winds and fought with clubs and rocks throughout the city, grimly and out of control. Demonstrators chanted "The whole world is watching" on national television, and Mayor Daley shouted obscenities at a platform speaker. Acrid fumes of tear gas drifted into the convention hall as Hubert Humphrey was being nominated. The consensus on which democratic government depended seemed to be coming apart.

Violence as Ideology

The 1960s were a decade of violence, often pointless violence—like the bombing at the University of Wisconsin that killed a young instructor. But even random violence, it was quite seriously argued in intellectual circles, was in itself purposeful; more, it was transcendental, cleansing and liberating. The creed of violence was part of the baggage of the existentialist movement, descended from Hegel and Fichte and their exaltation of the German state. It worked its way into French existentialist thought via Nietzsche, who was transported by visions of

> the superb blond beast wandering in search of prey and carnage.
> . . . The terrible gaiety and profound joy felt by all heroes in all destruction, in all the pleasures of victory and cruelty.

Georges Sorel cited Nietzsche admiringly in his *Reflections on Violence* (1915). Sorel insisted that socialism could come only as a "catastrophe," for

> it is to violence that Socialism owes those high ethical values by means of which it brings *salvation* to the modern world.
> Proletarian violence produces an entirely epic state of mind. [Sorel's italics.]

Sartre thought Sorel a Fascist, but they shared the Nietzschean fascination with violence as a form of philosophic statement. Violence was the central experience of the Resistance, the high point in the lives of a whole generation of French intellectuals. Simone de Beauvoir's thinly fictionalized account of Sartre's circle immediately after the war, *The Mandarins,* describes their sense of the suffocating banality of peacetime existence, their longing for the sharp moral distinctions of wartime, for the sense of living on the knife's edge, for the intensification of experience that came with risking and dispensing death. Being French and intellectuals, they concocted universal doctrine from their plight: a man's existence required self-creation through violence. As Sartre said about the Algerian war, "This irrepressible violence is neither sound nor fury, nor the resurrection of savage instincts, nor even the effect of resentment: it is man recreating himself." Social constraints are of no sway. Sartre insisted that man "invents his own law"; humanity "begins with rebellion." "The perfect moment" was achieved only in the terrorist group, where man achieved the pinnacle of existence by losing himself entirely in the "group-in-focus" and its code of violence. The protagonist in one of Sartre's plays achieves his humanity by killing two of his brethren.

Norman Mailer brought Sorel and Sartre, brightly packaged and precooked, to a broad American audience. In his essay "The White Negro," Mailer extols the "hipster," the "philosophic psychopath" who scales the existentialist summits by indulging his impulse to violence.

> The strength of the psychopath is that he knows (where most of us can only guess) what is good for him and what is bad for him. . . . The psychopath murders—if he has the courage—out of the necessity to purge his violence. . . . It can of course be suggested that it takes little courage for two eighteen-year-old hoodlums, let us say, to beat in the brains of a candy-store keeper, and indeed the act, even by the logic of the psychopath, is not likely to prove very therapeutic, for the victim is not an immediate equal. Still courage of a sort is necessary, for one murders not only a weak fifty-year-old man but an institution as well, one violates private property, one enters into a special relation with the police and introduces a dangerous element into one's life. The hoodlum is therefore daring the unknown, and no matter how brutal the act, it is not altogether cowardly.

Later, in *The American Dream*, Mailer's hero, Stephen Rojack, a teacher of existential psychology, seeks a "more authentic self"—Heidegger's phrase—liberated from "the rot and gas of compromise, the stink of old fears, the mildew of discipline, all the biles of habit." During the war, Rojack trained his gun on a German machine gunner, looked into the man's eyes, and then, when he failed to shoot, lost "The Presence." He regains his authenticity by strangling his wife. For a while he contemplates mutilating and eating the corpse, but, fortunately for the reader, even Mailer recognizes limits to the demands of philosophy. In real life Mailer stabbed his second wife, but did not kill her, thus achieving, presumably, only a blemished authenticity himself.

All of this was, of course, greatly appealing to the fledgling revolutionaries of the 1960s; it was what Julian Benda, in his *Treason of the Clerks,* called "the intellectual organization of political hatreds." Frantz Fanon's *The Wretched of the Earth* was a sacred text for revolutionaries, black and white. It was written during the Algerian war by a black psychiatrist, was much admired by Sartre, and was viewed as a practical guide, second only to Mao's *Little Red Book,* by the Panthers and their black janissaries in the revolutionary movement.

> National liberation [Fanon wrote], national renaissance, the restoration of nationhood to the people, commonwealth: whatever may be the headings used or the new formulas introduced, decolonization is always a violent phenomenon. . . . The naked truth of decolonization evokes for us the searing bullets and bloodstained knives which emanate from it. For if the last shall be first, this will only come about after a murderous and decisive struggle between the two protagonists.

Fanon's words were a banner for black men who felt their manhood challenged by racism, or perceived racism. Violence, particularly against whites, or better, white police, was an existential affirmation—in Mailer's terms, a discovery of authenticity. For Eldridge Cleaver, his first encounter with the Black Panthers was a kind of epiphany.

> Suddenly the room fell silent. . . . From the tensions showing on the faces of the people before me, I thought the cops were invading the meeting, but there was a deep female gleam leaping out of one of the women's eyes that no cop who ever lived could elicit. I recognized that gleam out of the recesses of my soul, even though I had never seen it before in my life: the total admiration of a black woman for a black man. I spun around in my seat and saw the most beautiful sight I had ever seen: four black men wearing black berets, powder blue shirts, black leather jackets, black trousers, shiny black shoes —and each with a gun! In front was Huey P. Newton, with a riot pump shotgun in his right hand, barrel pointed down to the floor. Beside him was Bobby Seale, the handle of a .45 caliber automatic showing from its holster on his right hip, just below the hem of his jacket. A few steps behind Seale was Bobby Hutton, the barrel of his shotgun at his feet. Next to him was Sherwin Forte, an M1 carbine with a banana clip cradled in his arms.

Newton and Seale evoked emotion akin to worship. Here is Cleaver again:

> At that moment a beefy cop stepped forward. He undid the little strap holding his pistol to his holster and started shouting at Huey. . . .

Huey walked to within a few feet of the cop and said, "What's the matter, you got an itchy finger?"

The cop made no reply.

"You want to draw your gun?" Huey asked him. . . .

"OK," Huey said, "you big, fat, racist pig, draw your gun!"

The cop made no move.

"Draw it, you cowardly dog!" Huey pumped a round into the chamber of the shotgun. "I'm waiting," he said, and stood there waiting for the cop to draw. . . .

Then the cop facing Huey gave it up. He heaved a heavy sigh and lowered his head. Huey literally laughed in his face then went off up the street at a jaunty pace, disappearing in a blaze of dazzling sunlight.

"Work out, soul brother!" I was shouting to myself. "You're the baddest motherfucker I've ever seen!"

White radical students tinkered with bombs and held turgid debates on the redemptive nature of terrorism, but actual violence was confined to a disturbed fringe. The black spokesmen hammering at the theme of violence were much more in the mainstream. Newton preached Mao's maxims: "To get rid of the gun, it is necessary to pick up a gun." "Political power grows out of the barrel of a gun." Malcolm X shouted, "The ballot or the bullet" to put "iron in a young nigger's blood." Carmichael pounded away at "Black Power." Cleaver wrote: "The genie of black revolutionary violence is here. . . . A fire rages in the hearts of black people today: total liberty for black people or total destruction for America."

There was a sharp increase in black crime, an upsurge so severe that it virtually paralyzed most major cities, undermining any attempt at renewal or reclamation, and rendering large urban areas virtually uninhabitable. There has always been a strong thread of violence in the black underclass community. Charles Silberman points out the significance of the legend of Stackolee, a black mythic hero, who is a kind of Paul Bunyan of mad dog killers. ("Stackolee" was also the name of a hit 1960s rock and roll song; few whites would have understood the significance of the name.) But the rhetoric of violence almost certainly reinforced and ratified a slum youngster's worst impulses. Panther Bobby Hutton, who was later killed by the Oakland police, orated at a rally:

In school, when a little white liberal walked by, I used to come up with my knife and say, "Give me your lunch money or I'll cut your guts out." And he'd give me his lunch money. Pretty soon, I'd say, "Tomorrow, you bring me two dollars." And the next day, he'd bring me two dollars. Because that two dollars was *mine.* Mine because of four hundred years of racism and oppression. When I take two dollars from you, pig, you don't say nothing.

Cleaver said: "I look with respect on a guy . . . who doesn't go around begging and instead walks into a store and says, 'Stick 'em up, mother-fucker.' " Even rape, according to Cleaver, was "an insurrectionary act."

I arrived at the conclusion that, as a matter of principle, it was of paramount importance for me to have an antagonistic, ruthless attitude toward white women. . . . I had stepped outside of the white man's law, which I repudiated with scorn and self-satisfaction.

It is impossible to be precise, of course, about the link between the violent rhetoric and the upswing in crime. The link with a series of murderous ambushes of policemen—both black and white—by so-called black revolutionaries that began in New York City in 1968 seems clear, however. And the slogan "Burn, baby, burn" was part of the inflammatory mix that erupted each year into summer city riots.

Riots

The ghetto riots are still not completely understood. They were not race riots in the sense of blacks pitted against whites, as in the Chicago riots of 1919 or the Detroit riot in 1943. If they were intended as a form of social protest, the mode of expression was bizarre. The damage was almost totally confined to black neighborhoods, and the people killed or injured were overwhelmingly black. In the early stages of most riots, there was some attempt to distinguish between black- and white-owned stores, but as the disturbances wore on, damage was inflicted indiscriminately. The Kerner Commission appointed by Lyndon Johnson developed a "frustration" theory of rioting by focusing on the relatively high educational level of riot arrestees. The path out of the ghetto, they reasoned, was closed to even the most success-oriented blacks, causing them to rise up and express their frustration in unfocused violence. But reanalysis of the commission's own data casts doubt on their theory. The rioters were actually the least educated and least socialized youth—the unruly *lumpenproletariat* that Marx held in such scorn. Better-educated blacks tended to join in the looting late in the riots when store windows were lying irresistibly open for the picking; but, of course, that was just at the point when police were beginning to re-establish control, and older and better-educated blacks were easier to catch than street-quick youngsters.

Edward Banfield and other neo-conservative scholars have tended to dismiss the riots as mere hoodlumism—rioting for "fun and profit." There is considerable evidence to support their point of view. Rioters in Watts threw rocks into crowds of blacks. During a disturbance in Harlem, a black bus driver took an elaborate detour around the riot area and told a white reporter, "These crazy kids don't care who their brick hits." Reporters consistently remarked on the "carnival atmosphere" that pervaded many of the riots. One wrote that it was more like a "contest between two athletic teams with supporters cheering and egg-ing on the contestants." After King's death, a Washington rioter shouted that it was "early Easter shopping," and another, asked why he was looting a store, replied "because Whatsisname was killed." Televi-sion coverage probably contributed materially to the rate of outbreaks, as youths in peaceful cities felt their manhood challenged. By 1967, there was a tendency by local stations to dub any transitory outbreak of vandalism a "riot." The largely successful tactics used in New York City to contain riots showed an acute awareness of the faddish conta-giousness of incidents. Police would cordon off disturbed areas with military precision, would try to avoid pitched battles with individual rioters, and would bring incidents under control with the sheer weight of massed uniforms. As soon as an incident was controlled, sanitation crews would be on the streets sweeping up the debris, often at three or four in the morning, so the area looked relatively normal by daybreak.

But the "fun and profit" theory of the riots is too glib. Even if nonideological underclass hoodlums did most of the actual rioting, the outbreaks themselves were almost all closely connected with underlying civil rights issues, connected in ways undefinable and imprecise to be sure, but connected nevertheless. My firsthand experience of a riot was in the 1967 disturbance in Newark. The precipitating incident was the rough handling of an arrested driver as in Watts; but the arrest was merely the incendiary occasion. It was preceded by months of tense negotiations over the proposed clearance of a large section of one of Newark's worst slums in order to build a state medical school, and the controversy occurred during a time of steadily deteriorating relations between the black community and the predominantly Italian and Irish —and thoroughly corrupt—city administration and police force.

The decision to locate the medical school in central Newark proceeded from impeccably liberal motives. The trustees much preferred a suburban location, but the state and city governments pressured for the Newark site in the hope that the school would provide the foundation on which to build an economic recovery. The trustees reluctantly agreed to the Newark site on the condition that a suburban-scale tract of land be provided, necessitating major clearance. The decision to provide the land was never properly communicated to the affected residents, partly because the city administration intended to renege on the deal and clear a much smaller site once the school was committed.

When word of the slum clearance project leaked out, it was seized upon by assorted groups that had been competing to organize Newark's black community on behalf of a goulash of revolutionary and political schemes. There was a militant local chapter of CORE, a "black liberation army" outpost of a "Colonel Hassan," the Community Action Program, and an SDS chapter that had been attempting to prove that white students could organize effectively among working-class blacks. News of the clearance project coincided with a number of incidents of apparent police brutality and the cold-shouldering of several popular blacks for ranking jobs in the school system and the police department. There were meetings, rallies, a proliferation of leaflets; spokesmen for the poor sought to outdo each other demonstrating their militancy.

On Wednesday evening, July 12, the police arrested John Smith, a black taxi driver, for allegedly driving erratically. Police said Smith was abusive and violent; Smith claimed to have been beaten without provocation. It is undisputed that Smith had to be taken to a hospital after his arrest with a concussion and a fractured rib. The arrest and the struggle were witnessed by a crowd in front of a black housing project. CORE immediately organized a demonstration in front of the precinct to protest police brutality. When Smith was taken to the hospital, the rumor spread that he had been killed. The crowd grew larger and more unruly. Someone threw a Molotov cocktail. When police sallied out of the station, they were met with a hail of missiles. By midnight, crowds of teenagers were forming and reforming in hit-and-run tactics, harassing the police with rocks and bottles. A convoy of twenty-five black taxi drivers double-parked outside the precinct. Police reinforcements with helmets and nightsticks finally succeeded in clearing the crowds from in front of the station, but as the teenagers filtered into the adjacent streets, looting began. When police did not attempt to intervene, the looting intensified before dying out about four in the morning. By five o'clock, with the city apparently calm, the administration declared the incident over.

Thursday morning, the mayor met with civil rights leaders and acceded to their major demands—invoking disciplinary procedures against the police involved in the arrest and promoting a black lieutenant to the rank of captain. But much to the alarm of city officials, leaflets had already been passed out calling for a mass nighttime rally. The leaflets were reportedly printed by the Community Action agency and distributed by the SDS chapter. Pickets formed outside the precinct that night. A civil rights leader announced the promotion of the black lieutenant. When he finished speaking, a crowd across the street bombarded the station house with bricks, bottles, and garbage. A woman with a long pole walked around the precinct house breaking windows. Heavy police reinforcements eventually cleared the neighborhood around the precinct, but as calm returned to the station house, looting broke out on Springfield Avenue, the main business street in the black section. Bands of eight to fifteen youths roamed the avenue, breaking windows, overturning cars, and setting fires. Police hesitated to react, afraid of provoking violence. When the crowds saw there were no reprisals, they began to help themselves from store windows. Firemen were stoned when they attempted to respond to fires. At 2:20 a.m., the mayor telephoned the state governor and reported that he had lost control of the city.

The state responded by dispatching six hundred state troopers and thirty-five hundred National Guardsmen to the city, but Friday night was still the worst night of looting. Ominously, a Sears store was broken into, and twenty-four rifles were stolen. On Saturday, the National Guardsmen effectively blockaded the black area with command posts and half-track tanks at most major intersections. The looting diminished, and the riot evolved into spreading incidents of arson, sniper fire, and deadly gun battles between police and National Guardsmen and real or imagined snipers. Most of the bystander deaths occurred on Friday and Saturday.

I had been working with the governor's office, and was asked to come up to the state command post in an armory in central Newark late Saturday. Driving into Newark was surreal. The sky was lit with scattered fires, gunfire crackled sporadically through the streets, from time to time erupting into deafening cannonades. Because of a curfew, no one was permitted on the streets except for police and military, but twice I saw lone strollers, seemingly bent on routine business. At one point, when I stopped for a red light, a state trooper with a rifle took cover behind my car. I waited for the light to change before driving on; it seemed only polite. The trooper scurried away to other cover.

Inside the armory was barely organized chaos. The local police, the state police, and the guardsmen all operated on different radio frequencies and couldn't communicate with each other on patrol. I busied myself, along with several other minor functionaries, relaying messages from one set of phones to the other, so at least the commanders could communicate. The Newark police had not been able to produce maps of the city for use by the outside forces, so the patrols would frequently get lost. At one point, while we were working the phones, a young boy taking out garbage was caught in a crossfire between state police and guardsmen. Both thought they were shooting at a sniper; quite likely they were responding to each other's gunfire. It took an agonizingly long time, perhaps fifteen minutes, perhaps less, to convince them to hold their fire. The boy died.

The sniper incidents were grossly overstated by frightened and untrained guardsmen. Much of the return fire was at phantoms. There was also extensive evidence that local police shot up black-owned businesses that had been spared by the rioters and blamed the shooting incidents on alleged snipers. But there *were* snipers. A uniformed police detective and a fire captain were both killed by small-caliber rifle bullets. Early Sunday morning, several of us were driven to a nearby friend's apartment in a police car; the windshield had been shot away earlier in the evening. Later I saw a sniper. The apartment building overlooked a housing project. A man with a rifle came out on the roof and fired down into the street. Police came running from all directions, some of them firing wildly at the building. A woman with eight children was killed looking out a window in that building. I don't know if the killing occurred during the incident I saw or not.

Sunday was relatively calm. We worked to deliver food to distribution stations in the riot-torn areas, which were already suffering serious shortages of fresh milk and other basics. There were scattered incidents that night, but the riot was effectively over Monday morning. Troop withdrawals began Monday and continued through Tuesday. By Wednesday the city was functioning normally.

To write off the disturbances merely as an outbreak of hoodlumism trivializes what happened. Almost certainly, a number of the transient outbreaks in smaller cities that were indiscriminately labeled "riots" by a breathless press were nothing more than sprees by juvenile delinquents. Newark, and I assume Watts and Detroit, were much more than that. My strong impression was that a very large number of blacks—stable blacks, middle-class blacks, blacks who were terrified of the shooting and the burning—saw the riot as a message to the city administration, to the police, to whites in general. It was not a message that could be easily reduced to a point-by-point program or a set of specific demands. In fact, the "demands" that typically grew out of riots were as trivializing in their own way as neo-conservative white scoffing. The message was simply that blacks were to be taken seriously from then on.

White liberals and black "spokesmen" quickly enveloped the central message in a cloud of posturings and chicaneries. Immediately after the disturbances subsided, the state government and the black leaders formed negotiating committees to air grievances and to develop an official response to the riot. The resolution of the issues relating to the medical school held center stage in the discussions, but working groups were developed around a host of other issues—police/community relations, employment programs, antipoverty funding, insurance for stores in ghetto areas, small business development loans. Some things were accomplished, but not much. The medical site was reduced, and an agreement of sorts was reached that construction could proceed. The issue of slum clearance was mooted the following spring after King's death. Central Newark was so gutted by fire that it was for all practical purposes abandoned. Even the huge housing projects were mostly vacated—including the one where I saw the sniper—and they now stand with boarded windows, megalithic monuments, looming uselessly.

The committees dragged on for months. I participated in several of them. On the official side, the attitude was overtly intense and concerned. Periodically, when discussions would founder, the black spokesmen would threaten another riot, and the official representatives would shake their heads grimly and plunge onward with the negotiations. My strong impression was that almost no one believed the threats. Clearly, if groups of official-looking blacks walked around Newark's worst areas telling youngsters to riot, some windows would have been broken. But none of the "spokesmen" seemed truly in touch with events, in the sense that any one of them really understood how the tensions had transmuted into a full-scale riot, or knew who was really involved, or commanded a mass following that would rise up or cool down as ordered. For the most part, they represented no one, nor had they been elected to anything by anyone; they had merely been recognized by the whites. They happened to be there and were eager to speak, so they were spokesmen: several ministers, one or two fire-eating radicals—one of whom was a Yale law school graduate—an assortment of poverty and civil rights bureaucrats and, saddest and most interesting, a handful of opportunists, seizing upon the moment to improve their chances to get a state job, get a grant, get a political appointment, or simply to bask in the fleeting spotlight of prominence.

The state officials needed the discussions as much as the black spokesmen. They needed someone to talk to, they needed to create an impression of motion and progress, they needed the intense discussions as a kind of self-verification. For as surely as the black leaders knew they were poseurs, the officials understood deep down that none of their programs, however cleverly labeled or brilliantly reasoned, would have averted the riot, or would avert a riot in the future if it was destined to happen, or indeed would make very much difference at all to anyone. The negotiations were a variety of theater, a mutually necessary charlatanism. Otherwise, the riot, searing event though it was, would have ended in a vacuum of anticlimax. The ritual of negotiations allowed it to trickle away, with a minimum of embarrassment, into the safety of winter.

Violence as Theater

The reawakening of moral zeal was the finest achievement of the civil rights movement. The stark courage of the SNCC kids, the mute force of a quarter million marchers, the cadenced rhythms of the black spirituals, the shining, transcendent, glory of stoic resistance to hoses, clubs, and dogs, all stirred sensibilities dulled by the technocratic reductionist creed. It was moral zeal that nourished the best impulses of Lyndon Johnson's Great Society, for all its arrogance and overreachings. It was moral zeal that channeled the disruptive instincts of bursting youth into outrage at the cold savagery of remote-control war. Sadly, by the late 1960s, through a kind of Gresham's law of motive and emotion, soul-felt protest at genuine injustice was being drowned out by the cawing of revolutionary dilettantes. Moral fops minced and clowned. Zeal was a thrill, protest was theater.

Black Panthers became star guests at fashionable New York cocktail parties, and Tom Wolfe announced radical chic. He chronicles the Panthers' arrival at Leonard Bernstein's apartment in 1968:

> Christ, if the Panthers don't know how to get it all together, as they say, the tight pants, the tight black turtlenecks, the leather coats, Cuban shades, Afros. But real Afros, not the ones that have been shaped and trimmed like a topiary hedge and sprayed until they have a sheen like acrylic wall-to-wall, but natural, scraggly . . . wild. . . .
>
> *These are no civil rights Negroes wearing gray suits three sizes too big—*
>
> —no more interminable Urban League banquets in hotel ballrooms where they try to alternate the blacks and whites around the table as if they were stringing Arapaho beads—
>
> —these are real men!
>
> Shoot-outs, revolutions, pictures in *Life* magazine of policemen grabbing Panthers like they were Vietcong—somehow it all runs together in the head with the whole thing of how *beautiful* they are. *Sharp as a blade.* The Panther women—there are three or four of them on hand, wives of the Panther 21 defendants, and they are so lean, so *lithe,* as they say, with tight pants and Yoruba-style head-dresses, almost like turbans, as if they'd stepped out of the pages of *Vogue,* although no doubt *Vogue* got it from them.

Radical chic posed fascinating problems. Did one serve Roquefort cheese balls and asparagus tips to revolutionaries? Was it grapes or lettuce that Cesar Chavez was boycotting? The fashion for revolution spread beyond the leisured elite. The Catholic Diocese of Brooklyn pumped money into various protest organizations, and young priests took time off for community organizing. Riots were treated as almost an acceptable mode of expression. Hubert Humphrey announced that if he had to put up with conditions in the slums, he "would lead a mighty good revolt." Protestant audiences in New York applauded the castigations of James Forman and seriously debated his demands for billions in reparations. Businessmen solemnly sported black and white "Give a Damn" buttons. Suburbanites in slacks descended upon Harlem five thousand strong to clean and paint for the residents.

White liberals saw the pathologies of the ghetto through a romantic haze and extolled its music, its warmth, its aliveness—missing the child abuse, the brutality, the abandonment, the drunkenness, the drug addiction, the disease. Textbooks were written on "Black English"—that is, ungrammatical English—and it was quite seriously proposed that teachers attend training programs so they could speak "Black English" to their students. Norman Mailer's envious description of ghetto life was more insulting than any Southern redneck's.

> The Negro (all exceptions admitted) could rarely afford the sophisticated inhibitions of civilization, and so he kept for his survival the art of the primitive, he lived in the enormous present, he subsisted from his Saturday night kicks, relinquishing the pleasures of the mind for the more obligatory pleasures of the body, and in his music he gave voice to the character and quality of his existence, to his rage, and the infinite varieties of joy, lust, languor, growl, cramp, pinch, scream, and despair of his orgasm.

Even prison and prisoners were romanticized. Black prisoners were dubbed "political prisoners," the victims of white repression, and white liberals—Tom Wicker and Jessica Mitford, among others—drew portraits of black prisoners as strong, warm, intelligent, decent men set upon by sadistic and small-minded keepers. (Not that that is never true. There are sadistic prison staffs; I've known some extraordinary prisoners.) George Jackson's *Prison Letters* made him a cult hero—the archetype of the oppressed revolutionary, in prison eleven years "for the original offense of stealing $70," as Mitford put it. In fact, his offense was armed robbery, and his sentence was regularly extended because of his repeated implication in prison violence.

White radicals adopted the same swaggering, Wild West rhetorical stance as the blacks. A white underground newspaper writer, for instance, lashed back at what he perceived as black racism.

> I must revolt against your racism, your scorn of everything white, just as I revolt against the racism of white America. I will not let you put me in a bag. . . . I won't let even a black person, no matter how hard-bent he be on black liberation, squeeze me back into

honkiedom. If I have to shoot a black racist one of these days, well, baby, that's part of the struggle.

The intense self-consciousness of university communities compounded the theatricality of campus incidents. Students "liberated" Columbia University's campus by holding sit-ins in major buildings in the spring of 1968. The administration first called the police and then changed their minds, so the police hovered on the fringes of the campus for days, fuming at the taunts of the students, as the faculty met in an hysterical round-the-clock conclave debating first principles ("The purpose of a university . . . "), posturing, shouting, weeping, vilifying the administration as Nazis and the university president as Hitler. Dwight Macdonald, an aging arbiter of Upper West Side revolutionary fashion, received a call from a friend:

> "You must come right away, Dwight. It's a revolution. You may never get another chance to see one." I came up and he was right. I've never been in or near a revolution before; I guess I like them. There was a spirit of daring and experiment, the kind of expansive mood of liberation from an oppressive and, worse, boring tyranny that Stendhal describes in the Milanese population after Napoleon's army had driven out the Austrians.

The operative word here, of course, is "boring."

Politicians, civil rights leaders, and radicals converged on the campus. Roy Innis from CORE. Tom Hayden from SDS. Charles 37X Kenyatta, leader of the "Mau-Maus," roamed on the fringes with a band of black high school youngsters. The *New York Review of Books,* caught up in the spirit of liberation, published designs for Molotov cocktails. Normally sensible politicians, like Percy Sutton and Charles Rangel, rushed to declare their solidarity with the students—"Whatever you do, we're with you." Ultimately the buildings were cleared by the police, with a considerable amount of vindictive violence, which, to be fair, the students had done their best to provoke. Interestingly, the black students, who had occupied Hamilton Hall, gave up their building peacefully after a brief negotiation with the administration. With relatively more to gain from a Columbia education than the white students, they were less prepared to jeopardize their futures pursuing a revolutionary chimera.

The New York City police, the country's most practiced in dealing with large-scale demonstrations, developed a wearied cynicism. Demonstrators, particularly antiwar demonstrators, were most interested in television coverage, they found, so the police would meet with leaders beforehand, explain the positioning of the cameras, and show them where to stand for maximum coverage during an arrest. If the demonstrators wished to resist arrest, the police would suggest that they simply lie down when the arrest began and they would be carried to the police vans in full view of the cameras without risk of injury and with minimum disruption of the police's own work schedules—but still genuine resisters, flying V signs, with the security of knowing that a "resisting arrest" charge was guaranteed as part of the bargain.

The television cameras were ubiquitous. A revealing AP Wirephoto shows a reportedly seriously injured woman lying in the street on her face during the Newark riot, with a television reporter kneeling to work a microphone to her mouth so she could be interviewed. I was the New York City welfare director at the turn of the decade when welfare demonstrations were still common, although without the flair and drama of the massive welfare rights marches of 1966 and 1967. The demonstrations followed a ritual dictated by the availability of the cameras. The demonstrators would arrive at a welfare center, often with considerable advance notice. There would be a period of aimless milling. Then someone would shout, "The TV is here." The demonstration would immediately take shape, the radical workers would march off their work stations, the leaders of the demonstration and the center director would engage in an apparently heated, but highly conventionalized shouting match, perhaps some files would be strewn about, and perhaps an arrest or two would be made. People would wave their fists for the cameras and be interviewed. Everyone would hurry home to watch themselves on the early news. Welfare demonstrations hardly ever made the late news anymore.

The tidal wave of moral outrage that had swept the country out of its lassitude of conscience was, by the end of the decade, breaking into driblets of petulant narcissism and mindless exhibitionism. Radical students proclaimed the "Days of Rage" in Chicago in 1969. Forlorn little groups of tatterdemalion youngsters spent a few days performing acts of petty vandalism and being chased by police around the city streets. Yippie leaders Abbie Hoffman and Jerry Rubin called a pointless demonstration in Grand Central Station in New York. City officials ignored them, assuming that no one would come. But a metropolitan area rock station broadcast news of the demonstration for several days, and at the appointed time, tens of thousands of suburban high school students were disgorged from arriving trains. There was no organization, no objective, no leadership, no plan at all. The police surrounded the station but were equally unprepared. The packed youngsters grew unruly. A mob clambered onto the glass ceiling of the information booth. The police command, fearful that the booth's collapse would precipitate a panic, ordered the station cleared. The men surged forward, free-lancing through the crowd with their nightsticks. The command utterly lost control, and a number of youngsters were injured in the ensuing melee.

By the end of the decade only the ugliness was left. The official response to the "revolution" had become openly vindictive. Chicago police riddled Panther Fred Hampton's body with bullets, although there is evidence that he was sleeping when they raided his apartment. National Guardsmen fired into antiwar demonstrators at Kent State, killing four students and wounding eight. The charm of Woodstock degenerated into the violence at Altamont. Predators roamed among the flower children in Haight-Ashbury and the East Village. It was discovered that drugs really did cause psychosis. The trial in New Haven in 1971 of prominent Black Panthers on charges of torturing and murdering a dull-normal black youth, a Panther camp follower, was an epitaph for the decade. There was no question that the torture and murder took place, or that it was done by Panthers. The issue was merely whether the top Panther leadership was involved. Thousands of students in a festive mood descended on the city. Angry black residents barred them from black neighborhoods. "We've got to live here after you've had your fun!" The president of Yale doubted pompously whether a Black Panther could receive a fair trial anywhere in the country. Tom Hayden proclaimed that it was "a trial of whether there is anything left in America worth defending." Abbie Hoffman, arms flung high over the crowd, shouted, "We ain't never, never, never, gonna grow up!" A pasty-faced youngster in a Columbia T-shirt brandished a broomstick on the edge of the crowd and whined, "I want to kill a pig, I want to kill a pig."

The revolution had become tawdry and, even worse, boring. The radicals were facing their thirties and adulthood. Blacks were still an underclass, and the war was still raging. The greening of America was a childish dream, and most of the country was tiring of the revolutionaries' antics. One of the few political achievements of the radicals, in fact, may have been twice to ensure the election of Richard Nixon as President of the United States.

VII

NIXON

When Richard Nixon assumed the presidency in 1969, elected by the barest of pluralities, the country was divided as it had not been for a century. Sadly, neither Nixon nor his enemies were prepared for conciliation. The Kennedys and their legions of retainers, ADA Democrats like Schlesinger and Galbraith, committed liberals, intellectuals in general, the managements of the Washington *Post* and the *New York Times,* all loathed Richard Nixon; and he returned their loathing with an aggrieved and clumsy hatred, the embittered truculence of the scorned outsider. The liberal distaste for Nixon dated from the very beginning of his political career. They still remembered the below-the-belt style of his congressional race against the popular Jerry Voorhis, his savaging of Helen Gahagan Douglas, his pursuit of Alger Hiss—rankling all the more because Hiss seems really to have been a Communist agent—and the lugubrious appeal of his "Checkers" speech. "No class," was John Kennedy's verdict. "No style, no style at all," pronounced the Washington *Post*'s Benjamin Bradlee.

The personality that Nixon projected in his public career was thoroughly unattractive. The smothering pieties contrasted unpleasantly with the ruthlessness of his campaigns. The forced joviality and the reflex smile—at the most inappropriate times—gave an impression of falsity, of a peculiar incompleteness beneath the studio makeup. His public statements often had a double-entendre quality, the sly dig slipped into a sentence of statuesque statesmanship—like his response to Lyndon Johnson's bombing halt in Vietnam during the 1968 campaign:

129

I am told that this spurt of activity [to agree to a bombing halt] is a cynical, last-minute attempt by President Johnson to salvage the candidacy of Mr. Humphrey. This I do not believe.

The speech announcing the incursion into Cambodia in 1970 was vintage Nixon—the unerring instinct for the maudlin, the self-conscious pretensions to greatness, the self-pity.

Whether my party gains in November is nothing compared to the lives of 400,000 brave Americans fighting for our country. . . . Whether I may be a one-term President is insignificant compared to whether by our failure to act in this crisis the United States proves itself to be unworthy to lead the forces of freedom in this critical period in world history. I would rather be a one-term President and do what I believe is right than to be a two-term President at the cost of seeing America become a second-rate power and to see the Nation accept the first defeat in its proud 190 year history.

Even his admirers conceded that Nixon had a mean streak, the meanness of a small man from pinched circumstances. Brooding over the stings and scars of a long and embattled career, he compiled his lists of enemies with the obsessive precision of an accountant, moving with vindictive glee at every opportunity to avenge old wrongs. Oddly, he always exercised his meanness at a distance. For all the back-alley rough-and-tumble of his early campaigns and his grim capacity to "tough it out" in public, whether in negotiating with the Russians or enduring the long torment of the Watergate investigations, he took full flight at the prospect of personal confrontation, even with his own subordinates. When he asked his cabinet to resign en masse after his 1972 election victory, the request was so mumbled and ambiguous that after the cabinet meeting ended, Nixon's chief of staff, H. R. Haldeman, held the cabinet in the room and said, "I'm not sure you people understood what the President meant. . . . He *wanted your resignations.*" In the abstract, the decision was taken toughly, even cruelly; but the message was delivered by remote control.

Looming over all else was Nixon's fatal instinct for self-destruction. It stemmed from the scrambling and mistrustful side of his personality, the part of him that was the failed grocer's son, who awoke to dark, flapping night thoughts, and lay trapped and sweating amid concentric rings of doubts, slights, and supposed humiliations. Nixon flogged himself up the ladder of public office. Even at the pinnacle, he could never achieve the careless ease of a Kennedy, and he resentfully knew it. In his own mind, he was convinced that people who glittered, who could walk into a room gracefully, smile dazzlingly, make conversation easily and wittily—writers, editors, intellectuals, the Kennedy set—hated him and his achievements not because of his policies, but only because he was not one of them, and could never become one of them, and had struggled and clawed to triumph over all of them. There was no small amount of truth to his conviction; and to use Nixon's own nasty phrase, the constant pricking of inferiority was like picking off a scab. The narrowness of his spirit did not allow him to bask in his victories; he wanted to grind them into the faces of his tormentors like bits of glass. And he did so in a way that destroyed himself, almost as if, pathetically, he believed in his heart that his enemies were right, and so he fashioned for them the means of his own destruction—the deliberately insulting nomination of G. Harrold Carswell to the Supreme Court that ended his tenuous honeymoon with Congress; the clumsily provocative impoundments controversy that ruined his opportunity for refashioning social programs; the stupidity of Watergate when a stunning electoral victory was already assured; and, finally, his paralytic inability to destroy the tapes until he handed over the stored evidence that would drive him from office as a virtual criminal, in shame before the stricken faces of his daughters, his ears ringing with the choral gloats of everyone he hated.

A caricature works when it's true. The liberal caricature of Nixon sustained its force over so long a period because of its basis in truth. But a caricature is also a distortion of reality, suppressing all but the facts that strike the eye of the cartoonist. There was much greater breadth and depth to Richard Nixon than orthodox liberal ideology would allow. A host of close observers—Theodore H. White, Eliot Richardson, Henry Kissinger, Daniel Patrick Moynihan, William Safire—attest to the unusual sweep and clarity of Nixon's mind. He had the bold courage for the brilliant stroke, for the dazzling reversal and slashing attack that confounded and put to flight his opposition. Kissinger writes of Nixon's "decisiveness," his "extraordinary instinct for the jugular" cutting through "tactics or the meticulous accumulation of nuance," his ability to "understand the essence of an opportunity and push for it consistently." The policy masterstrokes of his first term—the opening to China, détente with Russia, wage and price controls, floating the dollar, even his Vietnam policy—were not all ultimately successful by any means, but uniformly displayed a daring and imaginative pragmatism that was impressive by any standard.

His knowledge of foreign affairs was profound. Ever the assiduous learner, he had used his years traveling as vice president and later when he was out of office to develop an intimate acquaintance with most of the major countries of the world and a subtle sense of the ebbs and flows of geopolitical power. He seems to have been trusted and respected by de Gaulle, for example, as few recent presidents had been. Brezhnev and Kosygin dropped the Kremlin's usual bullying tactics while Nixon was President, and dealt with him as an equal in understanding and tenacity —an attitude conspicuously lacking during Jimmy Carter's presidency. Nixon's ability to sustain aggressive military action in Southeast Asia at the same time as he pursued détente with the Soviet Union didn't stem from rashness or confusion, as his critics would have it, but from a confident calculation of Soviet psychology and self-interest. Henry Kissinger's contributions to Nixon's foreign policy were, of course, immense, but Kissinger has always been the first to concede that the leading ideas were as much Nixon's as his own. The concept of the rapprochement with China—the enduring monument to Nixon's presidency—was Nixon's from the outset. He first bruited the idea of a triangular U.S.-U.S.S.R.-China diplomacy in a *Foreign Affairs* article in 1967, at a time when the notion seemed so unrealistic as to draw little comment. The Chinese leadership, surely among the most capable and pragmatic in the world, made their high regard for Nixon known even at the height of the Watergate scandal, and in 1982, although still in disgrace at home, Nixon was pointedly invited by the Chinese to attend the celebration of the tenth anniversary of the Shanghai Communiqué, the official agreement to normalize American-Chinese relations.

There was a human side of Nixon, too, difficult as it sometimes was to find it beneath the carefully crafted mannequin shell. He was apparently exceptionally sensitive to the emotional and personal needs of his closest aides and often, despite his poor relations with the press in general, was strikingly considerate of individual reporters. He was deeply loyal to his top staff, and his inability to cast them aside as the contours of the Watergate scandal first emerged sucked him deeper into the quagmire. His worries for his own men are a persistent theme of the Watergate tapes, and the only redeeming one. He could be compassionate. When he made his final appeal for his Family Assistance Plan, he rose early in the morning and wrote the speech himself. As he talked about ending the stigma of being poor, he was talking about his childhood and his own family, and Moynihan, for one, was delighted and surprised to discover that the President felt deeply about what he was saying. Mary McGrory, a long-time adversary, called the speech "magnificent." Accounts of Nixon's early-morning visit to antiwar students protesting at the Lincoln Memorial often portray him as boorish and vulgar. But that is part of the anti-Nixon mythology. He was awkward and uncomfortable, to be sure, but he really was worried, it seems, about what was happening to the country's young people and wanted to reach out, in however fumbling a way. And there were his daughters. Covering the 1968 convention, Norman Mailer was stunned when he met the Nixon daughters in the flesh. There they were, he wrote, a reality he couldn't deny. Graceful, intelligent, charming young women, who clearly had a warm and loving relationship with their father. How could *Richard Nixon* have such daughters?

During his first term, his administration had purpose and theme. Nixon believed in original sin. This most deeply flawed of men knew that people were not perfectible. He knew that Dewey's vision of each man's reaching his full potential with an assist from a benevolent government was not achievable; that some people on welfare would cheat, and that if the accessibility and flexibility of the system were increased greatly, cheating would increase greatly; that some Vietnamese guerrilla fighters were peasant heroes, but that others were cynical adventurists; that no government, particularly a Soviet government, could be trusted to act except in its own self-interest. The progressive impulses of the 1960s were not totally alien to Nixon, as a number of his policy initiatives indicated, but his predisposition was toward the dour, Puritan view of social progress. The history of American social thought is a swinging back and forth between the Puritan position and the optimism of benevolent progressivism. The Puritan view holds sway, I think, when the nation is concentrating on building its wealth and power, as in the post-World War II period and in the late-nineteenth-century era of Social Darwinism. Optimistic progressivism tends to dominate during periods when gains are being consolidated after a new plateau of wealth has been achieved, and issues of distributive justice again begin to receive attention. The pre-World War I Progressive era and the late 1960s were such times. I believe Nixon understood his presidential election victories as a signal that the tide was shifting back again. I suspect liberals knew it as well, if only half-consciously, and resented Nixon the more for it. Their resentment was hardly dulled by Nixon's delight in rubbing the liberal nose in the fact that the majority of the country seemed ready to adopt the Nixonian view of the world.

The Real Majority

Nixon's national landslide in 1972 underscored the shift in the country's sentiment and demonstrated with unmistakable force the gap that had opened between the intellectual left of the Democratic party and the vast majority of voters. After Eugene McCarthy's antiwar movement against Lyndon Johnson split the party in 1968, and Nixon defeated Hubert Humphrey's liberal-centrist coalition, the Democrats were effectively taken over by a left-wing minority. The rise of the left after 1968 was a natural playing-out of the politics of morality. There was a plausible case that the Democrats had lost in 1968 because they had compromised on principle. In this view, Humphrey was a trimmer. His break with Johnson on the war was too late and too equivocal. The commitment to civil rights was not total; the party was dominated by white males and political bosses and had yet to erase the stain of the failure to seat the Mississippi civil rights/SNCC delegation in the 1964 convention. The savage battling in Chicago, the argument went, was bloody testimony to the party's hostility to youth, gays, women, and minorities of all kinds.

The "New Politics," as the politics of morality came to be called, was expressed through loosely flowing organizations like the New Democratic Coalition, built around sets of more or less related issues, in contrast to the traditional interest-based politics of American parties. The leadership tended to be veterans of campus antiwar demonstrations, the civil rights struggle, and the newer environmental movement, with a good sprinkling of former Peace Corps volunteers, antipoverty warriors, and welfare rights campaigners. The most politically savvy came from the McCarthy campaign and the Kennedy staff—Robert's rather than John's. The autoworkers, or at least their professional staff, were an important source of financial and intellectual support, as were the state and municipal unions; most unions, however, stayed uninvolved, and the AFL, or trade-union, side of labor was openly hostile. The movement was serious and professional enough to strike a real scare into experienced politicians. McCarthy's kids, "all neat and clean for Gene," proved a formidable organizing force. The development of wholly new campaign techniques based on television, detailed polling, and scientific voter segmentation made it practical simply to bypass traditional party organizations. John Lindsay's mayoral victory in New York City in 1969, after he had been repudiated in his own party primary, was something of a high point. Jack Newfield wrote in the *Village Voice:* "[Lindsay] has stopped the backlash at the banks of the Hudson with his New Politics combination of an independent political campaign, expert media, hundreds of student activists, and antiwar conviction. ... He's invented the scale model for a national New Politics campaign in 1972."

There was a grab bag of "movement" issues—abortion, gay rights, minimum wages for farm workers, pollution—but it was the continued failure to end the war in Vietnam that was the source of organizing strength. Dissatisfaction with the war was sufficiently widespread that it is possible to imagine that if American casualties had continued unabated, the antiwar forces could have brought down another administration. But Nixon outmaneuvered his opposition and defanged the war issue by sharply reducing the American presence in Vietnam in favor of local troops. As the number of Americans killed or wounded dwindled to the vanishing point, the war became just another distant savagery between alien peoples. Despite continued strong opposition in the Senate, it quietly slipped from the top spot on the national political agenda. When draft call-ups were ended in 1971, the campus demonstrations came to an abrupt end. The moral indignation of the campus radicals was, after all, laced with a healthy dose of self-interest.

Once the Vietnam issue was contained, the New Politics collapsed. In the dazzle of their own rhetoric, the New Left leaders forgot the most fundamental rule of politics—do your arithmetic. John Kenneth Galbraith had not done his sums when he intoned in 1972: "George McGovern will appeal to the unrich, unpowerful, and unprivileged majority and, therefore, he will be elected President." Whatever the numbers of the "unrich, unpowerful, and unprivileged," they couldn't swing an election even if they voted, which members of underclasses rarely do, and George McGovern, as it turned out, appealed to almost no one at all, except enough of Galbraith's fellow Massachusetts intellectuals to carry that one lonesome state. The vast majority of Americans in the early 1970s, in fact, considered themselves quite well off and were reasonably happy with their lot. They were troubled by many of the things they saw going on in the country, to be sure, but what troubled them was for the most part precisely the policies and attitudes espoused by the New Left.

There is an odd and inverse symmetry between personal and abstract systems of morality. The greater the stress on concrete values of family, hard work, sexual morality, and conventional religious ethics, the greater, it seems, is the acceptance of an amoral, realpolitik posture in international relations. Kant stressed that the golden rule had no application between nations. On the other hand, the most fervent advocates of morality between nations and racial groups are often the most ready to derogate long-standing personal values. When breaking with tradition, perhaps, the tendency is to break with it across the board. In any case, the New Left advocates of international peace and racial and sexual justice were wont to link these wholly admirable objectives with attacks on conventional values and systems of personal morality, and they pressed them with a stridency and self-righteous scorn that thoroughly antagonized the great middle classes of the country. The great majority of American women, for example, were in favor of equal rights with men, particularly equal pay for equal work, but they were not prepared to agree that keeping house and raising kids were tasks best left to menials. Most people could agree that homosexuals shouldn't be victimized or discriminated against, but they didn't want their children being told that homosexuality was as good a choice of life-style as any other. Almost everyone accepted that the unemployed needed money and help in finding jobs, but they were annoyed when welfare reformers insisted that people shouldn't take jobs that weren't "meaningful."

For all the media adulation of the "Forerunners" and the "New Consciousness," the typical American voter was not a shaggy twenty-year-old or an angst-ridden philosophy professor, but was more like a forty-seven-year-old housewife, married to a machinist in Dayton, Ohio. As Ben Wattenberg and Richard Scammon wrote perceptively in *The Real Majority,* a basic text in the Nixon White House:

> To know that the lady in Dayton is afraid to walk the streets alone at night, to know that she has a mixed view about blacks and civil rights because before moving to the suburbs she lived in a neighborhood that became all black, to know that her brother-in-law is a policeman, to know that she does not have the money to move again if her new neighborhood deteriorates, to know that she is deeply distressed because her son goes to a community college where LSD

has been found on campus—to know all this is the beginning of contemporary political wisdom.

It was a bit of wisdom that the national media and the Democratic intellectual leadership did not understand nearly as well as Richard Nixon. During the riots outside the Chicago convention, one television commentator, deeply distressed, shouted, "They are beating up our children!" He was right. The youngsters battling the police in Chicago were overwhelmingly the children of the upper middle classes, who were attending the best, and most expensive, private colleges in the country. The Dayton housewife, on the other hand, saw rich kids throwing rocks at her sister's husband.

The great majority most parted company from the liberal elite in their view of blacks and civil rights. I learned to appreciate the gap between liberal doctrine and reality about 1970—from my oldest son, who was then six or seven. We lived in the city, and one day while on a walk, we heard loud sounds of people fighting. Michael shook his head and said, "Those black people sure fight a lot." My reflex response was, "You can't see them, you don't know they're black." His look was withering. *"Dad."* I shrank to about half normal size—the voices were clearly black, of course—and when I recovered, pressed the topic a bit. It soon emerged that he had worked out a rather careful set of distinctions. About half his playmates and best friends were black so he wasn't a racist. He knew that all black kids did not steal bikes, but he also knew that, in his experience, the kids who stole bikes were black. He knew that some of his black friends were smarter in school than he was, but he also knew that the disruptive kids, and the kids who couldn't or wouldn't do the work, were black. He knew that white kids didn't steal your lunch money, but he had learned the hard way to be on his guard when he met black kids he didn't know on his way to school.*

The surveys collected by Scammon and Wattenberg showed that most people in the country had a fairly discriminating set of views about race based on practical experience not unlike my son's. There was a proportion of pure bigots, to be sure, but they were clearly not

---

*We lived in a university community in West Philadelphia that was superficially highly integrated; but the blacks tended to be lower- or working-class and the whites highly educated, so the class differences were vast. Lower-class ethnic groups—white or black—rarely integrate spontaneously. Much of the urban "integration" of recent years has been accomplished by upper-class whites returning to the central city, which, perversely, helps reinforce impressions of racial stereotypes.

a majority; George Wallace got only 13 percent of the vote in 1968. Most people in pre-election surveys thought that Nixon would not increase the pace of civil rights change, but importantly, they thought that he would not *decrease* it either, a moderate position, in short, that counted heavily in his favor. An overwhelming majority supported civil rights, felt badly about racial discrimination in the past, and favored government intervention to clean up slums. But the same people were thoroughly exasperated with the social tensions that had paralleled the civil rights movement. The average New York City taxpayer, to take an example, had lost patience with preachments about equal job opportunities. He knew that in 1958 there were only about 150,000 people on welfare in the city. And a decade later, he knew that there were 1.5 *million* people on welfare, that they were almost all black, and that it cost more than $1 billion a year to support them despite the fact that employment and economic growth in the city were at all-time highs. The same New Yorker knew that in the 1950s he never thought twice about riding the subway at night or walking in the park and that now he was afraid to do so. He also knew that almost all the new crime in the city was committed by blacks, and he didn't like it when liberal politicians tried to tell him that it wasn't so. And he was particularly angry when he was told that his concern for his own safety and his insistence on law and order in his neighborhood meant that he was a bigot.

The crime issue, even more than welfare, was a wedge splitting apart blacks and whites. Shortly after he had taken office, Nixon proposed a series of supposedly tough new anticrime measures. They were immediately attacked by civil rights leaders as "racist" and "antiblack." It was an extraordinarily ill-considered reaction. The measures themselves were of little moment and, as cynics predicted, were quite ineffectual. But by insisting that anticrime measures were inherently antiblack, the civil rights spokesmen confirmed what middle-class whites had suspected all along—that crime was a black problem. And by claiming that crime control was a form of discrimination, they seemed to be saying that black youngsters could act as antisocially as they pleased—beating up old ladies was a civil right. Such statements not only inflamed white antagonisms, they also demonstrated the vast distance between official black spokesmen and the great mass of working blacks. The old lady who got beaten up was, in the great majority of cases, a black old lady, and the prime beneficiaries of effective crime control would have been working-class blacks.* It took almost another decade for black politicians to realize that a tough anticrime stance was a most effective appeal to the black voter.

Given the mood of the country, his own conservative proclivities, and his attachment to the traditionalist virtues of hard work, thrift, and self-reliance, Nixon might have been expected to orchestrate a wholesale abandonment of the egalitarian goals of Lyndon Johnson's Great Society. The fact that he did not do so was very much to his credit. Indeed, he launched a program of his own that was in many ways superior to Johnson's, and he received neither credit nor cooperation from liberals in doing so.

Nixon as Social Reformer

Early in 1971, after Nixon's Family Assistance Plan (FAP) had failed for the second time to pass the Senate, the *New York Times* wrote, "Even Richard Nixon came out for income maintenance payments that would be paid to desperately poor families with no questions asked." In his chronicle of the effort to pass FAP, Daniel Patrick Moynihan amends the *Times* statement. "Not 'even,' " he writes. "Among presidents, 'only.' " Moynihan is correct. Nixon's record on social legislation bears comparison with that of any other President. The Kennedy and Johnson technocratic strategy for ending poverty was essentially a service strategy. The premise of their antipoverty program was that specialists in community organization, mental health, job training, social work —that is, college-educated white people—could work some alchemy upon the poor that would make them rise up and become nonpoor. Nixon adopted an income strategy. The fastest way to raise people out of poverty was to give them money—an absolutely direct approach, both conservative and radical at the same time, considerably more expensive than a service strategy, but less bureaucratizing and much less patronizing. It was a profound change in the relation between the federal government and its citizens, and one that was oddly unremarked upon. If liberals gave Nixon little credit for his reforms, conservatives assign little blame to him now, when the scale of transfer payments has

*Black civil rights leaders were not elected, of course, but were merely recognized by whites. They were, not unreasonably, typically more responsive to a white civil rights constituency than to the black electorate. Charles Hamilton has theorized that the "recognition" process retarded black political development.

become an economic problem of significant proportions.

The Nixon program was developed early in his first term and, with the exception of Family Assistance, was passed by Congress substantially as proposed. It is indicative of the congressional understanding of Nixon's strategy that one of its cornerstones, the effective elimination of federal income tax on the poor, was passed without controversy and almost without comment. In its first year, the tax change had the effect of a $625-million transfer payment to poor families; by 1972, the cost was $2 billion—much more, that is, than the entire Office of Economic Opportunity appropriation, even in its halcyon days, and none of it diverted to professional salaries.

Coverage under unemployment insurance was substantially broadened and a national "trigger" was introduced so the duration of benefits would increase whenever unemployment rose above a specified level. The food stamp program was extended throughout the country and eligibility requirements were simplified. In three years, food stamp recipients increased from less than five million to eleven million, and spending, virtually all of which was a direct transfer to the poor, rose from $250 million in 1969 to $2.2 billion in 1971, a ninefold increase. Most significant of all, in terms of both its economic impact and its effect in reducing poverty, Social Security payments were increased substantially and indexed to inflation to preserve their purchasing power. The largest group of poor, recall, were older white women, not black or Hispanic welfare mothers.

Finally, and at least indirectly related to the income strategy, Nixon greatly increased federal aid to cities and states. The period of fastest growth in aid to cities was not during Lyndon Johnson's presidency, as conventional wisdom has it, but during Richard Nixon's first term. A significant part of the increase was in the form of unrestricted revenue-sharing grants—long a liberal objective—with the remainder concentrated in housing, employment, and the pollution-control programs. Almost as important, rule changes made the grants more predictable and reduced the level of bureaucratic control that could be exercised from Washington. All this, by the way, from an administration Richard Rovere in 1971 dubbed "stridently right-wing."

The failure to pass the Family Assistance Plan demonstrated the loss of compass for the achievable by the political left-of-center. The basic welfare program, or Aid to Families with Dependent Children, was, and remains to this day a mess. The eligibility criteria are voluminous, byzantine, and internally contradictory. Benefits vary widely from state to state. With some exceptions, aid is generally not available to intact families, creating an inducement for parents either to separate or to lie to the welfare investigator. Worse, when Nixon took office, the program had become racially divisive. Poor whites were much less likely to be on welfare than blacks: because both parents were in the home in a much higher percentage of the cases, because family income was more often just slightly over the welfare eligibility level, and because whites were not nearly as willing to apply for welfare as blacks or Puerto Ricans, regardless of eligibility. A de facto color criterion for receipt of federal income support was a depressing, even frightening, portent for racial harmony.

Nixon proposed a set of truly radical changes. First there would be a national floor on welfare benefits that at a stroke would triple or quadruple the incomes of the very poorest people in the country, dependent blacks in the Deep South. More important, Nixon proposed to recast welfare support into the form of a negative income tax. All families would be eligible, regardless of their marital or employment status, depending only on their income. From a base grant of $1600 for a family of four with no outside income, the FAP grant would taper off as outside income rose, cutting off completely when total money income reached about $4000. About fourteen million additional families would become eligible for assistance, almost all of them working poor in intact families. There were work requirements for employable heads of families, essentially no different from the ones that were already law. There were additional funds for job training and day care and a fund to ensure that all states would save at least some money compared to the previous program. The additional cost was estimated to be $5 billion in the first year.

Nixon and Daniel Patrick Moynihan, who was his domestic adviser, calculated that enough moderate Republicans would follow the President's lead on FAP that, together with the liberal Democrats, they could pass the program over the objections of the rock-hard conservatives in both parties. It was a tactic that could have been pursued only by an administration with impeccable conservative credentials; a liberal Democratic administration could never have passed FAP in the 1970s. As expected, the Southern opposition was immediate. Representative Phil Landrum's comment was typical: "There's not going to be anybody left to roll these wheelbarrows and press these shirts. They're all going to be on welfare." The rumblings on the right were worrisome, but they could be managed. Nixon and Moynihan did not anticipate, however, that moderate Democrats would sit on their hands—out of fear of conceding social points to a Republican—or that the party's left would attack the proposals with a vehemence that bordered on frenzy. The National Welfare Rights Organization said that FAP was an "act of political repression" and that the work requirement was "genocide." John Lindsay said that work requirements were "from the dark ages." Senator Fred Harris wanted a minimum grant of $2500 with tapering-off provisions covering seventy-five million people at a cost of $20 billion. Harris voted to kill the President's bill in committee. Senator McCarthy wanted a minimum grant of $5000, covering the majority of the people in the country, at a cost of $100 billion. He also voted to kill the FAP bill. George McGovern wanted universal family allowances at a cost of $35 to $55 billion, and opposed FAP. When the bill finally died, the welfare rights lobbyists popped champagne corks and declared themselves "jubilant." The Southern conservatives who controlled the Senate Finance Committee, meanwhile, watched these liberal gyrations with ill-concealed pleasure, and then, once the FAP struggle was over, proceeded to pass welfare eligibility restrictions and work requirements that were far more draconian than anything in the current law or the even milder provisions of FAP, much to the horror of the "victorious" left.

Despite its penchant for high-minded moralizing, the liberal opposition was irresponsible. After the last great spasm of antiwar protest that accompanied the invasion of Cambodia in 1970, social militancy degenerated into self-interested showmanship. It felt good to yell for more, and every petty interest group tried to convert its claims into moral imperatives. Union bargaining rights for local government civil service employees was one of the demands of the Poor People's March on Washington, for example. When Nixon reduced the mandatory social services required in state welfare programs from fourteen to three, the move was loudly attacked by social workers as a repressive step, a "sharp attack on the family" designed to "make the poor poorer." It was nothing of the kind; the new rules were perfectly consistent with the shift from a services to an income strategy against poverty. It *was* a sharp attack, however, on the pocketbooks of social workers, who had increased both their numbers and their dependency on the federal government manyfold in the previous decade. Catching the mood, Congress passed the

Child Development Act of 1971, a genuinely revolutionary bill, of shadowy intellectual provenance, but strongly supported by militant feminists and organized social workers, that would have provided government day care for most children in the country. Passage of the bill was irresponsible, because Congress did not intend that it should become law. Although the legislation passed both houses by more than two-thirds majorities, there was no serious attempt at override when Nixon vetoed it. Congress was playing for the gallery; the bill would never have passed if Nixon's veto had not been a certainty.

Perhaps if political fashion had been less expressive and rhetoric less shrill, Nixon's social initiatives might have achieved a broader base of centrist support. But the superheated atmosphere of the early 1970s was hardly suited for dispassionate discussion of programmatic reform. With characteristic fatalism, Nixon expected little praise for his program, and told his advisers at the outset that they would receive no credit from liberals no matter what they did. But it seems clear that by the end of the first term he had begun to weary of the battle for his domestic agenda and was more prepared simply to return spite with spite. In any case, he always viewed domestic concerns as a secondary theme of his presidency. Foreign affairs was the arena where he intended to make a lasting mark on history. The furor of the debate surrounding Nixon's management of the American commitment in Vietnam made the fireworks on the domestic side seem mere flickerings by comparison.

Vietnam

By the time Nixon took office, the debate on the war in Vietnam had come to be framed in moral terms to an extent not seen in America since the Mexican and Civil Wars. Just as in the civil rights movement, transcendent moral concepts directly confronted traditional politics— in this instance, conventional notions of national self-interest and global jockeying for power. The rapidly elaborating theories of civil disobedience sharpened the clash, while the fissures along age-related lines added to its stridency. The moral criticisms of U.S. policy were rejected out of hand by Nixon and Henry Kissinger, who, as foreign policy aide, managed the day-to-day diplomacy of the war. For one thing, in their view, there was a meretricious ring to moral preachments in the mouths of Democratic liberals. Vietnam was, after all, the liberals' war. It wasn't Richard Nixon who sent a half million men to be pinned down in the jungle. The commitment was made by the cocktail-party guerrilla fighters of 1961, like Rostow, Taylor, and Schlesinger, and the brilliant young men who prated their ignorant theories of counterinsurgency in those glorious days when the White House crackled with vicarious Green Beret virility and touch football teams clashed playfully on the lawn. Now that the war was messy and protracted and ugly, and it was clear that the outcome, as in all wars, depended more or less directly on how determinedly Americans and Vietnamese killed each other, the erstwhile jungle warriors had withdrawn grandly to high towers of moral dudgeon to assail Nixon's militarism and to invent histories that proved how smoothly John Kennedy would have cleaned it all up.

More fundamentally, both Nixon and Kissinger took a "European" view of international politics, which essentially held that moral concepts were irrelevant and dangerous in the great contests between nations. Kissinger, the professor of international relations, most articulately defended the position. Ironically, his view was avowedly an existentialist one, with the difference that Kissinger had actually read his Kant and Hegel and Heidegger while the campus protesters had not. In the existentialist formulation, international politics flows like a river without a destination. Guided only by interest, the helmsman picks a course through the rapids and vortices, backpaddling as necessary, with an eye as far as possible on the rocks that lie ahead. It was a view radically different from the typically American conception of world politics as a global sporting event with rules and scores, good sides and bad sides, a final whistle, and providentially determined results. Kissinger was continually exasperated by what he called the American "disillusion with imperfect outcomes," or the "inability to understand the possibility of tragedy," or the "illusion that our exertions had a terminal point." On the other hand, he insisted that the existentialist attitude did not preclude normative conceptions of world order. But the grand conceptions would be grounded on principles of safety and wealth, not on notions of abstract goodness.

By conventional standards of diplomacy, the Nixon-Kissinger performance in extricating America from Vietnam was brilliant. Their essentially pessimistic expectations of the world served them well. American policy was reoriented toward far more limited objectives than under Kennedy or Johnson—simply getting out with the South Vietnamese government intact—and, despite the domestic turbulence of the early 1970s, proceeded to develop in a virtually straight line. Two dazzling strokes—the concordance with China and the détente with Russia—effectively isolated the North Vietnamese. The upgrading of the South's military capacity, the withdrawal of American ground troops, and the end of the draft, all dampened domestic protest sufficiently to give the President a freer negotiating hand. Removal of restrictions on bombing the North and the willingness to pursue the North's troops across international borders increased the pressure on Ho to negotiate in earnest. Kissinger, in fact, probably cared little about the objective outcome in Vietnam. With his eye fixed on a looming global confrontation over the oil resources of the Middle East, his concern was to re-establish American skillfulness in the use of power.

The Nixon-Kissinger policy was a daring one, as Leslie Gelb has pointed out, with more short-term risks than Lyndon Johnson's steady, but conceptually static, escalation. It also came close to succeeding. A critical assumption was that after a ceasefire was negotiated, U.S. air power would punish the North for any violations of its terms. When Congress prevented the use of that power in 1975, the North ignored the ceasefire and quickly completed its conquest—marching into Saigon as American officials and their Vietnamese retainers scrambled for helicopters on the roof of the embassy compound.

The best argument in justification of the essential cynicism of the Nixon-Kissinger war policy was the even greater cynicism of North Vietnam. The American press was late to realize that much of what John Kennedy called Communist aggression in Vietnam was in fact an indigenous uprising against the Diem tyranny. The image of the black-pajamaed freedom fighter then dominated press and literary reporting —Frances FitzGerald's *Fire in the Lake* is a good example—long after it ceased to represent reality. In fact, the regular army of the North took control of the war away from the Southern-based Viet Cong during the turmoil that followed the fall of Diem. In late 1964, the North launched the first conventional phase of the war with a classic infantry campaign aimed at cutting the South in half and isolating Saigon. The campaign ended when the Americans inflicted a major defeat on the Northern troops after a ten-day pitched battle in the Ia Drang valley in 1965. The North then went on the tactical defensive, rebuilding its strength and allowing the Viet Cong to take the initiative in a series of harassing operations, until the great Tet offensive of 1968. Tet was another military failure for the North, although an enormous psychological victory. Interestingly, Giap used Viet Cong troops to man the front line during

Tet, which destroyed the indigenous Communist infrastructure and left the North in uncontested control of the war. Whether such a result was intended is a matter of speculation, although there is ample precedent —one is reminded of the Russian use of Polish partisans as shock troops during the Warsaw Uprising.

The cynicism of the third great conventional assault—the twelve-division Eastertide offensive of 1972—surprised even Kissinger. It was launched against the backdrop of the secret negotiations Kissinger had been conducting with Le Duc Tho in Paris since 1969, and which had tested to the utmost Nixon's forbearance. Kissinger had offered basically every peace formula suggested by the American peace party,* while the North had steadfastly insisted on nothing less than immediate hegemony, which Kissinger could not offer and only a small minority on the American left were prepared to concede. At the same time, the official negotiators from the North repeatedly furnished American reporters with statements that appeared much more forthcoming than their secret negotiating posture, fueling an American outcry against Nixon's apparent intransigence. Then in the fall of 1971, Le Duc Tho unexpectedly canceled a scheduled session and refused repeated requests for further meetings. It gradually became clear that, with Nixon's "Vietnamization" program at a fragile stage and only 69,000 American troops still in the country, the North had decided on one last test of arms. When the attack came in March, it was again a purely conventional one: the first major trophy of the offensive, the provincial capital of Quang Tri, was taken by a tank assault after a heavy artillery barrage. Nixon responded with heavy air attacks on the North and the aerial mining of the Hanoi-Haiphong harbor. With close American air support, the South's troops turned in a surprisingly good account of themselves, and the offensive ground to a halt almost immediately. Within weeks, Le Duc Tho indicated his willingness to resume serious negotiations, and by the fall accepted essentially the offer Kissinger had made the previous year.†

*Within the first eight months of Nixon's term, Kissinger had offered Le Duc Tho all of the elements of the peace platform that had been *defeated* at the 1968 Democratic convention as too dovish—i.e., essentially the McGovern platform. It was rejected almost without discussion.
†Seymour Hersh argues that Kissinger in fact made a substantial concealed concession to the North in the wake of the spring offensive—permitting the North to keep their troops in the South after the offensive was halted. If Hersh is correct, it would seem to be another example of Nixon's and Kissinger's willingness to conciliate. But true to liberal dogma, Hersh insists that the American policy was one of obdurate warmongering. In his book *The Price of Power*, he cites the Nixon-Kissinger response to the North's 1972 offensive—which he concedes was a massive, conventional surprise attack—as an example of *American* escalation.

The last stage of the war, the successful assault from the North in 1975, could have been used to illustrate U.S. Army Field Manual procedures. It was described by the North Vietnamese general, Van Tien Dung.

> Because we concentrated the majority of our forces in the main area of the campaign, we achieved superiority over the enemy in this area. As for infantry, the ratio was 5.5 of our troops for each enemy soldier. As for tanks and army vehicles, the ratio was 1.2 to 1. In heavy artillery, the ratio was 2.1 to 1.

Dung's account might have been written by Patton.

> The Army II Corps . . . covering a distance of 900 kms . . . had been ordered to report in Bien Hoa and Ba Ria in eighteen days. . . . All 2000 vehicles of the army corps had to cross six big rivers while having to fight the enemy en route. . . . Cadres of the front staff . . . could not draw maps quickly enough to keep up with the advance of our forces.

When the North's troops finally encircled Saigon, they had amassed fifteen divisions against the defender's five, and the result was a foregone conclusion. The same conservative tactic of massed armor and infantry was used when the North rolled into Laos and Cambodia in 1978 and 1979. Hardly the guerrilla legend of the silent knife-thrust in the jungle night.

Nixon's grasp of the realpolitik of the war was far more clearheaded than that of the liberal opposition. Contrast, for example, the reaction of the American peace party to the 1972 bombing campaign with that of China and Russia. China issued a brief statement condemning the attacks but stressed that it intended to continue the "process of normalizing relations" with the United States. The Soviet Union received Nixon in Moscow for détente discussions at the height of the bombing despite damage to Soviet ships in the Haiphong harbor. Nixon contended, probably correctly, that he would never have been received so deferentially had the North put American troops to flight in Vietnam. At home, on the other hand, Democratic senators condemned the campaign as "folly" (Kennedy); "reckless and wrong" (Proxmire); "Congress must not allow it" (McGovern); "protracting the war" (Mansfield); "jeopardizing the security interest of the United States" (Muskie). The *New York Times* called it a "desperate gamble" and called upon Congress to "save the President from himself and the nation from

disaster." The Washington *Post* decided that Nixon had "lost touch
with reality" and demanded that he be turned out of office at the coming
election. The reaction was a replay, in short, of the storm of protests that
followed Nixon's offensive against North Vietnamese staging areas in
Cambodia in 1970—while in both instances the attitude in the Communist capitals seemed to be that American counterattacks were a hazard
reasonably to be expected when one waged conventional war against the
United States.

The most detailed moral indictment of the Nixon-Kissinger Vietnam
policy is that in William Shawcross's book *Sideshow,* on the expansion
of the war into Cambodia. Kissinger has rebutted Shawcross in his
memoirs, and I think has much the better of the argument. Shawcross
argues, first, that the bombing and invasion of the North Vietnamese
staging areas was ineffective, which begs the moral question. Secondly,
he suggests that the U.S. attacks pushed the war west into Cambodia
and drew that hapless nation into the conflict; and finally, he blames the
U.S. involvement for professionalizing the war in Cambodia, thus inten-
sifying its final horrors. Kissinger's view is that North Vietnam, not the
United States, widened the war. Up to 40,000 North Vietnamese had
been massed in Cambodia preparing for yet another conventional assault on the South Vietnamese and the Americans, who had already
commenced their withdrawal. By attacking the Cambodian "sanctu-
aries," the United States delayed the North's conventional assault, allowing U.S. withdrawal and Vietnamization to proceed. The argument
turns at bottom on whether the war had become a conventional one, as
Kissinger insists, or was still a democratic indigenous uprising, the view
implicit in Shawcross. The facts by 1970, it seems, were substantially on
Kissinger's side.

The view of the war as a peasant uprising had remarkable staying
power. As late as 1975, the *New York Times* argued against helping the
Cambodian government fight the Khmer Rouge on the grounds that the
insurgents were probably more representative of the people. The Khmer
Rouge regime, it turned out, exercised its writ with a genocidal repres-
siveness not seen since the Nazis marched into Poland. They did so, that
is, until they were in turn swallowed up by the ever voracious North
Vietnamese, who, as soon as they consolidated their victory in the
South, sent their tanks rolling over their erstwhile Khmer Rouge allies.

In the realpolitik view, the grievous sin of the war was to become
involved without understanding the consequences of involvement—the

cavalier commitment of the Kennedy administration was the root immorality. The sin was compounded by a reluctance to use power, which
skewed the contest into a prolonged war of attrition. The final immorality, if that word is applicable, was the abdication of responsibility in
1975. The clinching argument is that all the dire predictions of the
realpolitik practitioners came true. The domino theory was a fact—Laos
and Cambodia fell immediately and the rest of Southeast Asia shud-
dered. And although it took several years before the antiwar parties
would admit it, the Communist conquerors behaved with a malevolence
beyond the nightmares of any knee-jerk conservative. The predicted
bloodbath happened, complete with concentration camps, "re-educa-
tion" centers, and the heartbreaking plight of hundreds of thousands of
boat people, risking pirates, starvation, and the high seas rather than the
dictatorship at home. Finally, as Kissinger put it:

> The collapse in 1975 not only led to genocidal horrors in Indochina;
> from Angola to Ethiopia to Iran to Afghanistan, it ushered in a
> period of American humiliation, an unprecedented Soviet geopoliti-
> cal offensive all over the globe, and pervasive insecurity, instability,
> and crisis.

And yet. And yet. The realpolitik arguments are uncomfortably pat.
War has always been an instrument of policy, but how does one decide
which policies justify killing people, and how many people can, with
proportion, be killed? By the 1970s, the tons and tons of bombs dropped
from B-52s on peasant villages, the savageries of napalm attacks, the
sickening details of the massacre at My Lai, the bright blood on the
nightly television screens, the shots and screams at Kent State had all
compounded into a palpable, almost overwhelming, evil. And the stakes
in Vietnam, whatever the retrospective clarity of realpolitik, had become
so abstract, the daily ebb and flow of the conflict so amorphous and
apparently pointless, that the moral clamor would not down.

The burden of the moral blame does not lie with Nixon and Kissinger. The brutality was at its height when they assumed responsibility
for the war. It was already an academic question whether the cold
ferocity of the conquering North Vietnamese and Khmer Rouge would
have been softened by an easier victory. In 1968, I was convinced that
Nixon should simply quit the war, withdraw the troops—however
precipitately—and forget about Vietnam. I no longer believe that. The
actual withdrawal was about as direct and rapid as was possible, even

allowing for breakdowns like the failure of negotiations that led to the "Christmas bombing" of 1972—his fault, Kissinger acknowledges. But wherever fault lay, and however legitimate the ultimate resort to arms in behalf of policy, Vietnam raised squarely the question of limits. If the North Vietnamese simply refused to submit or negotiate—ever—how long could we have bombed them? The peace movement—for all the self-indulgent exhibitionism, the self-interested draft evasion, the woolly idealism, the intergenerational nose-tweaking—still raised sharply, insistently, the question of limits. Were there constraints that transcended policy?

Kissinger charges that "the foreign policy establishment" lost its nerve and morale over Vietnam. When the war did not produce the quick victory that the Green Beret fantasists expected, the establishment was traumatized by failure and discharged its shame and guilt in hysterical denunciations of Nixon. There is much truth in what he says, but I think the issue is more complicated still. I was involved in prison administration in the middle 1970s. I know of several instances where a psychologist or counselor attempted to treat a difficult prisoner, and where, after the expenditure of much time and emotional energy, the prisoner responded with outrageous behavior. The therapist had power to punish and properly did so. The prisoner responded more outrageously. The therapist, now fully committed, increased the punishment. Implacable, the prisoner raised the ante again, until, in the worst cases when the limits were not clear, the prisoner was brutalized, at least psychologically, and the therapist was degraded. Something similar happened in Vietnam. The foreign policy establishment was immobilized, not so much by failure of nerve, but by consciousness of its own degradation.

The feeling of degradation by the war was pervasive among liberals; it left psychological wounds that the furious denunciations of Nixon helped to cauterize. The need for cauterization, I suspect, also helps explain the willingness to pursue, even the enthusiasm for pursuing, the Watergate investigations to their bitter end. In a sense, as in the debate about Vietnam, Watergate was about limits, about where to strike the balance between the necessary and the permissible, drawing the line where the demands of realpolitik had to bow to the rules of acceptable political behavior. Watergate could not have happened, of course, if the Nixon White House had not carried its practice of political hardball to such gross extremes. But there had been opportunities for Watergate-type investigations before. No one inquired beyond Bobby Baker, for instance, to seek the sources of Lyndon Johnson's great wealth. The need to take a stand on moral grounds, regardless of the consequences, stemmed in part from the frustration of the search for limits that had been such a devastating failure for citizens of conscience during the war in Vietnam.

Watergate

When Richard Nixon was inaugurated for his second term in 1973, his admirers could plausibly argue that he had secured his place as one of the great Presidents. The war in Vietnam had ended without a humiliating American defeat. The ice floes that had encased the postwar confrontation between Communism and the West had been shattered. China, for decades America's bitterest enemy, now more nearly resembled an ally. A major new arms limitation treaty was only the most visible fruit of the new détente with Russia. America enjoyed preeminent influence in the Middle East. The economy was booming again—Nixon was the only postwar President skillful enough to orchestrate an economic upturn with a national election—while inflation had been checked by wage and price controls. The share of the federal budget devoted to social programs and income transfers had risen sharply, while the proportion going to arms programs was rapidly declining. A major new program to alleviate water and air pollution was in the offing. Schools in the South had been quietly integrated. The campuses were peaceful. Perhaps most important for Nixon, the spectral presence of John Kennedy had been thoroughly exorcised. Nixon's popularity ratings were consistently higher than any achieved by Kennedy, and his 1972 election victory, if not quite the greatest in history as he had hoped, was still a smashing vindication of both his policies and his ability to read the public mind.

Within months, he was a hunted man, crashing in breathless flight through the underbrush of Watergate revelations—burglaries, wiretaps, bribery, misuse of power—his enemies in full cry, tendrils of his own lies and deceptions coiling about his feet, until the hounds were upon him and he fell. The pursuit lasted about a year and a half, during which time Nixon gradually ceased to function as President, leaving the country rudderless during great crises like the oil price shocks. Congress attempted to take over the conduct of foreign affairs, and without an executive counterweight, policy yawed and heaved dangerously, until the nation simply withdrew from the world arena and the opportunity was lost for rebuilding American authority after the settlement in Vietnam. Worst of all, Watergate dashed the fragile hope that Nixon could use his sweeping electoral victory to rebuild a centrist social consensus and stabilize the tremor-splintered political foundations of the country. Nixon destroyed himself, undermined the authority of the presidency for a long time to come, and left scar tissue on the body politic that will take decades to fade away.

Without the contention between Nixon and the liberal, "national" press,* the Watergate revelations might never have come to light. Throughout Nixon's first term, journalists, especially print journalists, were feeling increasingly impotent, if the intense self-examinations recorded in the *Columbia Journalism Review* are a useful gauge. They had been late to understand the escalation in Vietnam; in Tom Wicker's view, they had let Johnson use them. Spiro Agnew's charge that they were out of touch had stung, particularly when establishment stalwarts, like Theodore H. White, conceded that Agnew was probably right. (White noted that neither he nor any of his journalist friends were shocked, or even surprised, when his son carried a Viet Cong banner in a peace march; outside the Eastern seaboard or California, the reaction might have been violent.) The national media were outraged by the invasion of Cambodia in 1970 and the "spring bombing" in 1972 and predicted dire electoral consequences. They were wrong both times; Nixon was the better judge of the minds of the people "Out There," in White's phrase. During the 1972 election campaign, Nixon was almost contemptuous of the media establishment. His appeal was carried directly to voters through local television; reporters were kept busy and off balance with an endless stream of prepackaged handouts; and the candidate himself was simply inaccessible. He didn't need the national media, and he let them know it. In the contest between Nixon and the press, he was the clear winner, until he handed them the issue of Watergate.

*Almost all newspapers in the country were staunch Nixon loyalists. But there are a few papers with national circulations—the Washington *Post,* the *New York Times,* the Los Angeles *Times,* perhaps the St. Louis *Post-Dispatch*—which together with the three national television networks exercise a disproportionate impact on the opinions of the educated professionals and those on the campuses. Their views tended toward Kennedy liberalism, and they disliked Nixon. Nixon and Agnew charged that they were an incestuous elite, talking only to each other, viewing America through a distorted lens.

When Watergate was about three years past, I was living in London and several English friends asked if Nixon had been the victim of an American press vendetta. It was a question that troubled me, and I wondered about it, too. In government, I had learned the power of a misinformed reporter and had been alarmed by the competitive investigative zeal that infected the journalistic ranks after Watergate. When I awarded a public contract in the 1970s, I laid down elaborate audit trails, because I *assumed* I would be accused of taking a bribe—and the accusations came more than once. I had good relations with the press, and the stories were in each case quickly killed, but I thought the process was demeaning. I didn't trust the righteous swelling of prosecutorial chests, and I knew people who had been caught in the sudden shift of standards after Watergate.

Public service increasingly seemed a snare. In New Jersey I once heard a county official, who had a reputation for honesty, explain to a contractor the procedures for bidding on work in his county. The official was stressing that his county was clean. There was no bribery, in the sense that a payment could influence the award of a contract. But contractors and architects were expected to make contributions to the party in power based on a percentage of the work they did. The party accounting rules were strict, the official claimed, and no one lined his pockets. The contractor, I recall, was pleased at the prospect of dealing in an "honest" environment. Perhaps I was jaded, but it didn't occur to me that the practice being described was probably felonious. I detested politicians who took money for themselves, as some New Jersey politicians, and later Spiro Agnew, were notorious for doing. They gave all of us in government a bad name. But the politicians I respected all worked hard developing party contributions. It was a shock a few years later to see men being indicted, in some cases even going to jail, for conduct that had seemed a normal part of the political process, and frightening to hear some of the righteous self-trumpeting of the post-Watergate prosecutors.

I never liked Nixon and didn't vote for him even in 1972. (It was easy to vote for McGovern; I was sure he had no chance of winning.) But pulling down a President shouldn't be a sporting event, and I was disturbed by the gleeful malice with which so many of my friends pounced on each new Watergate revelation. Nixon had beaten the liberals in the election, but now they were going to take the country back. The *New York Times* editorials treated him as something reptilian.

While Nixon was still President, Robert Redford was already filming *All the President's Men* in front of the White House, as if in anticipatory celebration. He seemed surrounded by Kennedys. Ted Kennedy had been a prime mover in starting the Senate Watergate investigations. Archibald Cox, the special prosecutor, was a friend of the Kennedy family and invited a number of Kennedys to his swearing-in. John Doar, who headed the House investigation, was a long-time Kennedy associate. Benjamin Bradlee, whose Washington *Post* did the most to uncover the Watergate story, was one of John Kennedy's closest friends and a longtime Nixon-hater.

There was so much hypocrisy—for instance, the press reactions to the expletives on the Watergate tapes. In my experience, almost all politicians and *all* newspapermen talked like that. Sam Ervin's sarcastic grilling of Watergate witnesses was good fun for a time, but then it began to seem like bullying. The congressmen and senators on the Watergate committees who expressed shock that Nixon had accepted questionable campaign contributions—from the dairy industry, for instance—had, in a depressingly large number of cases, done exactly the same thing themselves. Yet they sat there, puffing their cheeks in phony outrage. Once the smell of blood was in the air, prosecutors were relentless and there was little concern for the rights of Watergate defendants. Nixon's friend Charles "Bebe" Rebozo, for instance, was investigated for more than a year. According to the special prosecutor's office, 123 persons were interviewed or questioned, or gave testimony to the grand jury, in the quest for a charge against Rebozo. Two hundred subpoenas for documents were issued, agents analyzed "thousands of pages of records from more than 240 sources," and

> secondary sources also were . . . exhaustively utilized. This included records from banks, accountants, attorneys, various business partners and associates, business firms and so forth. Second, voluminous records were reviewed of telephone calls, travel, meetings with Administration officials, and correspondence with various persons.

The report concluded, disappointedly, that "there is plainly no basis for any indictments."

Still, the answer to my English friends was that, for all the excess of zeal, for all the liberal malice and unseemly glee, for all the air of vendetta, in the final analysis Nixon had done it to himself. Much of the Watergate charges was dross. It was arguably not a crime to wiretap to discover leaks of national security information. The Pentagon Papers *were* classified, and the Chinese had threatened to break off negotiations if Nixon couldn't keep secrets. The campaign fund-raising had been awesomely efficient but probably not illegal, except for some technical violations of an extremely intricate new law. But the fact still remained that the President was involved in a serious felony. Neither Nixon nor his immediate staff knew of the Watergate burglary in advance. John Mitchell knew of it, it seems, only in principle. But they all knew about it immediately afterwards. They knew Mitchell had authorized such goings-on, and they tried to cover it up. The President himself supervised the operation. Bribes were paid. Perjury was encouraged, even rehearsed, in the President's office. The FBI and the CIA were suborned to assist in the deception. The burglary was stupid. The cover-up was a crime, and it was the President's, and he deserved impeachment for it.

Just why Nixon did it still awaits a satisfactory explanation. If he had acted immediately, fired Mitchell, had an open investigation, there would have been a temporary flap; but he would have been re-elected, and the burglary would have been just an odd historical footnote. Perhaps he couldn't risk it. There were already too many unburied cadavers —the Ellsburg burglary, the excess of Tom Huston's internal security operation, Donald Segretti's campaign "ratfuckers." Perhaps. But my own guess is Nixon just didn't know how to be a winner. Deep down, his instincts were to lose—to lose fighting to the last breath, flailing, kicking, and clawing, even as the enemy dragged him down. The early preparations for the second administration—cleaning the opposition out of the agencies, planning revenge on the national media, tightening up on internal dissent—were all evidence that, at the very pinnacle, the mean-spirited side of Nixon was still in control. One can feel pity for him, but more for the country.

Since Watergate, revelations of wrongdoing in other administrations have come to light. The Church committee's exposures of dirty tricks at the CIA. John Kennedy's personal life. The shadowy Mafia connections with his Cuban policy. Wiretapping and bugging by both Kennedys and Lyndon Johnson. The murky sources of Lyndon Johnson's fortune. Pre-Nixon campaign hardball. It puts Nixon's behavior in context, but it is all irrelevant to the question of his guilt. A line had to be drawn somewhere. Similarly, even if most of the post-Watergate prosecutorial scourges were driven by self-aggrandizing hypocrisy, as

I'm inclined to believe, it was still a necessary purgative. The system for building local party war chests in New Jersey may not have been intrinsically dishonest, but the loose money sloshing around undermined probity and misserved the public. It was morally obtuse on my part not to recognize it at the time.

Saddest of all, the real losers in the Watergate debacle were the middle Americans who had kept their heads down during the excesses of the 1960s, who worried about their sons and daughters, who were frightened by the breakdown of family and traditional values, and who relied on men like Nixon and Agnew to help the country reassert its old morality. And now Nixon was a perjurer, and Spiro Agnew had sat in his vice-presidential office and taken money out of brown paper bags. The rest of the decade would be a difficult time, and the pillars people had expected to lean upon had rotted away.

VIII

THE COLLAPSE OF THE KEYNESIAN CONSENSUS

When Nixon took over as President in 1969, he faced difficult economic problems, but not ones that seemed unfathomable or unmanageable. The economy was clearly overheated, in part because of Johnson's attempt to finance the war in Vietnam without tax increases, but primarily because the long Kennedy/Heller expansionary run was finally bumping against classic business-cycle bottlenecks. Unemployment was down to 3.5 percent of the labor force, about a half percentage *below* what economists felt was a reasonable full employment rate for the United States; factory capacity utilization was so high that old and inefficient plants were being pulled back into production; and prices had started to rise. In five years inflation had shot up from only 1.3 percent to 5.4 percent, a rate that seemed wildly out of control to a nation accustomed to price stability. Forces were already in motion to lock in the inflationary burst. The 1966 transit strike settlement in New York City was the first decisive break with Johnson's voluntary wage-price guidelines, and since then the cracks in the policy had become gaping. With another round of nationwide bargaining looming, the major unions had served notice that they wanted big increases, and as long as the labor supply stayed so tight, they were almost certain to get them.

But the problems, serious as they were, still fit within the preconceptions of mainstream economics. The overheating had been predictable, and the modern "neoclassic/Keynesian synthesis" had an arsenal of solutions ready at hand. Despite his conservative rhetoric, Nixon was as committed to Keynesian demand-management principles as

Kennedy, and probably understood them better. He hired good economists for key posts—Arthur Burns, Herbert Stein, George Shultz—and
set about applying the standard Keynesian prescriptions for bringing a
runaway boom under control. The federal budget was brought into
surplus, primarily by reducing defense spending; the growth of the
money supply was dampened to raise interest rates; and the rate of
increase in local government spending was slowed. The economy came
to an abrupt halt—rather more jerkily than the planners hoped—and
there was a recession in 1970. Unemployment jumped to 5 percent,
which was supposed to happen. Disquietingly, however, the rate at
which prices were increasing speeded up, to almost 6 percent in 1970,
and that was *not* supposed to happen. Macroeconomic dogma said that
unemployment and inflation moved in opposite directions. The whole
point of risking the political consequences of higher unemployment was
to slow down the rise in prices. An ugly neologism, "stagflation," began
to appear in political news analyses, along with a growing murmur of
uncharacteristic self-questioning within the economics profession.

In early 1971, Nixon's political advisers started to panic. The administration had come through the 1970 midterm elections in reasonably good shape, but as both recession and inflation continued unabated,
their polls showed that public confidence was rapidly waning. With little
more than a year before the re-election campaign would begin in earnest,
something had to be done. After brooding for some months, Nixon
announced in August a sweeping "New Economic Policy"—a dash to
the left paralleling Lenin's dash to the right fifty years before. The dollar
was devalued, its link with gold was effectively cut, wages and prices
were frozen for ninety days, and a Cost of Living Council was established to administer wage and price controls during a hopefully short,
but unspecified, period after the freeze ended. The cheapened dollar
would stimulate American exports, the break with gold meant that the
dwindling Fort Knox gold hoard would cease to be a constraint on
monetary policy, and the wage-price freeze would allow the administration to pump up the economy without worrying about inflation. It was
an extraordinary demonstration of Nixon's capacity to shed doctrinal
ballast in a crisis.

The new policies were extraordinarily successful throughout 1972
and contributed significantly to Nixon's crushing re-election victory in
the fall. Price inflation dropped to a manageable 3.3 percent, although
wages grew more than twice that fast. Exports moved from a deficit into

a healthy surplus, unemployment dropped below 5 percent at the end of the year, and the economy surged forward at an overall growth rate in excess of 6 percent, one of the strongest showings of the postwar period. It was one of the few times a President had managed to coordinate an economic resurgence with a re-election campaign. It was also a wholly unsustainable performance. During the next two years, as the economy was pounded by external shocks and torn by internal stresses, policy came completely unstuck, along with Nixon's political career.

In the first place, it proved much easier to impose wage-price controls than to take them off, the more so since they proved immensely popular with the electorate. But with the economy running flat out, wages still rising rapidly, the federal budget in a stimulative deficit position, and easy credit—interest rates were at their lowest level since 1965—inflationary pressures were inevitable. The controls could bottle them up but couldn't mandate them away. At the same time, it was clear that controls couldn't last forever. The bare-bones Cost of Living Council had given way to a three-thousand-member Price Commission that was supposed to review and approve pay and pricing decisions for all major businesses in the country. Backlogs, legal tangles, and paperwork snarls were building fast, and businesses were starting to make production decisions by sniffing the bureaucratic breezes from the Price Commission. Only the most committed ideologues were prepared to argue that the resulting allocation decisions were even reasonably efficient. John Dunlop, the Price Commission director and a liberal Democrat, already feared that by adding to supply bottlenecks, the controls were making inflationary pressures worse than ever.

Then bad luck caused a spiral in food prices. U.S. corn production fell by 18 percent because of drought in the Midwest. Adverse weather conditions throughout Asia ruined grain crops in the Soviet Union and India, at a time when the U.S. buffer stocks had been allowed to run down to save on farm price supports. The anchovies which had always arrived each summer off the coast of Peru mysteriously disappeared, and an important source of animal oil-meal feed was lost. (Economists love telling about the disappearing anchovies. It was important, but not *that* important—about 1 percent of animal feed supplies—but in concert with everything else, it hurt.) The Soviet Union beat the capitalists at their own game and masked a huge increase in grain imports with a shrewdly coordinated series of purchases through agents and front organizations. By the time the U.S. government realized what was happening, Soviet purchases had risen from just over one million metric tons to almost twenty million tons, and at rock-bottom U.S.-subsidized prices, about half the world level. Wholesale wheat prices shot up from less than $2 to $6 a bushel. Consumer food prices went up 20 percent in 1973.

The Arab oil embargo during the 1973 Yom Kippur War was the *coup de grace*. The price of Saudi marker crude rose from $1.77 a barrel in October 1973 to $10 in early 1974. A clumsy attempt to allocate supplies led to hoarding and crisis buying. Nixon had attempted to decontrol prices in early 1973, but a rapid burst of price increases had led him to reimpose a freeze in June. From that point, his energies were increasingly consumed by the Watergate investigations. His decision not to press for an extension of price control authority was motivated in part by the necessity of maintaining relations with congressional conservatives, who would be his last line of defense in an impeachment trial.

Wage and price controls were officially ended in April 1974. From February to August, wholesale prices rose at an annual rate of 35 percent. For the full year, consumer prices rose 11 percent and wholesale prices 18.8 percent, truly catastrophic increases. The Federal Reserve clamped down hard on the money supply to choke off the inflation. In the ensuing credit crunch, interest rates rose to an unimaginable 11 percent, the highest to that point in the twentieth century. Industrial production was flat in 1974, and collapsed in 1975. Unemployment rose to 8.5 percent in 1975, the highest since before World War II. Real gross national product went off the cliff, falling more than 2 percent in 1974 and almost 3 percent in 1975.

The "Great Recession" of 1974 and 1975 was the worst since the Depression. It set the pattern for the jagged series of hopeful economic surges and sickening plummets back into the depths that have marked the American economy and bedevilled the entire world ever since. Most frighteningly, relentless inflation, impervious to received policy, shattered the confidence of economists and political managers. Surrounded by sudden instability, public men displayed a level of uncertainty and insecurity that had not been seen in more than thirty years.

Inflation

Inflation is a state of general price increases; but not all price increases are evidence of inflation. If a plant virus were to wipe out a large portion of the world coffee crop, for instance, coffee prices would rise sharply as consumers bid for the available supplies. Most economists would not call the coffee price rise an example of inflation, even though it would have some effect on the consumer price index. But if the Brazilian government attempted to make up for the loss of coffee revenue by vastly increasing the amount of cruzeiros in circulation, it is likely that cruzeiro prices in Brazil would rise rapidly and the value of the cruzeiro would fall in the international money markets. All economists would then call the Brazilian price rise inflation.

Price inflation tends to accompany the last stages of an upswing in the business cycle for two related, if conceptually distinct, reasons. As economic activity reaches a peak, less efficient workers are drawn into the labor force, old machinery is taken out of mothballs to keep up with demand, and the tight labor supply allows unions to insist on bigger wage increases. Costs go up, and so do prices; there is "cost-push" inflation. On the other hand, a business expansion normally will be accompanied by a substantial amount of new credit creation, either consciously by the government or less consciously by the banking system.* Credit is money, and if the production boom should falter for any reason, there will be more money in the hands of the public than there are goods to buy at established prices. Prices will rise; we have "demand-pull" inflation. In a classic business cycle inflation, both elements will be present and inextricably intertwined. Sometimes one or the other will

*The process by which the banking system creates money warrants a footnote. If I deposit $100 in a checking account and the bank lends $50 of it to my neighbor, and he also puts it into his checking account, we jointly have $150 in our checking accounts, and the banking system has created money. If my neighbor's bank relends part of the $50, there will be even more money created, and so on. The Federal Reserve Bank, America's central bank, limits the amount of new money that can be created by requiring banks to hold a portion of their deposits in reserve. If banks have to hold 20 percent of each deposit in reserve, for instance, my initial $100 can be parlayed into a maximum of $500 if it is lent and re-lent to the fullest extent possible—$100 ÷ .20 = $500. [The skeptical reader can confirm the formula by working out $100 + (.80 × $100) + .80 (.80 × $100) . . . etc.] The lower the reserve requirement, the more money can be generated out of the same deposit. By changing reserve requirements, the Federal Reserve can limit or expand the ability of the banking system to create money. Typically, however, the Federal Reserve creates or annihilates money by buying or selling from its huge portfolio of government securities. If the Federal Reserve buys government securities from the public, it pays with its own checks—just numbers on paper or on computer tape, materialized out of nothing. When the public deposits the checks in the banking system, the volume of bank money increases, and will increase even more so as the banks start lending it. In effect, government bonds, which are not spendable, have been converted into checking accounts, which not only are spendable, but can hatch even more spending power through the lending and relending process. If the Federal Reserve wants to reduce the amount of money in circulation, it will *sell* securities from its portfolio, draining checking account money out of the banking system. The same multiplication process will now run in reverse, money will begin to dematerialize, and the total money supply will contract by some amount greater than the amount drained off by the Federal Reserve's security sales.

predominate. The inflation that followed the Arab oil embargo had substantial cost-push elements. The wage increases and easy credit policies during the period of wage-price controls generated demand-pull inflation when the controls were taken off.

In recent years, as inflation has gradually emerged as the world's most important economic problem, it has come to be regarded as the economic equivalent of the black plague. Inflation is, in fact, not always and everywhere a bad thing. In the icy depths of the Depression, when prices, wages, and national wealth were falling rapidly, a little inflation would have seemed like a saving ray of sunshine. Inflation operates as a tax on idle assets; people who keep their money in the sugar bowl during a time of high inflation see it gradually lose its value. In an economy with large amounts of frozen resources, inflation is often a handy way of rejiggering wealth so it can be used productively. Andrew Jackson and American farmers fought the Second Bank of the United States because it wouldn't give them enough inflation. Inflation released them from crushing burdens of debt and let them add to their farms or sell out at a profit to push on further West. The period of the most rapid expansion of the frontier in the mid-nineteenth century is replete with stories of farmers driving to buy their month's provisions with barrels, or even wagons, of wildcat bank notes. To the wide-horizoned American yeoman, a "sound currency," like the cross of gold, was a plutocratic weapon of oppression. More recently, and for similar reasons, a substantial dose of inflation was probably essential for rapidly industrializing countries like Brazil to achieve and move past the point of economic takeoff. Significantly, throughout the 1960s, just before it emerged as an economic superpower, Japan ran double-digit rates of inflation, the highest by far among the industrialized economies.

High and prolonged rates of inflation, however, can be every bit as damaging as a recession, although its effects are distributed differently. People holding money are penalized, and it is perhaps true—although as far as I know it has never been proved—that small savers and the proverbial widows and orphans lose the most. More fundamentally, long periods of inflation undermine stability and concepts of value. Investment money flows away from productive assets into inflation hedges—real estate, art, gold bars. Long-term interest rates rise to very high levels to compensate for the increased uncertainty, and as a consequence, long-term investment dries up. Keynes stressed that long-term investment is the basic driver of the economy. Without continued renewal of its physical assets—its plants, its capital equipment, its roads and bridges, its research and development facilities—a country loses its ability to compete. Something of this sort has happened to England over the last thirty years, and after more than a decade of relatively high inflation in the United States, the same ominous signs are in increasing evidence here.

The persistence of inflation in the 1970s created an intellectual crisis among mainstream economists, since it gave the lie to their alleged ability to fine-tune the economy. Worse, Milton Friedman and his Chicago "monetarist" school of economists argued that inflation inevitably followed expansionist demand-management policies. According to Friedman, the Keynesian policies of which Kennedy, Johnson, and even Nixon had been so proud would work only over the very short term, and would ultimately leave the economy in even worse shape than before.

Friedman's argument is that every country has a "natural rate" of unemployment that is determined in the final analysis by the abilities, the training, and the culture of its people. For social and political reasons, Keynesian demand-management policies are typically aimed at driving the rate of unemployment below this natural level. Inflationary government budget deficits* and easy credit policies were the means of doing so. The policies work over the short term because when prices begin to rise, wages at first lag behind. Workers are victimized by "money illusion"; they do not at first realize that their apparently healthy wage increases are being eaten up by even larger price increases. As long as wages lag behind prices, the cost of labor falls in relative

---

*The relation between inflation and government budget deficits also warrants a footnote. There are no inherent reasons why a government deficit should be inflationary. If government needs more money than it takes in as taxes, it borrows from the same capital markets as everyone else. If it borrows a lot, there will necessarily be less money for private investors to borrow. The consequences of that depend entirely on how the borrowed money is spent. In a socialist country, for instance, if the government spends the borrowed funds on a steel mill, the investment—at least in theory—could be as productive as if private investors had borrowed the money and built the steel mill. One of the objectives of Keynesian policy, however, is to keep the level of interest rates low to encourage investment. Keynesians, therefore, will usually attempt to match government deficits by an equivalent amount of new credit creation through the banking system (see previous footnote). The government's borrowing needs then can be met without crowding out private credit demands and causing interest rates to rise. Economists call the process by which government borrowing requirements are funded by new money creation "monetizing" the deficit—and that process generally *is* inflationary, at least over the longer term, depending, of course, on whether the economy is starting from a recession or is already growing rapidly. But it is the *combination* of deficits and easy monetary policy that is usually inflationary, not the deficits themselves.

terms, employment increases, and economists can crow about the success of their policies. Inevitably, workers realize that they are losing ground and insist on building inflationary expectations into their wage demands. Keeping down the rate of unemployment then requires even greater levels of stimulation from the government. Prices rise that much faster. Workers immediately try to lock in an even higher level of inflationary expectations, and so on, until soon the inflationary spiral whirls out of control.

Friedman's critique of demand-management policies has great force —which is not to say that his policy prescriptions have any closer connection with the real world than those of the Keynesians. A good case can be made that they have even less. But by the mid-1970s, there was consensus on at least one point: Inflation was a fact, deeply permeating the economy not only of America but of the whole world, and undercutting all the confident assumptions of the planning technocrats.

The Inflationary Process

One of the virtues of Friedman's analysis is that it calls attention to the deep-rooted character of inflationary mechanisms. When price inflation becomes a normal state of affairs, inflationary assumptions weave themselves throughout every day's transactions, and the inflationary process becomes so deeply embedded in the economy that it is beyond the reach of policy-tinkering by presidential advisers.

The machinery of wage inflation illustrates the point. The standard labor contract after World War II embodied the "General Motors Formula" achieved by the autoworkers after years of strikes and unrest. The contracts typically awarded three years of wage increases at an assumed rate of productivity increase. As far as it went, the principle was a sound one: if wages increase in step with productivity there will be no inflation because the growth of purchasing power will exactly match the new supplies of goods for sale. The fastest growing sectors of the economy after the war, however, were local government and services—from restaurants to finance—where productivity is much more difficult to define, much less measure. Service and public employees, particularly as they unionized, naturally kept an eye on the contracts won by their manufacturing brethren and fought for similar annual wage increases. To the extent they were not financed by increased productivity, higher service wages were paid for by higher prices and higher taxes, raising the cost of living for autoworkers and the cost of doing business for auto manufacturers.

By the mid-1950s, the standard manufacturing contract came to embody two elements: the productivity formula *and* a cost-of-living increase just to maintain purchasing power. The total increases were necessarily larger and rippled through to the service and government sectors just as before; higher costs in those sectors were then automatically reflected in the next round of manufacturing contracts. It is a process that works in only one direction. Matters went from bad to worse when productivity growth slowed down in the early 1970s. The productivity bonuses, recall, *anticipated* a standard rate of productivity increase. When those increases didn't materialize, the productivity raises translated directly into higher costs. Strict logic would have called for rescinding the productivity increases, but the elite of American manufacturing workers—the autoworkers, steelworkers, rubber workers—had come to expect them as a matter of right and were willing to fight to keep them. Over the last half of the 1970s, productivity grew not at all, wages grew by 7 to 8 percent, prices increased by 7 to 8 percent, and purchasing power grew not at all. Some economic laws cannot be broken.

Wages are just one source of inflationary bias; government policy is another. In the first place, the level of U.S. defense spending has always been high relative to its allies, consuming roughly twice the share of GNP as that of the major European countries and ten times as much as Japan. Defense spending, most economists agree, is normally inflationary. Payments to defense workers create purchasing power, but there are no corresponding goods produced for sale. Prices must necessarily rise in the rest of the economy. The Vietnam War intensified the inflationary pressures of military spending, but the pressures predated Vietnam and continue today.

A second inflationary impetus stems from the network of government subsidies. The tax deduction on home mortgage interest, for instance, allows the average family to pay about 10 to 15 percent more for a house than they otherwise could afford. In addition, federal interest-rate subsidies have made long-term cheap credit readily available, at least until recently. Long-term fixed-rate loans are a wonderful bargain for families who expect inflation to increase their nominal take-home pay, and they can bid up house prices accordingly. Rising home prices are reflected directly in the consumer price index. Changes in the consumer price index trigger cost-of-living clauses in labor contracts, and wages go up again.

The entire complex of social safety-net measures put in place since the Depression imparts an irresistible impulse toward inflation. The whole economic point of the "automatic stabilizers"—unemployment compensation, welfare benefits, food stamps—is to maintain purchasing power during recessions, when incomes, and at some point presumably prices, would otherwise be falling. The automatic stabilizers have served the economy well: for half a century we have avoided the gasping plunge of prices and incomes that almost destroyed the country in the 1930s, and much human misery has been averted. But by placing a floor beneath incomes, the stabilizers ensure that the momentum of prices is always up.

The method of making social welfare payments itself can add to inflation. Federal medical payments for the poor and the aged now exceed $70 billion. The payments are mostly based on "prevailing rates" —that is, they reimburse medical providers at whatever price they can collectively set, and with no effective limits on the services to be paid for. Not surprisingly, medical prices have been rising about twice as fast as prices generally. Similarly, Social Security benefits are formally indexed to inflation; as prices rise, benefits rise automatically, reinforcing inflation again. When the government must borrow even in nonrecessionary times to finance income-support payments—which are now more than $150 billion a year—the impact is inevitably inflationary. The borrowing must be financed by new money creation or by drawing funds away from private investment. In either case, consumer spending power is being created without corresponding production of goods. Prices must therefore rise.

Businessmen and bankers inveigh against inflation, but they have acquired the same stake in continually rising prices as everyone else. The federal government spends several billion dollars each year on farm price supports—perhaps for good reason, to prevent erratic production swings, for instance—but the result is to raise food prices. The real estate and home-building industries benefit from mortgage subsidies just as home buyers do. Business pricing policies have a pro-inflationary bias. Production budgets are planned for periods of several years and build in cost increases to pay for contracted wage increases or escalators in leases. If product prices fail to rise along with the anticipated costs, profits will suffer; deflation could bring bankruptcy. In the decade after 1965, American corporations increased their outstanding debt by $1 trillion—an increase four times bigger than the increase in federal debt, and at a rate twice that of GNP growth. Just as for the heavily mortgaged homeowner, continued inflation is the only hope for the overleveraged businessman to be able to pay off his debts. Bankers, in theory, are opposed to inflation because it undermines the worth of their outstanding loans, but better to be repaid with a devalued currency than not to be repaid at all. If large numbers of businesses could not service their debts because of deflation, banks would fail. The inflationary engine keeps churning.

In the 1950s, a favorite parlor game of the American left was to criticize the Big Three auto companies for providing an inferior product at an inflated price. They were right. When competition came first from Germany and then Japan, the American companies were shown up badly. Today the Japanese can manufacture a better quality midsize car than the Americans and ship it across the Pacific for about $1700 less than the cost of producing a comparable car in America. About half the difference is accounted for by high American wages—which the auto companies did not bother to control so long as they could raise prices at will—and about half by better Japanese management. The Japanese, of course, do not undersell American cars by $1700. They pocket the difference as added profit, so the high American prices operate as a floor. The reflex response from the American companies and unions is to ask the government to impose quotas to protect their inefficiencies and their high prices. Steel tells the same story. Foreign countries—Japan, Korea, perhaps Brazil—can produce better quality and cheaper steel than American companies can and are willing to sell it at cut rates. And so we have "antidumping" laws, "trigger prices," and import quotas, all intended to keep steel prices in America high.

Inflation is not a transient phenomenon. It will not go away after two years of tight monetary policy or a couple of federal budget surpluses. In the 1960s, economists convinced politicians and the public that they could solve most problems with a kind of brilliant intellectual jujitsu. Inflation is not that kind of problem. In certain important respects, in fact, the inflationary problem may reflect fundamentals of the economy and the world credit system that are not within the reach of a single government at all.

Long Cycles

One of the cherished delusions of Kennedy's economists was that in the 1960s the United States was entering upon a long period of economic stability. Since the economic machinery, they thought, had been rather completely analyzed and understood, and the best economic teachings finally absorbed by a considerable body of public men, only sensitive fine-tuning was required to keep the country on the wide track of stable growth, steady accumulation of wealth, and greater equality of distribution. This was what Kennedy had primarily in mind when he announced that the only remaining governmental problems were technical ones. Keynes himself harbored similar illusions in the 1930s, although being an Englishman of impeccably restrained tastes, he did not expect or desire perpetual growth. He assumed that the British economy would grow to the point where everybody had approximately enough, and then growth would simply stop. From that point, only sufficient effort would be required to keep basic systems operating and in repair; idle time would presumably be occupied by the uplifting offerings of the BBC.

With the current loss of faith in the Kennedy-Keynes technocratic vision, there has been a flurry of interest in cyclical explanations of why economies grow and fail. Mainstream economics has always recognized business cycles—economic blips, occurring, on average, about every four years, caused by business inventory accumulations and sell-downs. The business cycles chronicled by the National Bureau of Economic Research have achieved a quasi-official status. The theories receiving recent prominence, however, postulate long, underlying economic rhythms of expansion and contraction that operate on multigenerational time scales and that, by implication, are beyond the reach of governmental fiscal and monetary manipulation. Most attention has focused on the so-called Kuznets long swings, named after Simon Kuznets, the Nobel-Prize-winning American economist, and the Kondratieff long waves, bearing the name of an obscure Russian agricultural economist, Nicolai Kondratieff, who disappeared and was presumably killed during Stalin's Great Purges. If we accept that theoretical economics is not a science, but rather an art of constructing provocative metaphors to advance our understanding of a complex reality, the concept of long cycles provides useful insights into the economic traumas of the 1970s and 1980s.

The Kuznets cycle is the shorter of the two. It is the economic reflection of the demographic ebbs and flows whose social effects (see Chapter IV) were suggested by Richard Easterlin, a student of Kuznets. Not surprisingly, residential housing construction tends to follow a twenty-year cycle coinciding with the population's reproductive cycle. The high rate of new family formation after World War II created the happy circumstance that relatively fewer workers competed for jobs at a time when vast new investments were required. The housing investment alone was massive, but the spin-offs from the nesting boom were probably even more important—new schools, new teacher colleges, new suburban highways, new shopping centers, second cars and station wagons, new fast-food industries, a home-entertainment industry. Together, the housing and family-related investments totaled about 10 to 15 percent of GNP for more than a decade, or about half of all domestic investment.

The aging of the baby boomers makes much of this investment obsolete. Vacant schools are now a blight. If, as Easterlin hypothesizes, the baby boom generation is cautious about reproducing itself, we can expect the 1980s to be a period of slow growth, the stagnation phase of a Kuznets cycle. Much will depend on imponderables. Will women start having children again? Will the graying of the population create as many industrial opportunities as its greening did? Obviously, tracking the progress of a Kuznets cycle is something less than a precise science. Nor is the concept of much use in defining macroeconomic policy, not least because it usually takes demographers five or ten years *after* the event to identify a trend change with confidence. The Kuznets insight is simply that basic forces, which are only imperfectly understood, can overwhelm short-term policy-related fluctuations. Kondratieff's long-wave theory has the same insight, but tracks economic tides that flow even deeper than Kuznets's, with crests and troughs about twice as far apart.

Just before he ran afoul of Stalin, Kondratieff published a famous article, "The Long Waves in Economic Life," in which he attempted to explain long-term swings in the prices of primary products, that is, raw materials and basic foodstuffs. He identified a forty-year cycle, or long wave, marked by at first a period of falling raw material prices, followed by another period of scarcity and intensive investment, and so on. Eighteenth-century England, for example, saw a period of rapidly rising fuel prices as the country became deforested and wood supplies ran out. Rising wood prices led to intensive development of coal mines and then to a period during which energy prices fell rapidly, coal power was substituted for human and animal power, and the modern concept of the factory was born. Walt Rostow has recently published an analysis of the world economy since 1790 in terms of Kondratieff cycles. According to Rostow, we are now approaching the end of the fifth cycle, which began roughly at the time of the Korean War, is marked by some twenty-five years of falling energy and food prices, and ends with a decade of scarcity, rising prices, and a near-frantic search for primary product substitutes.

The tenfold run-up of oil prices between 1973 and 1979 fits only too well with Kondratieff's basic concept. After the Middle Eastern oil fields were opened in the 1940s and 1950s, there was a continuing oil glut, falling real prices, rapid conversion of coal and steam power facilities to cleaner, cheaper, and more efficient oil, and, not unreasonably, progressively greater dependence on petroleum-based energy in all aspects of daily living. When the lifting cost of Saudi oil fell toward ten cents per barrel, the United States directed policy toward raising oil prices through import quotas and minimum price setting to maintain the competitiveness of Texan and Oklahoman wells. Amid such a glut, conservation would have seemed bizarre.

The United States in the 1950s and 1960s was an oil-based economy. Detroit produced cars with power, roominess, and tail fins; nobody cared about fuel efficiency. Suburbia was made possible by cheap gasoline. Architects designed glass-encased homes and skyscrapers. There was immense investment in electric utilities, virtually all of them burning petroleum. Electric power plants have large fixed costs and huge economies of scale, so average electricity prices fell, but profits rose, as power consumption rose. It was the best of all worlds, and utilities and their regulatory commissions bent their efforts toward increasing power usage by granting rate discounts for high consumption—some of which, unbelievably, are still in effect. Not surprisingly, by the end of the long Kennedy economic boom, it took more than twice as much energy as it had in 1950 to produce an extra unit of GNP.

The successful enforcement of the OPEC price cartel after the Yom Kippur War was, as everyone knows, the immediate cause of the oil price rises. But OPEC had been in existence since 1960 with little effect. OPEC suddenly grew teeth because world oil consumption had risen to such enormous levels that a marginal loss of supply could not easily be replaced. In the United States, the most profligate consumer of all, the appetite for oil virtually doubled during the 1960s, and as domestic resources were consumed, the country became increasingly dependent on foreign oil. By 1979, ten million barrels were being imported every day, or roughly half the nation's oil requirement and a quarter of its total energy supply. OPEC didn't cause the oil price rises. The intensive exploitation of oil-derived energy that followed upon falling oil prices eventually put pressures on supply, and that caused OPEC. In hindsight, it was all predictable.

The oil price rises had a direct impact on inflation, causing overall prices to rise by almost 4 percent per year through the latter half of the 1970s. The indirect effects, however, were far more serious, although impossible to calculate with precision. In the first place, as the search for oil shifted to marginal areas like the North Sea and Alaska, the production of each new barrel consumed more than ten times the capital consumed in the easily accessible Middle Eastern fields. Hundreds of billions of dollars were siphoned out of the investment market simply to replace Arabian oil with no gain in productivity. Even more important, enormous inventories of capital equipment became obsolete at a stroke. American automobile manufacturers are faced with the necessity of retooling their entire production lines at a cost of perhaps $75 billion to adapt to the new reality of high-priced gasoline. This enormous new investment will not increase the rate of new car production; it will only produce fewer, more expensive cars. All economic relations were thrown similarly out of kilter. The economic assumptions of the utility industry were disrupted. Airlines were immediately in distress. Shopping centers were suddenly poorly located. Homes needed insulation. All the careful assumptions of industrial engineers about the proper mix of machines and labor for maximum efficiency were invalidated overnight. American productivity growth came to a crunching halt. From that point, any wage increase translated directly into inflation.

Food supplies evidence a similar cycle. The United States is the Saudi Arabia of food. During the 1950s and 1960s, America combined its natural endowment of an enormous temperate growing zone with the awesome efficiency of its agricultural sector to increase vastly its output of grains and other staples and to lower their real prices. The development of hardier and more productive wheat strains was tantamount to the opening of new Middle Eastern oil fields. Government policies were based on the assumption of glut. Huge quantities of food were given away to poor countries, allowing them to enrich their diets without developing their own food supplies. The Soviet Union allowed its agricultural sector to deteriorate in favor of heavy industry. Peasants and workers the world over developed a taste for meat, although it takes almost three pounds of grain protein, in the form of animal feed, to produce a pound of meat protein. The heavy dependence on subsidized beef in countries like Brazil is the equivalent of encouraging tail-finned gas-guzzling cars. Predictably, when bad weather disrupted marginal supplies in the early 1970s, there were worldwide shortages and a rapid run-up in prices. In Kondratieff's formulation, the long wave that began with the modernization of American farm technology in the 1930s and 1940s has run its course; a period of scarcity and intensive development of alternative supplies should follow, with consequent lower productivity and higher prices, just as in the case of oil.

There are cycles in economic theory, too. Kondratieff's and Kuznets's long cycles are now as fashionable as Spengler's and Schumpeter's theories of decline in the 1930s. They are basically metaphors, however. Beyond the most obvious examples,* it takes considerable force-fitting to make the data work really well; when the analysis is extended back a wave or so, the data themselves become very shaky. The fewer the facts, the easier it is to construct sweeping theories—witness the proliferation of explanations for the origins of the universe. The resurgence of cyclical theory is a symptom of the loss of control felt by theoreticians and practitioners of economic management. It is both a healthy corrective to the technocratic arrogance of the 1960s and a sign of despair, a drifting into *schadenfreude,* a form of intellectual self-indulgence as dangerous as the hubris of the recent past. But the basic construct has the ring of truth, particularly when considering the implications of a fundamental change in the availability of a basic factor of production like energy. Significantly, the concept of alternating periods of glut and scarcity applies to another basic commodity, which is arguably even more fundamental to the process of global inflation than energy or labor. That commodity is money itself.

The Dollar Glut

It is only a slight exaggeration to characterize the position of the United States in the world over the past two decades as an importer of oil and

---

*Even the obvious examples don't always work that well. Almost as soon as the long-wave theory achieved prominence, oil and food supplies moved back into glut. Committed Kondratieffites, of course, insist that the gluts are only temporary.

finished manufactured goods and an exporter of food and dollars. American dollars became as essential a lubricant of the global economy as Saudi Arabian light crude. The American production of dollars has followed a Kondratieff cycle all its own, from a period of scarcity in the 1950s, to the beginnings of irritating excess in the 1960s, to a veritable flood of cheap dollars in the 1970s, fueling worldwide inflation and excessive dollar dependence. There is good reason to believe that the dollar will become scarcer in the 1980s—in other words, its price in terms of other currencies, particularly those of the developing countries, will rise over an extended period. Such a basic change in economic relations will be every bit as disruptive as the sudden run-up in oil prices, and perhaps more so. A brief sketch of the development of the world dollar market is essential to an understanding of the current situation.

Credit is a prerequisite of economic growth. When the industrialized economies, all save the United States, lay in smoking ruins after World War II, no one had confidence in either their governments or their currencies. Only the United States could supply the credit to finance recovery and reconstruction. In contrast to the bleak diplomatic record in dealing with previous great world crises—after World War I, for example—American leadership understood the nature of the challenge and devised uniquely intelligent and farsighted mechanisms to meet it. The emergence of Japan and Western Europe as the economic equals of America is the lasting adornment of American policy since mid-century.

Supplying credit was not a simple matter of making loans. The great fear of the devastated countries was that whatever hard currency they obtained would be sucked up by a great wave of exports from America's booming manufactories. The United States not only had to make loans and grants but had to ensure that the money stayed in the borrowing countries—more dollars had to flow out of America than flowed back in payment for exports. In technical terms, America had to run a persistent balance-of-payments deficit. A perennial U.S. international deficit would mean that other countries could accumulate larger and larger dollar balances, which they could use to finance international trade with each other, as well as with America, or which they could save as a store of wealth to back the issuance of their own currencies. The dollar replaced gold as the world's common money.

To achieve a persistent balance-of-payments deficit required a persistently overvalued dollar. The price of the dollar in terms of other currencies had to be maintained at a level slightly higher than the underlying economic facts justified. A high-priced dollar meant that American goods would appear very expensive to Europeans and Japanese and their products would appear correspondingly cheaper to Americans. Americans would therefore be encouraged to send their dollars overseas to buy foreign goods, and foreigners would be inclined to keep the dollars instead of sending them back in exchange for American exports. The accumulating balances of valuable dollars were the raw material for recreating the financial systems of the industrialized countries. As the German central bank, for example, acquired larger dollar reserves, it could safely extend the deutsche mark credits German industry needed to rebuild. Should anyone challenge the creditworthiness of the new deutsche marks, the central bank could buy them back with dollars. Holders of deutsche marks were thus assured that they had a safe currency.

The policy of maintaining an overvalued dollar was extraordinarily successful, but it came with a price. For Americans, the price was a gradual loss of international competitiveness in basic industries, which did not at first seem important, because the huge American economy could absorb whatever America produced. The price for Europeans was that they had to endure the preening of ugly Americans. The Almighty Dollar reigned supreme. America had preferential access to European and Japanese goods at cut rates. It was a golden age for the American tourist. The burdens of statesmanship were remarkably pleasant.

Maintaining an overvalued dollar for an extended period, however, meant that the world's governments had to agree to override some basic economic laws, which they successfully did for more than twenty years. According to classical economics, after the overvalued dollar caused foreigners to build up large dollar balances, speculators would begin to bet that the dollar would fall and would begin precautionary selling. As more and more dollars were offered for sale, their price *would* fall, which would generate faster selling and an even faster fall in prices until fundamental economic parities were restored. Speculative selling of dollars, precisely of this nature, began in the late 1950s on a large scale, much of it initiated by Swiss currency traders, the so-called gnomes of Zurich.

At first, the United States could choke off speculative assaults on the dollar simply by buying up any dollars offered for a fixed amount of gold —one ounce for $35, the price agreed at the monetary conference at Bretton Woods in 1944. As long as the United States held most of the world's monetary gold reserves, dollar raids were easily beaten down. But by the early 1960s, the American gold reserves had dwindled to only $15 billion, and the speculators, sniffing devaluation, were increasing the selling pressure. America had to turn to its allies for help. Governments with strong currencies, particularly Germany, helped staunch the out-flow of American gold reserves by intervening in the currency markets themselves and buying up huge amounts of dollars, propping up their artificially high price. One reason American economic managers were so tolerant of persistent trade deficits with Japan was that a cooperative Japanese government ensured that all the dollars their industries earned would simply disappear into the "black hole" of the Japanese central bank, never to be seen again on the world currency markets.

But by the mid-1960s, the allied governments, led by France under Charles de Gaulle, were increasingly unwilling to cooperate. Buying up the outflow of dollars to protect American gold reserves required them to issue excessive amounts of their own currencies, which kept their local inflation rates high. Even more important, an overvalued dollar, although a boon in the 1950s, was now beginning to hurt. American industry was expanding aggressively overseas and was rapidly acquiring foreign companies because an overvalued dollar let them buy on the cheap. De Gaulle complained bitterly that by supporting the price of the dollar, the allied governments were subsidizing the "expropriation of French industry."

The United States reacted to allied complaints with a mixture of irritation and hurt feelings. The whole point of American monetary policy, after all, had been to permit European and Japanese recovery. To American eyes, de Gaulle seemed an ungrateful churl. And much of the dollar outflow was caused by the large American overseas military establishment. If the allies didn't want to support the dollar, congress-men snorted, not entirely without justification, America could take its troops home and let the allies fend for themselves.

But the real reason America couldn't address its dollar problem was that it would have been too painful to do so. To stop speculation against the dollar, the United States would have had to maintain its interest rates higher than other countries and its inflation rate lower. Then the gnomes would keep their dollars instead of selling them. The high interest rates would slow down American growth. Americans would therefore spend less on imports and send fewer dollars overseas, which would have made the gnomes even happier. The way to satisfy the currency speculators and protect American gold reserves, in short, was to create an American recession, which American policymakers were not prepared to do. The trade-off between protecting American gold reserves and generating economic growth grew more and more difficult to manage throughout the Kennedy and Johnson administrations. Whenever the economic managers tried to stimulate the economy with lower interest rates or accepted slightly more inflation for the sake of higher employment, speculators would immediately begin to sell tens of billions of dollars, forcing the United States to buy them back with gold or to beg other governments to buy them and hold them instead. The gnomes of Zurich were the favorite whipping boys of American policymakers, and seemed to have a golden choke collar on the American economy.

Nixon smashed his way out of the dilemma with his New Economic Policy in 1971. He and his Texas-sized Treasury secretary, John Connally, simply announced that they would no longer pay gold for dollars. The price of the dollar could fall as far as it wanted—which it immediately did, by about 16 percent—and the currency speculators who held dollars could sell as they chose and take their losses, or eat their dollars, for all America cared. The cooperative allied governments, who had been holding dollars at America's behest, particularly the Japanese, saw the values of their reserves tumble overnight. The cheaper dollar made American exports more competitive, giving American industry a boost. With no worries about gold, and with wage-price controls to eliminate inflation, Nixon could gun up the money supply, drive down interest rates, and let the economy rip.

The industrialized countries screamed in outrage, but in the end could do little but swallow their losses and grumblingly accept the new dispensation. The dollar had been the world's monetary unit for too long. Virtually all world trade was denominated in dollars. Countries quoted prices to each other in dollars and used dollars to support their own currencies. To substitute another currency, say the deutsche mark, as the world monetary unit, would have required the Germans to supply the world banking system with vastly greater amounts of deutsche marks, with unhappy consequences for German inflation. The dollar remained the world's reserve currency, gold or no gold, and Nixon and Connally won their gamble, because the rest of the world had nowhere else to go.

It was a boom time for American banks. With the gold restraint removed, there was no effective limit on the amount of dollars that could be held overseas—the so-called Eurodollars.* And since the reserve requirements and other lending restraints that the Federal Reserve applied at home were of no effect overseas, the banks could lend and relend their dollars without limit. In theory, the world dollar supply could grow to infinity; the overseas branches of American banks had become the Saudi Arabia of dollars. Not surprisingly, the value of the dollar continued to slip under the pressure of such relentless dollar creation and sank like a stone during the early years of the Carter administration. But the falling dollar was of little consequence so long as dollars could be pumped into the world economy faster than the traders could bid them down. Gold hit $800 an ounce in 1978, up from $35 in 1971.

The OPEC oil price increases in 1973 were a massive dose of adrenalin for the Eurodollar markets. Most economists expected a prolonged world recession to follow from the price increases. The 1974–1975 slowdown was severe, but not nearly as bad as was feared, particularly in the oil-poor developing countries. The global private Eurodollar banking system effectively cushioned the shock. What happened was that people in Iowa, for instance, suddenly had to send their profits and savings to Arab sheiks to pay the increased oil prices. Savings held in Iowa banks went down, so Iowa banks had less to lend to local business, and Iowa had a recession. The Arabs couldn't immediately spend the billions flowing into their coffers, however, so they deposited them at interest in the Eurodollar banks. The Eurodollar banks had no mechanism for getting the dollars back to small businesses in Iowa and so were potentially in the position of holding large interest-bearing deposits with nowhere to lend them. Fortuitously, or so it seemed, developing countries like Brazil and Korea needed to purchase large amounts of oil to

---

*Eurodollars are simply dollars held offshore by American bank branches or by foreign banks. Since they may be lent and re-lent by banks of many countries, they are outside the control of any national monetary authority, with obvious worrisome implications for managing the world's money supply and vast potential for generating world inflation. Ironically, the concept of a Eurodollar seems to have been invented by Moscow. In the 1950s, the Soviet state bank needed to hold dollar deposits to pay for commodity imports, but was wary of maintaining them in America because of Cold War tensions. An apparatchik had the bright idea of asking London banks, which theretofore had done business only in pounds sterling, to hold deposits in dollars, and the Eurodollar market was born.

Before there were Eurodollars, overseas dollar balances were held by government central banks, usually in the form of U.S. Treasury securities. They had an impact on world inflation, therefore, only to the extent that the central banks chose to use their dollar balances as reserves for currency creation. The creation of a Eurodollar market effectively permitted the operation of a supranational banking system with the ability to increase the world's money supply at will as lending opportunities presented themselves.

fuel their local economies and didn't have the dollar earnings to pay for it. They appeared promptly at the Eurobank lending windows, borrowed the Arab deposits, and paid them right back to the Arabs for more oil. The dollars went full circle; the Arabs, in effect, financed their price increases themselves.

The banking system took great pride in its performance in "recycling the petrodollars." And, in truth, the system proved far more resilient than most economists had expected. The marvel of private enterprise is that it creates solutions before anyone understands them. The recycling process happened because individual bankers made individual loans with only the dimmest perception of the deep new flows of the world dollar tides. The bankers may not have understood what was going on —for all their retrospective preening—but the system worked far better than if the world had waited for government experts to figure out what to do, at least for the short term.

The apparent painlessness of the dollar recycling masked its immense inflationary consequences. Recall that dollars multiply as they are lent. Assume the Arab sheiks received $1 billion from America in payment for oil and deposited it with a Eurobank. The Eurobank then lent the billion to Brazil, which also used it to buy Arab oil. The Arabs now have *$2* billion. They could deposit the money again and it could be recycled again, making the Arab deposits that much bigger, and so on ad infinitum. America accelerated the process by allowing its money supply at home to grow rapidly enough to make up for the outflow of dollars overseas and finance its huge appetite for oil. With no gold reserve discipline to limit the production of dollars, America could cushion the oil price shock simply by printing enough dollars to pay the Arabs whatever they wanted. The gimmick was that the more dollars were printed, the faster their value would drop, until the OPEC nations found they couldn't raise oil prices fast enough to keep up with dollar depreciation. America could produce dollars faster than OPEC could produce oil, and the price increases were simply inflated away.

When it came time for the developing countries to repay their dollar debts, they—not surprisingly—did not have the dollar resources to do so. So they borrowed again in somewhat larger amounts to cover both principal and interest on the first loans and usually at somewhat higher interest rates. More dollars were created to cover the refinancing. The Arabs grew increasingly restive as the value of their dollar deposits steadily eroded away. When the turmoil in Iran disrupted marginal oil supplies once again, they seized the opportunity to triple oil prices. The borrowing requirements of the oil-poor nations increased vastly once again, and the banking system responded with vast new outpourings of dollars.

This time the system reached its limit. If dollars multiply endlessly, they will eventually go the way of the Argentine peso. The expansion of the world's Eurodollar supply had become geometric, reaching $1 trillion in the early 1980s.* The world's monetary system is built on confidence. If runaway growth of the world dollar supply undermines confidence in its value as currency, a financing crisis could be precipitated. Dollars can disappear into nothing as easily as they are created out of nothing. If a dollar in a checking account is re-lent twice, it has the effective purchasing power of three dollars. If, because of a confidence crisis, it should be re-lent only once, its purchasing power will have been reduced by a third, to only two dollars. If people became unwilling to accept dollars in exchange for goods, the turnover velocity of dollars would slow down. A rapid slowing down would cause the supply of dollars to contract, and sufficient dollars would not be available to refinance developing country debt. Countries would default. Banks could fail. Credit availability would dry up. International trade could grind to a halt as the world became illiquid. There could be a hair-curling depression.

As this is being written in early 1983, the situation is very dangerous. Developing countries—Brazil, Argentina, Mexico, Korea, the Philippines, Poland, Hungary, Rumania—owe some $600 billion, about half of it to private banks, and the rest to Western governments. Those are very large numbers. Some countries have already defaulted—in fact, that is, whatever euphemisms have been used. Most international bankers are confident that they will muddle through. If the defaults only come one at a time . . . if there are no major new disruptions in oil supplies for a while . . . if the Saudis are not overthrown by Islamic fanatics . . . if interest rates can drop long enough to ease the developing country debt-service problems . . . if world economic growth can start up again without inflation . . . if central bankers keep cool heads and

---

*Actually the amount on deposit in international banks approached $2 trillion in 1982, but about half of that simply represented deposits that banks hold with other banks. The assumption is that unless a dollar finds its way out of the system into the hands of private individuals or companies, it does not function as money. The $1 trillion figure is net of interbank deposits. Economists disagree on the significance of the gross figure for world inflation.

submerge national chauvinisms to deal with the common problem
. . . if, if.

The business cycle is characteristic of private enterprise systems.
Businessmen seeking profit sense opportunities and move to fill voids
much faster than government bureaucrats. The banks' response to the
dollar recycling problem is an example of the wonderful responsiveness
and flexibility of private enterprise. When profits seem easy, however,
whether the product is Hula Hoops, video games, or dollars, businessmen will typically produce an excess. The economy has to slow down
periodically to work off unwise inventory accumulations. Since the
banks were competing against each other for the profitable Eurodollar
lending, it was impracticable to orchestrate a concerted slowdown in the
pace of dollar creation until a crisis stage was reached. In the last stages
of the dollar buildup, hundreds of smaller banks, with little understanding of the perils of international lending, came plunging into the market.
No bank wanted to be the last lender who got stuck with a bad loan,
but each loan officer, striving to make his annual profit targets, hoped
to be next to last. Restoring order to the system and working off the
dollar glut without precipitating world depression and revolutionary
chaos in the developing countries will require immense ingenuity on the
part of central bankers and finance ministries of the industrialized countries, wisdom and forbearance in the industrializing Third World, and
statesmanship by all of the big international banks. A tall order perhaps.
Fast merry-go-rounds are fun until they stop abruptly.

The End of Liberalism

In the spring of 1975, New York City ran out of money and defaulted
on its debts. The financing problem was, in many respects, a microcosm
a hundred times smaller of the world liquidity problem of 1982–1983.
At a deeper level, the city's fiscal collapse symbolized the exhaustion of
the great liberal impulse that had inspirited public policy for forty years.
Faced suddenly with scarcity of resources and rising public demands,
city policymakers lost conviction and direction and proved quite unable
to cope. City fecklessness was roundly deplored, and deservedly so. But
the collapse in the city was not a unique event; by the end of the decade,
America's leaders, indeed, the leaders of almost all the major nations,
were foundering amid coils of similar construction.

The central theme of New York's disaster was excess. The public sector—the welfare, health, and educational establishments—were expanded excessively, and citizens became excessively reliant on them and demanding of them. As the service and public sectors expanded, productivity dropped and the economic base deteriorated. To support itself and the needs of an increasingly dependent and passive citizenry, the government's share of the economic product of the city had to be progressively increased. That fact, together with the increasing unruliness and indiscipline of its work force, the declining standards of performance, and the increasing sharpness of demands for shorter hours and higher wages, made the city a steadily less attractive site for economic activity of almost any sort. When the declining economic base could no longer support the city's expansive public tastes, bankers competed to supply the deficit. The loans were justified by hopeful economic prognostications; when they failed to eventuate, more lending at higher rates was required to refinance the first round of loans and so on until the bubble burst in 1975. A parable for our times.

Kondratieff's metaphor is apposite to the rise and fall of political philosophies. When the great liberal vision first glinted off the rigidly parsimonious political system of a Calvin Coolidge or a Herbert Hoover, the new possibilities were of the scale unveiled by the conversion from wood to fossil fuels. There followed the same cycle of cautious experimentation and ever more hopeful results, succeeded by optimistic commitment and technocratic exuberance, until finally working hypotheses hardened into blind dogma and principle was submerged by the plunge into glut—excesses of oil, grain, or dollars, an excessive public sector, excessive dependence, excessive inflation, excessive reach into private lives, excesses of promises and expectations. Sometime in the late 1970s or the early 1980s, somewhere, that is, between the collapse of New York City and the spectral looming of global default, the long wave crested and the period of readjustment began.

IX

THE HEAVENLY CITY
OF THE LIBERAL PHILOSOPHERS

The principles that governed modern American-style liberalism achieved a coherent canonical organization in the 1970s, particularly in John Rawls's brilliant, if, to my view, flawed, *A Theory of Justice* (1971) as well as in more tendentious but still thoughtful works like Ronald Dworkin's *Taking Rights Seriously* (1977). The formalization of liberal philosophy coincided with the eclipse of its political influence. "Life is a swallow and theory a snail." The first-term Richard Nixon—the Family Assistance Nixon—was the last President to attempt to put liberal political principles on a sustainable operating basis, and his commitment was ambivalent, to say the least. Gerald Ford's short presidency was a holding operation, and while Jimmy Carter mouthed liberal slogans, he was from the beginning overwhelmed by events. The election of Ronald Reagan, even allowing for the inherent ambiguity of national politics, was as explicit a disavowal of liberal principles as we are likely to get. With the loss of liberalism's political sway, conservative academic intellectuals achieved new prominence. Friedrich Hayek, Keynes's great opponent in the 1930s, won a wide audience again after almost fifty years. Milton Friedman, in the wilderness for a quarter century, became something of a national oracle, while the black economist Thomas Sowell moved to the front ranks of the younger critics with his *Knowledge and Decisions* (1980).

Political theory is cyclic. The sweeping conquest of political liberalism received its impetus from the two great failures of conservatism— the Great Depression and American racial segregation. And it is liberalism's excesses that have breathed new life into political conservatives. My own view of the actual results of the liberal experiment, particularly in its later stages, is quite a critical one. But it is almost inconceivable that the nation would have been better served by an unbroken conservative reign from Hoover through Eisenhower to Reagan. Merely stating the alternative demonstrates its absurdity. Neither camp has a monopoly of virtue or wisdom. The fact that a style of thought is temporarily useful doesn't mean that it is universally valid.

John Kennedy's liberalism had its roots in Dewey's pragmatism, the philosophic equivalent of Yankee ingenuity. To a generation of postwar liberal intellectuals, Kennedy himself was the cult figure, the American as nonideological problem-solver. But when pragmatism was faced with the challenge of the civil rights movement, it proved to be lacking moral depth and relevance. The freedom fighters, the black revolutionaries, and the assorted liberationists of the late 1960s were making transcendent claims and required a transcendent grandiloquence to state them. The language of European existentialism and German idealism, with all its occasional dementedness, was more expressive of the social turmoil at the decade's turn than the cool reductionism of the pragmatists.

Rawls and the thinkers like Dworkin who follow him attempt to synthesize these two strands of thought into a single set of principles that combine absolute rationality with an insistence on moral values. The principles they derive may be fairly summarized, I think, as follows: The relations, rights, and obligations of the citizen must above all be *rational* and be capable of explicit and rational formulation; to the extent they cannot be rationally articulated they are devalued. Equality, efficiency, and liberty are all principle objectives of the state, but *equality* is to be preferred over efficiency or liberty. Indeed, the pursuit of equality will enhance the prospects of achieving both efficiency and liberty, at least on average. Finally, the first two principles—a rationally disposed society and an ordered preference among guiding values—lead to the third, which is that conflicts of values or interests may be best resolved by quasi-legal or quasi-judicial *rules* and procedures. In a rational society, proper procedures themselves are the best guarantors of desirable outcomes.

The rationality sought for is an economist's rationality, a reflection of the sweeping intellectual conquest of the Keynesian dispensation and of Robert McNamara's theoretic-choice models of analysis, still powerful influences despite the failures in Vietnam. Rawls's *Theory of Justice,* although a work of moral philosophy, builds its case from microeconomics. He assumes an "original position"—a group of people in pristine ignorance but of high intelligence—and then proceeds to derive the rules of justice and fairness that people in the original position would be most likely to adopt for themselves. Rawls takes as given, for example, what he calls the "difference principle"—since no one knows what his eventual position in society will be, there will be early agreement to limit the possible distance between the highest- and lowest-status individuals. He argues the point with marginal-utility analysis, indifference curves, the minimax rule from game theory, just as a Pentagon war gamesman would. The economics style of rationality is so intellectually entrenched that even Rawls's opponents, like Hayek and Sowell, both economists themselves, couch their attacks on him in the language of economics.

When the liberal philosophers write of equality, they mean equality in the strong sense, equality of outcome, not merely Jeffersonian equality of opportunity. The view of equality taken by Great Society liberals like Schlesinger or Galbraith was akin to that of the British Labour party, stronger than the Jeffersonian position, but still much weaker than that of Rawls and Dworkin. To a British socialist, equality means equality of provision, the upper classes properly looking after the lower classes, developing a system of state services, and, not incidentally, enhancing the power of the intellectuals who administer it. In his book *Equality,* R. H. Tawney, the great British socialist theoretician, who is making the case *for* equality, argues that most thinkers "greatly overestimate the plasticity of human nature," citing with admiration Cyril Burt's now discredited studies on inherited mental deficiencies, and states flatly that "inequality of power is the condition of liberty, since it is the condition of any effective action."

Rawls, by contrast, is not prepared to accept even the inequality of a meritocracy. He writes of the "obvious injustice" of a distribution of assets based on "natural talents and abilities," since "these factors are so arbitrary from a moral point of view." The conundrum faced by Rawls and other egalitarians, of course, is that the pursuit of equality in the strongest sense must at some point interfere with the individual liberties of some people, on the one hand, and with the efficiency of the common social enterprise on the other. Must a business hire a quota of minorities if better qualified white males are available? Should blacks or Hispanics receive preferential access to law school over whites who have higher scores on a reasonable aptitude test? Should white children be forced to attend schools in predominantly black neighborhoods? Rawls and Dworkin unhesitatingly respond to all these questions in the affirmative. Dworkin says bluntly that the concept of liberty is "nonsense on stilts"—using Bentham's phrase—and proceeds to show, most ingeniously, that the rights we are wont to call liberties can be better defended as rules of equality. Freedom of speech, for instance, confers the equal right to express one's point of view rather than a right to liberty of speech. Rawls concedes from the outset that his "difference principle" —that inequality cannot increase unless everybody benefits*—does not maximize efficiency, but he argues with admirable agility and at great length that the pursuit of equality will enhance the overall quality of society even if there are restrictions here and there.

Finally, the emphasis on legalistic rules and procedures that characterizes so much of liberal political philosophy is a distinctly American trait, one commented on by both de Tocqueville and Bryce. Two developments gave the tendency particular force in the 1960s and 1970s. Law was a natural field of graduate study for the vast numbers of young people finishing college with only vaguely defined career goals. There are as a consequence ten times as many lawyers per capita in the United States as in England and twenty times as many as in Japan. Just as important, the brilliant legal tactics of Thurgood Marshall and his colleagues at the NAACP Legal Defense Fund showed that the courts and the Constitution, particularly the Fourteenth Amendment, could be molded into a sinuously flexible tool that would prevail against the darkest and most virulent forces of prejudice and ignorance. In the heady aftermath of the civil rights movement, activist federal courts adopted a series of rule changes regarding discovery, the formation of plaintiff classes, the definition of justiciable controversies, and the granting of standing to sue that greatly enhanced their ability to intervene in social disputes of all kinds—welfare rules, prison discipline, highway construction and location, school suspension practices, the rights of employers, of women, of parents and children. It is difficult to find an issue that could *not* be given a constitutional gloss under the more expansive readings of that document.

Rawls and Dworkin both celebrate the triumph of legalism. To

---

*Rawls betrays the influence of the Dewey-eyed optimism of the 1960s here; as far as I can find, he never entertains the possibility that increased equality may make everyone *worse* off. His choices are only between various degrees of improvement.

Dworkin, the social ideal is reached when an all-powerful judge, whom he calls "Hercules," can resolve every question simply by deducing the correct rule from his true knowledge of the rights of men. Rawls goes even further, in a sense, because in his ideal society the rules will be so clear and so obviously deducible that no judge will be necessary: "Any doubts that [society's] members may entertain about the soundness of their moral sentiments . . . may be dispelled by seeing that their convictions match those which would be chosen in the original position." Indeed, when the common man is not only a king but a philosopher, we will have "social arrangements in which envy and destructive feelings are not likely to be strong. The concept of justice eliminates conditions which give rise to disruptive attitudes." The ultimate victory of the law and the courts will be the withering away of the courts themselves.

The three fundamental liberal principles—rationality, equality, and a reliance on rules—are intertwined and reinforcing and exercised great influence on social policy in the 1960s and 1970s. Obviously no one, least of all the federal government or the courts, ever tried literally to organize the political business of the country according to the precepts of John Rawls or Ronald Dworkin. But their writings, like those of most capable philosophers, expressed a prevailing intellectual temperament, even if leaders, judges, and political actors were only dimly aware of the effect it had on their approach to the problems of the day. The rest of this chapter will examine some striking instances of the power and limitations of the liberal principles in practice.

Discrimination

The great liberal achievement of the 1960s was the elimination of legalized racial discrimination. The obvious symbols of second-class citizenship in the South—separate sections in theaters and buses, whites-only rest rooms, segregated drinking fountains and restaurants, lack of access to libraries and parks—were all gone by about 1967 or 1968. Under federal protection, blacks in the South slowly began to exercise the franchise, and by the end of the decade there was a sprinkling of local black elected public officials. The dual school system was effectively eliminated in the early 1970s. In the 1968–1969 school year, only 32 percent of black children in the South attended desegregated schools (schools that were at least 10 percent white). By 1970–1971, 77 percent of black children were in desegregated schools, and 86 percent by 1974–

1975. President Eisenhower insisted that legislation could not change the "hearts and minds" of the people, but the experience in the South between 1965 and 1975 seems to prove him wrong. When the barriers fell, they fell almost completely. Blacks passed judgment on the new dispensation with their feet; after economic conditions in the North worsened in the mid-1970s, they began to remigrate to the South in large numbers. The net black migratory flow for the rest of the decade was from North to South for the first time in history.

As the economy grew rapidly, and the most flagrant employment discrimination was eliminated, blacks began rapidly to make up lost economic ground. During the 1960s, white income rose 31 percent, but black income rose 55 percent, more than three-quarters faster. The rate of college enrollments among whites remained constant after 1965, but the black enrollment rate doubled. The number of blacks in skilled blue-collar jobs doubled, and blacks increased their representation in professional occupations at a rate about two and a half times faster than whites. The gains should not be exaggerated; blacks were coming from very far back. The number of black engineers tripled in the 1960s, for instance, but there were very few black engineers to begin with, and blacks are still greatly underrepresented in the engineering profession. More troublesome, as the economy slowed at the end of the 1970s, the black gains began to slip away. Unemployment among black teenagers rose to rates almost triple that of white teenagers, and the percentage of blacks in poverty began actually to increase. In the North in the 1970s, the percentage of black children attending 90 percent black schools also increased. By 1975, the *majority* of black youngsters in the North were attending schools that would have been considered segregated in the South.

The economic success of blacks in the 1960s was a triumph of reason over prejudice. Blacks could not make progress until they were freed to do so. The simple rule that the color of a man's skin could not bar him from a job, nor his child from a school, nor his family from a restaurant, opened a new world of opportunity that blacks as a group quickly took advantage of. The black response to the dismantling of discriminatory barriers was so rapid and so broadly based that their recent economic slippage—with the goal seemingly in sight—has been frustrating in the extreme. The first assault on discrimination was so successful that there is a natural temptation to regard the present problems as evidence of continuing, or resurgent, discrimination, which must be rooted out the same way. Lester Thurow makes essentially this argument in his *Poverty and Discrimination* (1969). The argument has been restated with even more urgency in the recent and much-publicized *A Dream Deferred,* published by the liberal Center for the Study of Social Policy in Washington, D.C. Reality, unfortunately, is far more complex.

I sometimes ride the New York City subway late at night and occasionally find myself alone on a platform. It is an uneasy feeling— mid-forties in a business suit, easy prey. On one such night, a group of rowdy-looking Italian youths came down to the platform. They'd been drinking, I didn't like their company, and I stayed out of their way. But I wasn't worried about being mugged. On another occasion, two black youths came down to the platform when I was alone, and I became quite tense. A few minutes later, we were joined by a group of black men, in their thirties, it appeared, wearing working clothes. Reflexively, I moved closer to the black men, stopped worrying about being mugged, and relaxed with my newspaper. Clearly, I was engaged in prejudiced sorting here, making blanket judgments on the basis of race and age. The odds, in fact, were rather high that the two black youths harbored no ill intentions toward me. But my instincts were not irrational, nor were they based solely on race. Mugging in New York is overwhelmingly a crime committed by young black males. The chances that the two young men *might* be muggers was not trivial, and I had almost unconsciously interpreted signals from their dress and demeanor to mean that they were lower-class, which increased the chances even further. And statistically, I was quite correct that I had little to fear from black workingmen or white youths.

To take another example, one of my youngsters attended a public high school in New York for two years. Because of the way district lines fell, the school he should have gone to was almost entirely black. The school was dominated by lower-class black youths, there was little in the way of educational atmosphere, and it was frankly dangerous. I pulled every string I could and got him assigned to a school in another district that was more or less ethnically balanced and where there was a reasonable chance to get an education. Was that bigotry? I don't think so. The black parents in my neighborhood do the same thing, and do so desperately. The nightmare of working-class black parents is that their children will get sucked into the lower-class black subculture, that their sons will become drug addicts or criminals or get killed, and that their daughters will get pregnant and go on welfare. These are not, needless to say, fears born of prejudice and bigotry. The working-class black parents I know struggled hard to escape the ghetto themselves. It is their intimate knowledge of the subculture of violence and dissolution that causes them to fear it so.

Issues of social justice are complex; rationalist one-variable models misrepresent reality. In the case of race relations, it is not always obvious how to separate genuine discrimination from distinctions arising from other reasons. The bitterly drawn-out school desegregation battle in Boston is a case in point. It is clear from the public record that the Boston school authorities engaged in invidious racial discrimination. For example, a new high school was budgeted to replace an older school that was almost entirely white. By the time the new school was finished, the school it was designated to replace had become mostly black, so it was redesignated to replace another older school that was still white. But other parts of the record are open to multiple interpretations. Schools in black neighborhoods were underutilized and those in white neighborhoods were overcrowded. White parents, by and large, elected to have their children attend more distant white schools rather than send them to nearby black schools, and the school board accommodated them. In part, I'm sure, the white parents were motivated by simple racial bigotry, but their contention that the schools in black neighborhoods were bad schools was almost certainly not an invention. The court master who assembled the record in the case referred to the black schools as "troubled schools"; incidents of vandalism and petty crimes were frequent, and teachers were afraid to teach in the worst schools. Reasonable parents could refuse to send their children there without being guilty of bigotry.

A Dream Deferred is a classic example of the simplistic single-variable style of policy analysis, to an extent that seems almost anachronistic in the 1980s. Comparing the earnings of whites and blacks with the same number of years in school, it finds that "the financial rewards for black workers are less than for whites of comparable education . . . thus the reasons . . . seem to lie primarily in structural inequities." But counting *years* of school does not measure the quality of education. Blacks, on average, for reasons that have nothing to do with genetics, are less able students than whites and go to lower-quality high schools and colleges. In 1982, for example, 49 percent of black male college students had SAT scores of 700 or less (out of a possible 1600); only 14 percent of white male college students had scores that low. (Civil rights leaders often charge that such tests are culturally biassed. They may be right, but the point is irrelevant. SAT scores *are* a good predictor of academic performance; and there is no doubt that certain aspects of the black subculture will have to be modified if blacks are to forge ahead economically and academically.) Much of the recent penetration of blacks into the college ranks has been accomplished only by diluting the college curriculum—in some cases, as in the notorious New York City "Open Enrollment" experiment, down nearly to a high school level. The long-run advantages of a more schooled black population, I suspect, may outweigh the costs of temporarily debasing the city's university programs, but it is foolish to suppose that employers can't tell the difference between a low-quality and a high-quality diploma.

A Dream Deferred concludes with a call for greater interventions on behalf of blacks—more affirmative action programs and more social welfare. Their own statistics might have given the authors pause. In 1950, only 8 percent of black families were headed by a female. By 1960, that number had risen to 21 percent, and female-headed families accounted for 30 percent of all black families in poverty. By 1981, almost half of all black families were headed by females, and those families accounted for 70 percent of the black families in poverty and three-quarters of the black children in poverty. (Interestingly, white children in female-headed inner-city families are even more likely to be poor than black children in the same circumstances.) Clearly, social disorganization in a part of the black community has much to do with the stubbornness of black poverty and can hardly be blamed on increased discrimination since 1950. If anything, it lends force to the conservative argument that twenty years of open-handed welfare policies have undermined black family stability and traditions of self-reliance.

The further one probes behind the comparative economic data for blacks and whites, the less convincing a simple discrimination hypothesis turns out to be. Black *female* college graduates, for instance, have consistently earned more than white female college graduates, although no one would claim that the gap is caused by discrimination in favor of black women. Black teenage unemployment is at disastrously high levels, but in the 1940s and 1950s, when discrimination was presumably much more widespread than it is today, black teenage unemployment was consistently lower than that for whites. Black-owned banks are even more reluctant than white-owned banks to invest in inner-city neighborhoods, for the simple reason that inner-city neighborhoods are poor risks, and black banks cannot afford the losses. The discrimination model wholly fails to explain the difference between blacks of West Indian origin and native American blacks. West Indians, who are of the same African ethnic stock as American blacks, and who suffered under an even more brutal system of slavery, have incomes 52 percent higher than other blacks and below-average unemployment rates. Second-generation West Indians have incomes higher than the national average, even though by appearance and accent they should be indistinguishable from blacks of native American stock. Finally, when young professional blacks are matched against professional whites of the same age, with the same quality schooling, in the same region of the country, income differences disappear altogether. Indeed, the divergence between the upwardly mobile, middle-class black and the inner-city welfare mother has become so sharp in recent years that it raises the question of whether it is useful to speak of a "black community" as a statistical entity at all.

If blacks are compared with other ethnic groups who migrated en masse into American cities, their progress or lack of it becomes rather unremarkable. It took the Irish almost a hundred years after their arrival in the Northeastern cities to achieve economic parity with older white ethnic groups. By all accounts, the Irish slums were more violent and crime-ridden than today's black slums. On the Irish West Side of New York before World War I, mugging was a common offense, half of the families were fatherless, and virtually all of the orphans and public dependents were Irish, even though large numbers of German and Italian immigrants arrived even later than the Irish. For all the Irish religiosity, slum life seems to have broken down sexual morals. The city's prostitutes were Irish, and social workers were shocked to see open acts of sodomy between boys as young as seven or eight. The term "paddy wagon" attests to the police view of the "wild Irish." More than a thousand people were killed in the Irish riots of 1863, a number which is not even remotely approached by any of the black riots of the twentieth century. There are still one or two small pockets of unsocialized Irish not far from my neighborhood in Brooklyn. When my children are feeling particularly irritated by the antisocial behavior of lower-class blacks, we can take a walk past our little museum-piece Irish slum as an antidote for incipient racism.

The vast majority of blacks are still traversing the first couple of steps on the American social ladder—the children of laborers become skilled operatives; the children of skilled operatives become public school teachers; the children of public school teachers become lawyers, doctors, and university professors. Some individuals, and even some family trees, never make it out of the slums, but as more and more people do, slum dwellers become a dwindling minority and cease to exercise cultural influence. Racial discrimination accounts for the fact that blacks are beginning the process now instead of a hundred years ago. But totally eliminating racial discrimination will not magically convert working-class men and women into lawyers or create the intellectually stimulating home milieux that produce candidates to Harvard.

Racial prejudice is a terrible emotional burden to an upwardly mobile black, one that a white can only imagine. It starts early. At our local public school I'm convinced that the teachers expect less from black children, although most of the teachers would consider themselves liberals. A professional black needs constantly to prove himself. A partner in a New York law firm told me how their clients almost always look uncomfortable when they are assigned a black associate. They are afraid they will receive inadequate service, and the black associates must be aware of the feeling. The scorn which Thomas Sowell heaps on affirmative action programs stems in part, I suspect, from a fear that despite his formidable intellectual accomplishments people will assume that *he* achieved his present position through preferential treatment. There is, unfortunately, no way to eliminate the problem in the short term, and I suppose it will persist with diminishing force for another generation. Affirmative action programs are helpful to a point, for they provide opportunities to qualified blacks and help build the accustomed presence that will eventually overcome prejudice. Pressed too far, they are probably counterproductive, for they lend substance to the expectation that unqualified blacks are being pushed up to fill quotas and confirm prejudicial racial stereotypes.

The recent inroads made by women in law and finance are instructive in this regard. When I attended law school fifteen years ago, there were almost no women students. Women in finance were almost unheard of. Now women make up at least a third, and often half or more, of law school and MBA classes. Ten years ago, law firm clients raised eyebrows when they were assigned a woman associate. They no longer do, of course, because they take women lawyers for granted now—and increasingly, the client is apt to be a woman, too. At a major bank where I worked, more than half the new young officers hired over the past five years have been women. They perform obviously as well as men and seem to be moving up the promotional ladder as rapidly as men. A woman friend at the bank, in her mid-thirties, told me of the difficulty of getting the younger women officers to join women's support groups. The problems their older sisters had struggled with—performing in an all-male world, for instance—didn't exist for them. All of their academic and professional lives have been spent in a gender-integrated world. Women have made progress faster than blacks, of course, and for obvious reasons. Ethnicity is class-related; gender is not. There was always a large pool of middle- and upper-class women attending the best schools in the country; all that was required was a shift in career focus.

There is much residual discrimination, against women as well as against blacks. The flagrant discrimination by white male craft unions against both women and blacks is only the most notorious example. But rooting out the last remnants of discrimination will be much more difficult than just pulling down "whites-only" signs. When issues of race intersect with issues of class, when past wrongs intertwine with present rights, when simple justice compounds into complex injustices, simplistic solutions and simple principles, whatever their surface rationality, break down.

Changing People

Extreme rationality is irrational, and at the extreme, enforcing equality can generate dreadful inequalities. Tawney assumed that equality of result required inequality of power: in his view most people needed the state to take care of them. American advocates of participatory democracy sought to avoid the condescending strain that runs through traditional liberalism. Their romantic assumption was that the lower classes, particularly the black lower classes, could not only take care of themselves but were better endowed with perspicacity and insight than their putative superiors. But all egalitarians must eventually face the brute fact that the lower classes often don't behave very well. Life in the slums is, at least on average, more dissolute and present-centered, more prone to violence and disorganization, than even revolutionaries would like. The conundrum is solved, however, if people can be changed. And that explains the credulous enthusiasm of Charles Reich, Herbert Marcuse, and other radicals for technocratic programs to rehabilitate dropouts and criminals. Technocratic people-changing is, on the whole, as harmless as it is ineffectual. A few programs—jobs training and preschool education—are probably useful, but others raise troublesome issues.

Prison reform illustrates starkly the dilemmas that intractable human nature presents to liberal philosophers. Throughout the 1960s, there was a general easing of the rigors of confinement and a loosening of prison discipline in most state systems. Washington State, where I was the institutional and social services administrator in the mid-1970s, had been a leader in the reform movement. Dress and hair codes had been abolished, mail screening was dropped, disciplinary procedures were formalized and regulated, and prisoners were generally confined to their cells only at night, having the free run of the institution during the day. All of this was premised on the rehabilitative assumption that people will act responsibly if they are given responsibility for their own lives. The result was something of a disaster. For an extended period, at least one prisoner a month was murdered in Walla Walla state prison, the biggest and "heaviest" in the system. Relaxed mail and visiting privileges made it almost impossible to control drug traffic. Homosexual rape was an everyday event. A younger and weaker prisoner suffered nightmares of abuse until he either volunteered for segregation,* or "punked" for a stronger inmate—essentially became a prostitute and slave in return for protection. The "wolves," the strongest and cruelest inmates, ran the drug and protection rackets, traded or sold punks, and to a large extent determined the tempo of institutional life. Most of my administration was spent trying to inch back to more controls—we feared an explosive riot if we moved too quickly. We were never really successful. To my knowledge the problem exists to this day and now in fact seems typical of most large prisons in the country.

More controls were just one response to prison indiscipline. Another was more elaborate programs, particularly in states like California that could afford extensive rehabilitative superstructures, but in most other systems as well. After I had been in Washington for about a year, I received a complaint from a legal services lawyer about a behavior modification program at Walla Walla. A prisoner had sustained a fractured jaw. I spent a day at the program, most of it talking in a group with the inmates. There were ten men in the group, all of whom had

---

*Segregation is the traditional punishment and control device for unmanageable prisoners. It is, and is intended to be, time "in durance vile." The prisoner is typically alone in his cell, participates in no programs, and is released for only about an hour of exercise each day. An index of the loss of control inside prisons in the last decade is that in many large institutions the *majority* of prisoners in segregation are there at their own request for relief from the pressures of the main line.

appallingly bad records, as bad as any group in the prison. One or two I already knew from previous episodes of violence. They had all been involved in major violence or killings inside, and none of them had any chance of parole in the foreseeable future. All of them had volunteered for the program, in part it seems out of a spirit of machismo challenge —could they beat the program? To my surprise, they were the most orderly and polite group of inmates I'd ever met. There was no cursing, no interruptions. After a while I noticed that when one of the men wanted to speak, he'd make eye contact with the group leader, another inmate, who would signal him permission with his finger. The total effect was astonishing, and somewhat eerie.

The program was based on the simple premise that the inmates needed to learn self-control; they didn't need to "get in touch with their feelings" as some rehabilitative theories had it. It operated apart from the rest of the institution as a self-contained unit. There was an elaborate set of rules—rise early, watch educational television, clean up quickly, no smoking except in prescribed areas, complete participation in extended discussion groups, and so forth. Each violation was promptly punished, with prescribed penalties adopted by the group. Punishment was meted out by the group and meted out immediately. The punishments were trivial at first—loss of smoking privileges for an hour, perhaps—but became progressively stiffer and finally truly draconian— loss of recreation time, then confinement to a cell for progressively longer periods, then confinement in the dark, then being strapped to the cot, and finally, being strapped to the cot in the dark in a diaper.

The essential principle was that the mutinous group member never won. As the group explained it to me, a new participant would reflexively resist the group and would immediately lose. The toughest inmate was no match for the group. As punishment grew more severe, he would promise to amend his ways and be released from punishment. He would then offend immediately, and the punishment would be ratcheted up a notch. Eventually, for the sake of a respite, he would decide to *pretend* to comply. At that point he was hooked. After a relatively short period of complying with the rules, he invariably internalized them. Life was better with a structure, more peaceful, more pleasant. Within about a month, the recruit was a true believer, ready to enforce the system against a new rebel from the outside. The man whose jaw had been fractured argued passionately that he hadn't been hurt badly, that the jaw was almost healed, that the whole incident was his fault in the first place—he had assaulted the other inmates while trying to disrupt the program. He gestured dramatically out the window to the main yard and said, with a touch of scorn, that people like me thought a broken jaw was something terrible. Out there he had been in a dozen knife fights. A broken jaw was nothing.

I reviewed the men's records again with the warden. They had been an extremely difficult group of prisoners; for the warden, the program was a godsend. A review team from the National Institute of Mental Health had issued a glowing report the year before. I decided to let the program ride. A few months later, the legal services attorney called to tell me he had filed suit against the state. Inevitably, as I had lacked the imagination to anticipate, an inmate had entered the program and refused to break. The most extreme stage of the punishment had gone on for weeks before the attorney found out what was going on and intervened. We didn't immediately end the program, but installed an outside appeals process before the more serious punishments could be imposed. The program disintegrated at once. With an appeals process, a rebel had an opening to manipulate; if he had even an infinitesimal chance to win, the others couldn't control him. Shorn of its certainty, the group collapsed. After a few months, the men went back to the yard.

I visited other state systems to see how they controlled their most violent prisoners, the 10 percent or so who caused the worst problems. Everywhere the story was the same. A program would seem to work until it encountered an inmate with a truly strong personality. The ensuing contest of wills resulted in degradation all around, the inmate by the punishment, the staff by inflicting it. The worst case I saw was that of a young and inoffensive-looking inmate in Vacaville in California. He had killed two men on the yard. His arms were crisscrossed with the scars of suicide attempts. He had been administered anectine, a curare derivative—a practice since outlawed. Anectine is a drug that paralyzes breathing centers, causing suffocation and hallucinations of dying. It was the last resort in Vacaville's behavioral modification program. The young man described its horrors in hushed tones, then smiled a smile of gentle triumph. His second killing had been *after* the anectine treatment.

These were extreme cases. Prisons, even the notorious Vacaville, are not, in the main, playgrounds for mad scientists. Most "treatment" programs, almost *all* that I observed, are simply too ineffective to hold any terrors for the inmates. The brightest prisoners quickly learn the rehabilitative jargon and manipulate the programs with a casually mocking cynicism. One man, an intelligent, physically impressive, wonderfully charismatic black, explained to me how he had invented a bizarrely convoluted sexual history to keep the social workers interested. He was a bank robber, he said, because he was good at it, and he liked having and spending large amounts of money, amounts he could never conceivably earn. No social worker would accept that explanation, so he invented case material for them. And then, he laughed, he would begin to show insight into his problems. He always got an early parole date.

It is easy to abhor anectine treatment. Most progressive liberals would have condemned it as an example of oppression in a totalitarian institution. But it is a natural consequence of simplistic egalitarianism. Prison reform movements tended either to deny that prisoners required any controls at all—hence the daily violence of a Walla Walla—or to maintain that prisoners' problems could be "cured" by simple technocratic interventions—and the interventions eventually evolve to horrors like anectine treatment. It is inconsistent with the whole spirit of modern liberalism to accept that violent offenders are different from the rest of us in the essential respect that they are much more likely to hurt other people, and to accept that there may be very little we can do to make them change.

Simpleminded egalitarians deny the real differences between people, between social classes, and between ethnic groups. Blacks and Irish both have higher crime rates than Jews, and blacks currently have a higher crime rate than the Irish. The oral fluency of the Irish is a stereotype, but it seems to be a fact—or, perhaps more accurately, *was* a fact, before the Irish were assimilated into the middle classes. Germans, for some reason, once dominated swimming the way blacks now dominate basketball. Chinese have always been remarkably law-abiding, but the violent crime rate among recently arrived Hong King Chinese is quite high. Irish and French have extremely high rates of alcoholism; Italians and Jews don't. Japanese work harder and are more thrifty than almost anybody else. Japanese and Chinese perform exceptionally well in mathematics and physics. Cubans are successful businessmen, far more so than Puerto Ricans.

Egalitarians are right to insist that humans are plastic. Most ethnic differences blur with time and with progress up the economic ladder. IQ scores, for example, seem to be largely class-determined. Eastern European Jewish soldiers in World War I had one of the lowest average IQ scores of all the ethnic groups tested, a fact which was taken to "disprove the popular belief that the Jew is highly intelligent." (*German* Jews, who had emigrated some seventy-five years before, accounted for the intelligence stereotype.) In less than two generations, average Polish-American IQs rose a truly remarkable 24 points, from 85—barely normal—to 109, well above the norm. The IQ difference between blacks and whites today is only about fifteen points. The difference is real, but there is no reason to assume that it is permanent. But to insist that expungeable differences are trivial, or that they can be expunged with only a brief technocratic intervention—whether an educational program or an anec-tine treatment—is the error of simplistic egalitarianism.

There are times and places when simplistic egalitarianism is a necessary, indeed the only appropriate, position. The civil rights movement and the feminist movement drew much of their energy from simplistic egalitarianism. Women still don't always get paid the same as men for the same work, but the situation is changing rapidly, partly as a result of a sustained feminist commitment to simplistic egalitarianism. Women, on the other hand, are not, on average, as strong as men, particularly in the shoulders and arms. No woman managed to pass the New York City fire fighter's qualifying test, which required carrying an adult-weight dummy on a ladder. The test was therefore changed—to dragging a lighter dummy across the floor—so women could pass it, although it is occasionally necessary, if only rarely so, for fire fighters to carry unconscious adults on ladders. A similarly misguided egalitarian impulse from time to time attempts to make admission to New York's several elite scientific high schools turn on factors other than academic competence—on balanced ethnicity, for instance. When continued commitment to simplistic egalitarianism requires the denial of real and relevant criteria, we are reaching the point in the political cycle where the principle has begun to lose its usefulness.

The Legalitarian Society

The American predilection for rules is a long-standing one. One of the very first actions of the Puritan company that landed in America was to formulate their *Laws and Liberties,* the first written constitution in the English-speaking world. Later, as the founding fathers became deities, their Constitution and its system of law took on the nature of a divine bequest. A spokesman for the New York Bar intoned in 1913:

Our great and sacred Constitution, serene and inviolable, stretches its beneficent powers over our land . . . like the outstretched arm of God Himself . . . the people of the United States . . . ordained and established one Supreme Court—the most rational, considerate, discerning, veracious, impersonal power—the most candid, unaffected, conscientious, incorruptible power. . . . O Marvelous Constitution! Magic Parchment! Transforming Word! Maker, Monitor, Guardian of Mankind!

By the mid-1970s, the "Magic Parchment" had become somewhat tattered, while the veracity, the discernment, the impersonality, and the conscientiousness of the Supreme Court was under persistent challenge. For two decades, particularly during Earl Warren's tenure as chief justice, the Court had steadily expanded the reach of its rulings. The uneasiness stemmed from a feeling that in doing so it was implementing a vision of an ideal society which comported closely with that of the liberal philosophers like Rawls and Dworkin, and which was not shared by most Americans.

Judges cannot avoid making law. And, as the American legal realists pointed out, it is foolish to presume that a judge can interpret the Constitution or any other law without reference to his own personal, probably only half-articulated, values and beliefs. Historically, in both England and America, the courts have functioned as correctives to the political process; and from the time of Francis Bacon, the power of Anglo-American courts to set right abuses of the legislature or the executive has been broad. Even the most conservative critics of the Warren Court—Justice Rehnquist, for example—concede that the content of constitutional formulae will change with time. What was acceptable to Jefferson and Madison may not be tolerable today, and it is up to judges, to a large extent, to determine the tempo of the shift in standards. The problem of judicial statesmanship, one that Felix Frankfurter wrestled with for a half century, is to discharge the Court's creative political function without giving free rein to the merely personal or merely factional. The swelling chorus of complaint in the name of "strict construction"* and "judicial restraint" in the early 1970s evi-

---

*Conservative "strict-constructionists" are, of course, no less inclined than liberals to twist the Constitution to their own purposes or discard it completely when it doesn't fit their vision of the good society. The First Amendment, for example, says flatly that "Congress shall make no law respecting an establishment of religion . . . or abridging the freedom of speech." Today's conservative advocates of congressional action to ensure prayer in the schools seem as undeterred by the plain language of the amendment as were the anti-Communist crusaders of the 1950s.

denced a growing feeling that the Court had crossed the line that separates permissible creativity from capricious prescription. Taking the Warren Court's criminal-procedure, school, voting, and obscenity decisions as a whole, the conservative critics have a good case. More to the point, for the purposes of the present chapter, the problems of constitutional interpretation over the past decade indicate the limits of the ideal of organizing society according to legalistic rules.

Judicial activism is carried to excess only by degrees. An egregious wrong presents itself and cries out to be righted. The judges solve the problem and state a rule. Legal exegetes then parse and interpret the rule, and apply it to a broader and broader range of situations. In Ohio, police invaded the home of one Mrs. Mapp, apparently without a warrant, looking for an alleged subversive; they ripped apart the hapless lady's bedroom, searched through her bureau drawers and closets, and finally found some "lewd" pictures. She was arrested and convicted, and her possession of obscene materials was publicized throughout the community. The Supreme Court professed itself to be shocked by the police's behavior and so extended the federal "exclusionary" rule to all the courts in the country. Thenceforward, evidence could not be used if it was illegally obtained. The justices decided that the constitutional protection against "unreasonable searches and seizures" could be assured only by such a doctrine. Within just a few years, drug dealers, their lawyers, and the federal judiciary had spun out the exclusionary doctrine into a body of law that rivals scholastic theology in subtlety and complexity, baffling the ordinary citizen, who cannot understand what principle requires that drug dealers, who may have been caught with large quantities of drugs in their possession, should routinely be allowed to go free.

The issue is not whether there should be an exclusionary rule. It is clear from experience that without the threat of an exclusionary rule policemen will routinely abuse the rights of suspects. The issue is its mechanical application. There are a number of cases on record where police attempted to comply with the requirements for a warrant and where lower courts agreed that they had acted properly, but where the evidence was excluded on appeal. It seems absurd that an obviously guilty defendant should go free for a violation so technical that even courts disagree on whether it occurred. It is the mechanical application of rules in defiance of the dictates of common sense that is characteristic of the legalitarian society.

In the legalitarian ideal, rules are pressed to their logical extreme. In order to decide *Brown* v. *Board of Education,* the landmark school desegregation case, the justices needed to overturn a much older line of cases declaring that "separate but equal" facilities were constitutionally acceptable. They did so by finding that separate facilities were inherently discriminatory because they were apt to "generate a feeling of inferiority . . . that may affect [the children's] hearts and minds in a way unlikely ever to be undone." Over the course of fifteen years, as the courts were continually called upon to rule on the subtle evasions of school boards, North and South, the rule gradually evolved from one forbidding segregation to one requiring integration, on the dubious theory that an adequate education could not otherwise be obtained, however insulting such a generalization may be to blacks. By 1966, the federal courts had adopted the rule that the "racial mixing of students is a high priority educational goal."

A line was finally drawn in *Milliken* v. *Bradley* (1971), which involved de facto segregation in Detroit's schools. The lower courts admitted that, with all good faith, integration was impossible in Detroit—not because anyone had committed acts of discrimination, but simply because almost all the city's students were black. The district court and the court of appeals, therefore, on absolutely straightforward logic, ordered the surrounding suburban school districts to merge with the city's so white students could be imported into Detroit. The Supreme Court, with Thurgood Marshall in powerful dissent, overruled the court of appeals, on grounds that seem altogether flimsy. (They ruled, in effect, that the state board of education was not sufficiently involved in local district affairs to require it to carry out the order of merger.) Marshall's dissent is by far the better reasoned; the whole body of federal court decisions since *Brown* pointed ineluctably toward a requirement that districts merge where that is required to achieve racial mixing. The majority was dithering because they knew the courts had pressed beyond the line of political acceptability; to persist in the path of logic would eventually have jeopardized the power of the Court itself. The Court was probably correct to draw the line where they did, but it was, by strict logic, an arbitrary line. If the limits of the reaches of logic must be drawn arbitrarily, all previous extensions of logic are called into question.

A number of the Court's decisions from the 1960s and early 1970s seem clearly to be engrafting the then current liberal vision onto the

Constitution by bringing more and more segments of society under the sway of simple legalistic rules.* The results were often perverse. The one-man, one-vote rule has a superficial appeal, for as Chief Justice Warren wrote, "Legislators represent people, not trees or acres." But it betrays a simple faith in majoritarianism that is not apparent in the Constitution. James Madison argued in the Tenth Federalist Paper that the Constitution was designed to assure representation of competing interest groups, a concept rather radically different from that of the Court's. Ironically, the perennial local redistricting that the Court's decision requires offers unparalleled opportunities for gerrymandering, and majority rule is often in conflict with equal protection. The surface democracy achieved by breaking up the New York City school system into community districts under local majority control makes it much more difficult for blacks in mixed areas to be represented on local boards. Once again, the initial cases brought to the Court were examples of flagrant maldistricting, by the Alabama legislature among others; it was the attempt to formulate a simple general rule that would apply to all political institutions that led the Court into the thornbushes.

In a few notorious cases, it is difficult to find even shreds of constitutional support for the rules fabricated by the Court. *Roe* v. *Wade* (1973), the decision that fashioned a constitutional right to an abortion through the first trimester of pregnancy, is the purest example of the Court's reading its own political views into the Constitution.† In the wake of the decision, sympathetic legal scholars tried valiantly to construct a coherent theory of the case. It was no easy task, for as the *Harvard Law Review*'s commentator—who strongly supported the result in the case —wrote: "One reads the Court's explanation several times before becoming convinced that nothing has inadvertently been omitted . . . [for the opinion] offers no reason at all for what the Court has held."

---

*The *horror vacui* that sometimes seems to motivate federal judges is illustrated by this quotation from a decision by J. Skelly Wright, one of the most activist members of the judiciary. The decision concerned the right of a patient to refuse medical treatment. Judge Wright wrote: "Failure to 'declare the law' would not place the responsibility on the executive or legislative branches of government. Judicial abdication will create a legal vacuum to be filled only by the notions and remedies of the private parties themselves." He ordered the patient to be treated.

†Perhaps I should say that I personally favor freedom-of-choice abortion statutes. But there is a long leap between favoring legal abortions and maintaining that the Constitution requires them. I think it is precisely because of the fragility of the Court's reasoning that the abortion issue has not yet come to rest. Should an antiabortion amendment to the Constitution be passed, which is not inconceivable, legal abortion will become considerably less available than it was before *Roe*.

The precedent of the Court relied upon most heavily was *Griswold* v. *Connecticut,* a case that struck down a state statute prohibiting the sale of birth control devices. Relying upon *Griswold,* however, is bootstrap logic, for the Court could not agree on a theory even in *Griswold.* The argument that drew the most support from the *Griswold* Court (there was no majority opinion) was that the statute conflicted with a citizen's right to privacy. Privacy as such is not mentioned in the Constitution, but it was discovered lurking in the "penumbral emanations" of the Bill of Rights. As Justice Douglas put it, "specific guarantees in the Bill of Rights have penumbras, formed by emanations from those guarantees that help give them life and substance." The overwhelming impression from reading both cases is that the justices are saying that if the Constitution doesn't protect the right to buy contraceptives or have an abortion, then it *ought* to.

One of the dangers of legalistic rules is that they must be applied to specific cases by people at a vast remove from whoever it was who formulated them. When I was the welfare director in New York, to avoid the problem of duplicate applications we had a procedure requiring positive identification by clients, preferably a birth certificate, but with multiple alternatives. One day I got a call from a *Daily News* reporter to tell me that a woman with eight children and no hands had been rejected by three welfare centers for failure to show proper identification. Her birth certificate was in Cuba, and there was no mail service between the mainland and Cuba. The rejection was ridiculous, of course, but it illustrates how grossly rules may be misapplied. Welfare caseworkers were not generally cruel people. Their behavior toward the Cuban woman becomes explicable only in a rule-ridden system. A primary emphasis of welfare reform for the previous decade—particularly once the system became a testing ground for the managerial instincts of the federal courts—had been to remove any scope for caseworker discretion by making all decisions subject to a body of quasijudicial rules. It was a reforming impulse that sprang originally from civil rights motivations, on the suspicion that caseworkers were prejudiced. But after ten years of trying to formulate a new general rule for each new special circumstance, the rules themselves had become an impenetrable thicket. When one becomes accustomed to applying rules that have no apparent reason, it is easy to apply rules unreasonably, or even to assume rules that don't exist. To take another example, a correspondent in a New York newspaper wrote recently that he was horrified to see on a local cable television station a scene where six men apparently forced a woman to eat a dead rat, then dismembered her with a chain saw and cannibalized the body. When he called the state cable television commission to complain, he was told that "free speech" prohibited interference with the show. The official was quite probably wrong: his response was the anodyned reflex of one accustomed to applying rules that made little sense to ordinary people.

The Supreme Court's line of obscenity cases illustrates how rules can turn back upon themselves. Justice Brennan, who wrote almost all of the obscenity decisions, slogged manfully through mountains of pornography for more than a decade. With each new case, he would formulate a new rule, more elegant and more rational than the ones that had gone before. Each of his opinions betrays the fervent hope that he had finally disposed of the noisome issue. And each time a new case would present itself calling into question the logic that had seemed so hermetically sealed just one opinion before. Brennan finally threw up his hands. The courts couldn't do the job, he wrote: "One cannot say with certainty that material is obscene until at least five members of the court, applying inevitably obscure standards, have pronounced it so." The conclusion he reached, therefore, was that there should be no regulation of obscenity. If a subject could not be compressed within a framework of legal rules, then society was proscribed from dealing with it altogether. The logic of rules presses inevitably to the point where there are no rules.

The majority of the Court agreed with Brennan's premise but, wisely I think, rejected his conclusion and upheld the judgment of the local legislature on a "community standards" doctrine. For almost a decade thereafter, it has simply refused to review local antipornography legislation. In this connection, Dworkin's position on pornography regulation is interesting. Opposition to pornography regulation has long been a litmus-paper test of liberalism. In *Taking Rights Seriously,* however, Dworkin fudges the issue, for the right to purvey pornography appears to conflict with the right of women to be free of psychic and physical abuse—another of Dworkin's litmus-test rights. Dworkin's hedging is certainly reasonable; the vile pornography on display in most downtown areas portrays a diseased sexuality that panders to the vindictive hatred some men apparently feel toward women. But if Dworkin himself must fall back on an amorphous "community standards" doctrine—albeit his choice of a "reasonable man" or "reasonable woman" may differ from that of most people—the seamless logic of his legalitarian society begins to unravel. The rule-making of the liberal philosophers then becomes just another elaborate rationalization of intuitively favored outcomes, which is what conservatives suspected all along.

The Heavenly City

Writing of the eighteenth-century philosophes, Carl Becker says:

> This was Locke's great title to glory, that he made it possible for the eighteenth century to believe what it wanted to believe, namely, that . . . it was possible for men, "barely by the use of their natural facilities," to bring their ideas and their conduct, and hence the institutions by which they lived, into harmony with the universal natural order.

The surface skepticism, even cynicism, of Voltaire and Hume, the devotion to cold logic, Becker suggests, concealed a naive faith that humanity would achieve a "heavenly city" in some distant future where Reason and Science would reign supreme, and mankind, finally accepting rational principles, would live in everlasting peace and contentment—a vision as mystic and millenarian as St. Augustine's City of God thirteen centuries before. The future polity of John Rawls, where "envy and destructive feelings are not likely to be strong," and where the "conception of justice" reigns, is no less based on a pietistic confidence that Reason alone can discover the one, right, natural, and harmonious order of things and men. The bright world of rationality and equality, guarded by constitutional rules and procedures, is the heavenly city of the liberal philosophers.

Men are rational beings. Reason must be the first court of appeal, the primary basis for testing the validity of ideas and institutions. Racial segregation, discrimination against women, and the benighted economic practices that helped bring on the Depression were all failures of reason; and, to a large extent, it has been through the application of reason to human affairs that we have been able to make such recent progress as we have. But reason is also a fallible instrument, and too great a faith in the power of abstract reason can be as misleading and dangerous in its own way as blind prejudice. The Pavlovian theories of gradually escalated bombing favored by the defense intellectuals during the war in Vietnam and the simplistic models of human behavior that underlay the War on Poverty were eminently reasonable. The problem was their lack of connection with the real world.

Intellectual clarity is a prerequisite for dealing with difficult problems, whether of economics, racial discrimination, or pornography; but, at the same time, real life is too complex to be contained within rationalist models. Blue-collar bigotry is a major obstacle to urban school integration, but it is not the only obstacle, and social policy based on simple assumptions about the dynamics of ethnic integration is apt to be both ineffective and counterproductive. Obscenity regulation once may have been a straightforward matter of freedom of speech and artistic expression, but the perverted horrors that assault passersby from city newsstands seem to require other categories of analysis. Keynesian demand-management models helped point the way out of the frigid depths of the Depression, and rigorous monetarism may hold the key to controlling runaway inflation, but no economic theory exists that will permit the day-to-day fine-tuning of the economy that the electorate has been led to expect. The "economy" itself is a rationalist abstraction from an immensely complicated interplay of avarice, ignorance, and the basic requirements of human subsistence. Economic models from time to time provide striking insights that can be applied to the real world with great success, but we should not assume that we have thereby bottled the truth.

In every age, problems arise of such complexity, of such emotional resonance, that reason fails as a guide, and recourse must be had to unarticulated standards. The recent advances in biological science illustrate the point. It is now, happily, possible to fertilize a human egg in a laboratory and reimplant it in the mother, allowing a previously infertile woman to bear her own child. Since fertilization is a chancy affair, the scientists usually fertilize several eggs, which creates the possibility that some eggs will be fertilized but will not be reimplanted. On some occasions at least, the scientists have kept the extra fertilized eggs alive so they could observe the process of embryonic cell replication. Rationally, there is little to complain about. Abortion is acceptable in our society; the information gleaned from experimental embryos may be invaluable. Still, the notion is repellent. It seems simply wrong to grow human embryos in test tubes for the sake of experiment or observation. Some limits have to be set. There is still a field where standards hold sway, even if it is shrinking and shifting.

But there are no standards or principles that can withstand unrestrained reason. Keynes stated the ultimate ethic of the extreme rationalist.

> We entirely repudiated a personal liability on us to obey general rules. We claimed the right to judge every individual case on its own merits. . . . We repudiated entirely customary morals, convention, and traditional wisdom. We were, that is to say, in the strict sense of the term, immoralists . . . we recognized no moral obligation, no inner sanction, to conform or obey. Before heaven, we claimed to be our own judge in our own case.

Keynes was writing in the 1920s, an age excessively burdened with convention masquerading as truth, and one can sympathize with his view; but it is plainly no basis on which to organize society, as our own recent excursions into civil disobedience demonstrate. Keynes was no lover of anarchy, but the privilege of immoralism cannot be restricted to a narrow intellectual elite, as he presumably would have wished.

Extreme positions have a way of circling back upon themselves. When campus radicals and black revolutionaries attacked the aridity of the ruling technocratic rationalism in the 1960s, they pressed the rationalists' own weapons into service and, in doing so, assailed all standards and conventions, not just those which underlay the assumptions of the technocrats. Nixon and Agnew made political capital out of the assault on standards. Much of their appeal to the so-called silent majority was based on their recognition that the common man's cherished values were under siege. When Nixon and Agnew failed themselves to live up to the standards they preached, the way was paved for the simple moralisms of Jimmy Carter and, later, the even simpler ones of Ronald Reagan.

Edmund Burke was the great defender of traditions and institutions. He insisted that convention was the only basis for law; traditional institutions represented a form of collective "wisdom without reflection." Hayek takes the same position. Traditions evolve, he argues, through a marketplace of ideas; a kind of metaphysical supply-and-demand law shapes institutions to fit a myriad of social intricacies that no rationalist model of society can ever comprehend. Late in his life, even Keynes, the supreme rationalist, moved somewhat closer to this point of view. Commenting to Hayek on the latter's *The Road to Serfdom* in 1944, he wrote:

It is a grand book. . . . You will not expect me to accept all the economic dicta in it. But morally and philosophically I find myself in agreement with virtually the whole of it; and not only in agreement with it, but in a deeply moved agreement.

Turning to a few special points. . . . Moderate planning will be safe if those carrying it out are rightly orientated in their own minds and hearts to the moral issue. . . . What we need is the restoration of right moral thinking—a return to proper moral values in our social philosophy. . . . Dangerous acts can be done safely in a community which thinks and feels rightly, which would be the way to hell if they were executed by those who think and feel wrongly.

Plainly, there is force in the traditionalist position; but in their own way, Hayek's arguments are as one-sided and untenable as those of Dewey or the youthful Keynes. It required a decisive break with traditional institutions to begin the reform of American racial practices. The mismanagement of the British economy after World War I and of the American economy before World War II was rooted in excessive reliance on financial tradition. Burke was horrified at the notion of society without a queen, and his horror today seems comically quaint. But how do we know when tradition is merely the mask for ignorance? When do we grant legitimacy to an institution or a convention merely because it has endured? When do we discard long-standing values or beliefs because they don't measure up to our standard of reason? The issue, as lawyers would frame it, comes down to one of presumptions and burdens of proof, and there are no simple answers or simple rules that will point the way.

To return to the "long-wave" metaphor from the previous chapter: much of the history of political ideas may be read as the alternative waxing and waning of faith in reason and faith in tradition. Conservatives characteristically overweight the value of stability against the creative possibilities of stress and change; liberals make the opposite error. Prolonged stability can cause a society to calcify. An insistence on articulated rationality generates the examination of first principles that leads to healthy change. But the social bonds can be stretched only so far without breaking. During times of great stress, leaders need an intuitive grasp of social limits and a sense of justice that balances individual rights against the community's need for cohesion and consensus. The 1960s and the early 1970s were a time when institutions and traditions were subjected to the test of untrammeled reason; the intellectual housecleaning that resulted accomplished much good. The bias of the 1980s and 1990s, I suspect, will be swinging back toward granting greater deference to settled institutions and unarticulated standards. Cortez never found his El Dorado, but he helped open up a continent; it is not a measure of failure that the rationalists' heavenly city will remain locked in the inaccessible mists.

Ronald Reagan's election in 1980 is a harbinger of the shift back to more traditional value systems. Interestingly, the rationalist style of thought has become so pervasive that Reagan and his advisers—despite their attempts to distance themselves from the received liberal orthodoxy—slipped almost immediately into the rationalist traps that waylaid their predecessors.

X

⟨∽⟩

RATIONALISM RESURGENT

American voters were thoroughly sick of their own government when they elected Jimmy Carter President. The aura of sleaziness that surrounded Watergate was more dispiriting than the facts of the cover-up itself. Censoriousness was in style as the national media, liberal congressmen, and ambitious prosecutors and reporters competed with each other to dredge up new scandals. In part, the morbid fixation on wrongdoing in high places was a form of public purgation: congressmen and journalists recovered their moral stature in their own and their children's eyes by proving that they had been duped into going along with policy in Vietnam. In part, the revelations were simply too titillating to ignore. The exploding-cigar cartoon antics of the CIA's alleged attempts to assassinate Fidel Castro and John Kennedy's apparent liaison with a Mafia moll were staples of the supermarket tabloids.

Distaste for government made Jimmy Carter's candidacy for President possible. Although he was an able and intelligent man, he had no obvious qualifications for the office. He had been the successful proprietor of a medium-sized warehouse business and had served one term as governor of Georgia, a medium-sized state, with moderate distinction. His appeal was grounded on his very lack of acquaintance with official Washington: since he was virtually without experience, he was untainted by Washington's scandals. Even Gerald Ford, whose probity was beyond doubt, was tarred by his pardon of Richard Nixon. There was no evidence that the pardon was part of a deal for Nixon's resignation, but speculation could not be downed by simple denials.

To secure the nomination, Carter exploited the Democrats' new reformist rules even more systematically than George McGovern did in 1972. In a grueling twenty-month campaign, he entered thirty of thirty-one primaries and built a commanding lead before the professional politicians ("Jimmy Who?") began to take him seriously. By mid-summer, fully a month before the party convention, he had won enough delegate slates to sew up the top spot on the ticket. He began the presidential race itself with a seemingly insurmountable lead in the polls over Ford, and then almost succeeded in losing it. It was one thing to vote for a decent antiestablishment unknown in a state primary. It was quite another actually to make him President, based on little more than a promise never to lie. Carter finally squeezed home only by a hair's breadth on a voting base built up from solid support in the South, and from among labor and blacks, perhaps the last croaking hurrah of the old Democratic coalition.

Carter's sudden slippage in the last weeks of the presidential race reflected growing doubts about his capacity for office, a concern that turned out to be well-founded. His informality and lack of pomp in his first days in office—his walk to the inaugural, his relaxed official dinners, his jeans and cardigan—were a pleasant contrast to the imperial trappings that had grown up around the White House. But he never succeeded in establishing control over the political process and was from the outset engulfed by events. With the exception of the peace agreement he wrung from Israel and Egypt at Camp David, his administration was a failure in virtually every respect. His economic program veered erratically from stimulus to restraint, while his foreign policy lurched between naive optimism and truculent posturing. His energy program, the "Moral Equivalent of War" (dubbed MEOW by Russell Baker), was an object of ridicule. He blundered badly in initial arms control talks with the Soviet Union, and after a treaty was finally signed, it was repudiated by the Senate. The administration was unprepared and dithering at the collapse of Iran and the Russian move into Afghanistan. When the economy slipped back into recession after the second round of oil price increases in 1979, his own party split as Democrats around the country fled from the national ticket to protect their own seats. The failure of the helicopter mission to rescue the Iranian hostages was the knell for Carter's administration; from that point, he had no chance to win re-election. Intelligence, goodwill, and simple decency were not enough for a successful presidency.

Ronald Reagan appealed to a constituency that overlapped to a considerable extent with Jimmy Carter's original voting base. He was strong in the South and among Catholics and fundamentalist Christians. Although he was a much better known public figure than Carter had been in 1976, he was still an outsider to Washington politics and could lash away freely at the previous twenty years' administrations. Despite his penchant for display, he was amiable and informal, like Carter, and was given to the same homilies on family, patriotism, and respect for institutions and traditional values. The key difference was that while Carter's simple preachments concealed his lack of a clear and consistent vision for the national government, Reagan's expressed a political program aimed at nothing less than a thorough transformation of national policy.

The "thunder on the right" that accompanied Reagan's election— the fulminations of the Rev. Jerry Falwell and the Moral Majority, the creationist movement in biology teaching, the resurgence of hard-line 1950s-style anti-Communism, the skillful adaptation by conservative political action groups of the campaign tactics perfected by Gene McCarthy, George McGovern, and their cohorts in the New Democratic Coalition a decade before—all produced the impression of a retreat to atavistic, anti-intellectual politics. I think the impression is misleading, however disquieting the carryings-on of Reagan's supporters on the extreme right. The goals of Reagan's hoped-for political transformation, and in an important sense his methods, were, ironically, virtually identical with those of John Kennedy twenty years before.

Intellectuals of the right are as prone to simplistic rationalism as intellectuals of the left. Reagan is even less of an intellectual than Kennedy was, but enthusiastic academic theorists, although of quite a different political stripe, set the policy tone at the start of his administration just as they did in Kennedy's. The overriding objectives embraced by each administration were essentially the same: generate a lasting economic recovery, reassert dominance over the Soviet Union, and foster independence among the poor without relying on income transfers. As the basis of its policy, each administration adopted simple models of the national economy, global politics, and the social dynamics of poverty; and each assumed it could accomplish its goals by manipulating just a few of the variables disclosed by the favored models. The pendulum, perhaps, had swung completely from one side to the other, but it was the same pendulum, and the sounding chimes rang much the same as they ever had.

Complexity: Economics

The three pillars of Reagan's new economic policies were control of the money supply; "supply-side" tax incentives; and reduced government interference in the economy. If inflation could be controlled and the private economy unleashed, it was hoped, the nation could get back on the bullish growth track it had enjoyed during the 1960s. None of these policies is necessarily wrong. The Reagan error was to assume—apparently with genuine conviction—that if a limited number of economic buttons were pushed at the right time and in the right direction there would be an immediate and spectacular economic turnaround. Kennedy's theorists had the good luck to apply their simplistic models just as the global economy was launching into a long-term growth cycle; it was the misfortune of Reagan's intellectuals that their opportunity finally came as the world was sinking deep into a long recession. Both sets of policies doubtless reinforced trends that were already under way, although Reagan's economists no more caused the recession of the 1980s than Kennedy's caused the boom of the 1960s. The failure of the real world to conform to the "Reaganomic" worldview, however, was one more lesson in the limitations of rationalist models.

The focus on the money supply—the first cornerstone of conservative economics—is premised on the monetarist theories of Milton Friedman,* which maintain, generally, that changes in economic activity follow changes in the money supply with a predictable lag of about eighteen months. Friedman demonstrated the point with his massive *A*

---

*Friedman is an able and judicious economist who has made a number of major contributions to economic theory; but, as is the case with Keynes, Friedman the polemicist must be distinguished from Friedman the economist. And like latter-day Keynesians, Friedman's disciples tend to hawk aggressively simplistic versions of the master's views, which, unfortunately, are the ones with the most natural appeal to a political policymaker. Friedman and Keynes, in fact, would never have been as disdainful of each other's economics as their disciples are. The dispute between monetarists and Keynesians turns on a somewhat arcane point of investment theory. Empirical data gathered at Oxford University in the 1930s and 1940s seemed to show that investment responded primarily to changes in the long rate of interest, as Keynes had suggested; and, further, that readily available credit increased the demand for bonds and drove down the rate of interest, thus increasing investment and growth. Keynesians reasoned, therefore, that once monetary policy was loose enough to keep interest rates low, it was of little further interest. Any further tuning of the economy would have to be accomplished by fiscal policy. Friedman and his monetarists challenged the Keynesian empirical data. Monetarist studies suggest that easy money translates directly into the purchase of goods, not just bonds, and can therefore stimulate the economy without lowering interest rates. The increased activity could cause prices to rise and actually *raise* the interest rate because of inflationary expectations. There is plenty of evidence for both positions, none of it conclusive. It is entirely possible that each view is correct at some points in the business cycle and wrong at others.

Monetary History of the United States, in which he showed that over the last century there had been a more or less consistent relation between money availability and economic activity. Comparable surveys with, broadly speaking, comparable results, have been carried out in a number of other countries. Friedman has even challenged Keynes's analysis of the Depression: in the monetarist view, it was Federal Reserve misman-agement of the money supply, not inadequate demand, that caused the collapse. Keynesians—which is to say almost the entire body of aca-demic economists—responded to Friedman's theories with a predictable storm of denunciation and ridicule. The ensuing dispute between monetarists and Keynesians has been as heated, and sometimes as sub-stantive, as the arguments over the nature of the Trinity that sent third-century Greeks into the streets with bricks in their hands.

The debates have been so fierce because, just as in the ancient Mono-physite riots, the technical arguments mask basic differences in political principles. The essential premise of monetarism is that markets work, which is in fundamental opposition to the Keynesian assumption, rooted in the experience of the Depression, that they don't. The crucial policy conclusion that Friedman and his disciples draw from their re-searches is that if the government will merely assure a predictable supply of credit and then get out of the way, the rest of the economy will take care of itself. It is a position with obvious appeal to conserva-tive intellectuals and, of course, a direct threat to the economics-man-agement industry that has grown up in the government and the universi-ties since the Kennedy era. The monetarist position is at bottom an antirationalist one. Friedman, at least in his less polemical moments, insists that the economy is just too complex for elaborate fine-tuning strategies to work—that they are likely to do more damage than good. A consistent monetarist free market theorist needn't argue that things will always turn out well if his prescriptions are followed, but merely that the economy will be healthier in the long run than if the government attempts to direct events by *force majeure.*

The irony of the recent experiment with monetarism is how quickly the monetarists slipped from their antirationalist moorings into the rationalist policy trap, just as the pragmatists had a generation before. In the hands of Friedman's more enthusiastic disciples, monetarism was transmuted into the rationalist management tool par excellence. If eco-nomic activity really does follow changes in the money supply, the argument went, then precisely targeted changes in the money supply will produce precisely the desired levels of economic activity. Monetary policy thus becomes just another weapon of fine-tuning, not different in principle from those employed by Kennedy's Keynesians. The experiment was not a success. The Federal Reserve adopted the monetarist prescription—targeting the money supply rather than interest rates—in 1979 and effectively abandoned it three years later under pressure from the Reagan administration, which shed its commitment to monetarism as soon as the high interest rates that resulted from tight money supply management began to threaten its political standing.

The failure of naive monetarism is one more demonstration of the pitfalls of simplistic rationalist models. Correlations are not the same as causal mechanisms. As the poverty warriors discovered, the fact that almost all middle-income people can read doesn't mean that literacy training will make poor people middle-class. The causal relation between the money supply and the economy may in fact be the reverse of what the monetarists claim: even though changes in the money supply usually *precede* changes in other economic activity, they may not *cause* them. If the "animal spirits" of entrepreneurs move them to increase investment, they must first increase their credit lines at the banks; the increase in credit will increase the money supply well before the new investment begins to show up in national production statistics. It is the new investment that is the causal mechanism, however, not the change in money. In the real world, in all likelihood, the relation between the money supply and the rest of the economy is an intricate intertwining of mutual cause and effect that will vary with time and circumstances.

More important, as the monetarists, of all people, should have anticipated, market forces will quickly adjust to attempts at economic manipulation. Through a kind of Heisenberg principle, when pressure is put on one policy variable, its relation to the rest of the economy will almost certainly change. As soon as the Federal Reserve imposed tight controls on the availability of money, there were dramatic changes in the behavior of businessmen, banks, and consumers that undercut the Federal Reserve's policy initiatives. Businessmen invested heavily in electronic cash management techniques that greatly increased the *velocity* of money—a dollar spent twice has the same impact as two dollars spent once. The financial markets created new types of credit instruments—money market funds and "repurchase agreements," for instance—that functioned like bank money but were outside the Federal Reserve's monetary controls. Higher rates spurred banks into aggressive marketing of consumer loans and credit cards—and a credit card credit line has the same purchasing power as a checking account. As interest rates rose, huge amounts of Eurodollars came washing in and out of the country, in pursuit of fractional interest rate and foreign exchange profits, making day-to-day control of the money supply impossible.*

For three years, the Federal Reserve, red-faced and puffing like an overage butterfly collector, pursued will-o'-the-wisp money, valiantly updating its statistical definitions and its management tools with each new credit or cash-management wrinkle. The final straw came in 1982 when Congress authorized a rash of new savings instruments—All-Savers' Certificates, bank money-market accounts, NOW accounts—to help banks compete with money funds. As funds bounced back and forth between checking accounts and the new savings devices, the Federal Reserve, in effect, threw up its hands and admitted it no longer knew how to define spendable money. It is obviously folly to base national economic policy on an abstraction that defies definition. As gracefully as possible, the Federal Reserve announced that it would revert to its former practice of managing interest rate levels, although it would continue to accord respect to monetarist doctrine. The experiment in dogmatic monetarism was over.

The flirtation with simplistic supply-side theories produced similarly disappointing results. There is no question that there is some relationship between tax policies and investment, as the investment boom triggered by the Kennedy tax incentives demonstrated. There is also no question that American marginal tax rates, particularly on capital, are high relative to, say, Japan. And there is no question that there is some level of tax reduction that at some point will generate greater investment. But the naive assumption of Reagan's "Laffer-curve"† theorists

*Part of the volatility of international money movements reflects volatile foreign-exchange rates, another result of naive monetarist/free market theory. Friedman and his disciples long argued against fixed foreign-exchange rates on the theory that if governments allowed their currencies to float freely on the open markets, rates would quickly reach a state of stable equilibrium and fluctuate only as underlying economic reality required. In fact, free floating has created extreme foreign-exchange instability that vastly increases the complexity and dangers of international business and imposes a real burden on world trade. The monetarists argue that the world's governments have never allowed their currencies to float with perfect freedom—which is probably true, but theories that require perfect restraint are of little practical use in the real world.

†The so-called Laffer curve is named after economist Arthur Laffer, a Reagan adviser. He reasoned that if the tax rate were 100 percent, no one would work and there would consequently be no tax revenues. Therefore, there must be some tax rate of maximum efficiency such that a higher tax rate will reduce economic activity and consequently reduce total tax revenues. Laffer reasoned, apparently just on the basis of intuition, that the United States had exceeded the efficient tax rate, and convinced the administration that reductions in tax rates would *increase* tax revenues by moving the tax system closer to the point of maximum efficiency.

that marginal reductions in the top tax brackets would immediately call forth a surge in economic activity that would replace the lost tax revenues was just not true. Industrialists banked their tax breaks and sat on their hands waiting for demand to pick up before taking investment risks. The tax reductions translated into lost federal revenue and larger federal budget deficits.

Finally, the process of deregulating the economy proved much more complex than the administration expected. Plainly, the enthusiasm for government regulation of business and the environment was carried to excess in the 1970s. Even an interventionist economist like Lester Thurow concedes that it would be impossible to build the interstate highway system today because of the maze of regulations and the wealth of opportunities for blocking projects in the courts. But Reagan's deregulatory zealots discovered that a great mass of regulation is business-inspired. The self-interest of big business has long ceased to be identical with the cause of free enterprise. Strong business interests have fought each deregulation step, for example, in the trucking, airline, and banking industries. The steel industry fights against free trade, the banks against unregulated interest rates, airlines against competitive price-setting, the automobile, electronics, and apparel industries against unregulated foreign competition. The agricultural industries expect government price supports, and the major banks want government help with their risky foreign loans.

The demand for government protection is one more piece of accumulating evidence that America's industrial elite has become remarkably fat and lazy. Research and development expenditure in large companies, for instance, is only about a fourth as productive as small-company R&D, apparently because of the endless planning committees, management information specialists, auditing teams, and bureaucratic approval chains that plague the bigger firms.* Almost *all* new jobs created over the past decade have been created by small businesses, as the managers of America's smokestack industries have

*Ironically, despite its professed scorn of government, big business slavishly copied the budgeting, planning, and strategy formulation procedures developed at the Pentagon in the 1960s, with much the same results—bloated planning staffs, elegant strategies that relate only distantly to the real world, and vastly expensive and complex computerized information systems full of data that is either false or irrelevant. The same graduate schools of business and consulting firms that hawked the rationalist planning systems in the 1960s and 1970s are now just as aggressively trumpeting a wholly new set of slogans—hands-on, down-on-the-shop-floor, gut-feel management—in keeping with the sudden shift of national ethos. Watching middle-level executives scramble to adopt the new style is sometimes comic.

persistently demonstrated their inability to meet the challenge of foreign competition. The recent experience of the automobile manufacturers in shedding thousands of white-collar employees to drive down break-even points only serves to demonstrate how much unnecessary overhead large companies carry. One striking fact illustrates the extent to which government, business, and unions have conspired to undermine productivity. Fifty years ago, it took one year, almost to the day, to build the Empire State Building—from first shovel in the ground to tenants moved in. Today it would take at least four times as long, and the finished product would almost certainly be of much lower quality.

The disappointment of the naive hopes of Reagan's advisers doesn't invalidate certain of their central assumptions. The reliance on market forces to bring the supply and demand of petroleum into balance has proved far more successful than federal rationing, for example. By following monetarist prescription and tolerating high interest rates and a severe recession throughout 1981 and 1982, the Federal Reserve has wrung at least some of the inflationary impetus out of the economy, although the inflation bogey is by no means permanently downed. It is no policy breakthrough to slow inflation with a severe recession, of course; the challenge which the conservative economists have yet to meet, at least as of mid-1983, will be to keep inflation low during a period of sustained growth. Concentrating on tax incentives to encourage capital formation is almost certainly a proper course, given the historically low rates of savings and investment in the American economy. Lowering the capital gains tax in 1978 seems to have called forth a healthy surge of venture capital, for instance, although it took several years for the tax changes to make their effects felt. Finally, the stuttering attempts at deregulation merely underscore how important it has become to restore a measure of competitiveness to the economy and how difficult it will be.

There is at best only a groping understanding of the economic problems facing America and the world in the 1980s, but it is certain that there are immense dangers. The financial systems of the entire industrialized world are now so interconnected that the failure of major Third World borrowers could create global financial chaos. Economies could collapse with either sharp rises or sharp falls in oil prices. The level of hostility between trading nations is the greatest in decades. Recession has dogged the path of every major nation, reviving social dissension that had been muted by economic progress, widening the rift between blacks and whites in the United States, and raising the specter of revolution in Third World countries. Government budget deficits in almost every major country are endangering time-honored social insurance programs. It is not a time for simple answers, simple models, and simple slogans.

Complexity: The Military Balance

Ronald Reagan issued his rearmament call to a profoundly different world from the one that John Kennedy's trumpet had summoned to battle twenty years before. Kennedy's messianic zeal for converting the world to democracy had leached away into self-doubt and cynicism following the long and dispiriting war in Vietnam. Even more important, despite Kennedy's campaign rhetoric about a missile gap, in 1960 the United States enjoyed overwhelming military superiority over the Soviet Union. In 1980, there was at best a tenuous balance, with the Soviets enjoying clear superiority in most measures of conventional forces and certain classes of heavy missiles, and challenging the United States' lead in almost every other area.

The strategic map of the world has turned some startling somersaults. In the 1960s, America accused China of being one of the Communist puppet masters behind North Vietnam's war of conquest in the South. In 1979, China, by now virtually America's ally, attacked Hanoi's troops to quell the voracious Vietnamese imperial appetite. For its part, Vietnam, having long since discarded the black pajamas of its guerrilla-fighting past, now boasts the third largest standing army in the world, bigger even than that of the United States. In the United Nations, the United States and China are the leading spokesmen for the legitimacy of Khmer Rouge rule in Kampuchea—the same Khmer Rouge that the United States fought and condemned for genocidal butchery in the Cambodian wars of the early 1970s. In Europe, the biggest military worry is German pacifism, while socialist France is America's most resolute anti-Soviet ally. The oil shortage of the 1970s lent an entirely new edge to military planning. In 1960, the United States was, for all practical purposes, completely self-sufficient. There was no obvious way, for instance, that winning in Vietnam would have enriched America. The administration's military enthusiasm stemmed more from an abstract commitment to ideological conquest than from traditional motivations of power and wealth. In the 1980s, by contrast, the painful

vulnerability of the Middle Eastern oil fields is an overriding considera-
tion in Western military planning. There is an oddly nineteenth-century
ring to the debates in the Pentagon and in Congress on projecting forces
to secure and hold foreign natural resources.

Debates over military policy, even more than arguments over economics, tend to lapse into a quasi-religious clash of dogmas, because for
all the computerized gloss of defense planning exercises, they are
grounded in the final analysis on gross imponderables and airy speculation. Consider the nightmare scenario that haunts American military
planners: a preemptive strike by the Soviet Union against the U.S.
land-based missile forces. In theory, a Soviet first strike would kill
"only" about 10 percent of the U.S. population and, if it were coupled
with an evacuation of major Soviet cities, would sharply reduce our
ability to retaliate. The United States could respond with a submarine-
based missile strike against Soviet cities—submarine-based missiles are
not accurate enough to target against Soviet missiles—or do nothing. A
second Soviet attack would devastate America, so the rational course
would be to do nothing, leaving the Soviet Union with a free hand, for
example, in Western Europe or the Middle East.

In the real world, the threat of a Soviet first strike can almost—stress
the *almost*—be dismissed out of hand. No one has ever fired a missile
over the transpolar route that would be used in actual warfare, and the
gravitational anomalies and wind patterns are simply not known well
enough for the Soviets to count on the pinpoint accuracy required for
an antimissile strike. (Just as one example of the yawning gap between
theory and reality, the United States has never even successfully fired
a missile from one of its land-based silos; in only four attempts over the
years, *all* of the missiles have malfunctioned.) Nor could the Soviets
count on being able to evacuate their cities successfully. Paper plans are
one thing; actually moving millions of people on split-second notice is
quite another. Finally, for all the ominous character of the new generation of Soviet missiles, there are few indications that the Soviets are
actually planning a nuclear war. Their bomber and submarine fleets, for
instance, are typically maintained in a relatively low state of readiness.

Even the fundamental assumption that the Soviets have been aggressively outspending the United States on defense is open to question, for
it is almost impossible to make unambiguous comparisons of American
and Soviet force levels. If, in order to provide a common yardstick, the
high salary costs of the American forces are projected onto the much

larger Soviet army, the level of Soviet spending appears enormously inflated. On the other hand, since the Soviets lack a free-market price system, it is very difficult to arrive at an accurate ruble cost of, say, a truck. The ruble cost of American high-technology weapons is, for all practical purposes, infinite, since there is no way that the Soviets can buy them or build them. Nor is there any way to judge how many Soviet soldiers offset one of the United States' technically miraculous "smart" weapons.

Nevertheless, certain aspects of the Soviet buildup are extremely disquieting. They have strengthened their forces in Central Europe, for example, far beyond what could be required purely for defensive purposes. The Warsaw Pact countries have twice as many men under arms in Europe as the NATO countries, triple the number of tanks, twice as many aircraft, and an overwhelming superiority in short- and medium-range nuclear-tipped ballistic missiles. Once again, the apparent Soviet advantage is clouded by major imponderables: the doubtful loyalty of the East European troops; poor morale, alcoholism, and language problems, particularly among the Asian conscripts; perhaps serious logistic and control problems; and stodgy tactical doctrines. The consensus even among conservative military planners is that the prospect of a Soviet attack on Western Europe is quite remote; but defense officials would be derelict if they ignored the facts of the Soviet buildup.

Given the great imponderables of military strategy, the dogmatic sloganeering of both the left and the right holds unparalleled dangers. The reflex of the right is simply to step up American arms production until the Soviet Union is forced to bow to the sheer power of the American economy, and, in effect, drop out of the arms race. But there is no reason to suppose that the Soviet Union would not match an American buildup, even at a fearful cost to its civilian living standards. When the United States committed itself to the so-called MIRV technology in the 1970s—the installation of multiple warheads on a single missile, each of which can be independently targeted—the Soviets matched the American move tit for tat. The result was that each side added about five thousand warheads to its missile fleet throughout the decade, vastly increasing the risk to the entire world. The planned new generation of American missiles, the MX, will combine power and accuracy at a wholly new threshold and will undoubtedly provoke a matching Soviet effort. Even if the world avoids a holocaust, each country may manage to spend the other to its knees.

At the same time, the new Soviet threat is far too dangerous simply to ignore, as the left would seem to prefer. The very bleakness of the long-term economic outlook for the Soviet system adds to the risks. The Soviet Union is persistently unable to feed itself, has an aging and uncompetitive industrial base, increasingly restive consumers and sullen workers, and faces wholly unfavorable demographic trends. Pessimists within the Soviet government have reason to fear that they will sink into a semicolonial state of economic and technologic dependence, trapped between Europe and the United States to the West and the bursting economic powerhouse of Asia to the East. If militarists within the Soviet government perceive that the West is weak and irresolute, or open to nuclear bullying, traditional notions of power politics would call for the absorption of the Arabian peninsula and the expansion of Soviet sway in central Europe. The Soviet Union would then bargain from a position of strength for the food and technology it needs. To embark on such a course would be perilous in the extreme, but the notion is not so fantastic that it can be safely disregarded.

The arms race is insane. Countries are devoting critical social and economic resources to assure their ability to incinerate the world in a crisis. If the world is crazy, of course, it is folly to be sane, but the task of statesmen is to restore sanity by safe and digestible degrees. The Reagan administration's initial resort to Kennedy-style international machismo is hardly calculated to advance the pursuit of safety and stability. At the same time, it would be foolish to rely on the good faith and sound judgment of the Soviet Union. Working through the immense reservoirs of mistrust to bring the world's bristling armories under control will require wisdom, strength, and subtlety of a degree that has been displayed by no recent administration—except possibly for a short time (further to confound left/right ideologues) by that of Richard Nixon.

Complexity: Social Welfare

The assumption of Reagan's social welfare advisers has been that American income supports for the poor and the unemployed are quite high, but that a conspiracy of reporting—the exclusion of food stamp, medical assistance, and public housing benefits from welfare income statistics—has made them appear much lower than they actually are. High levels of income support, in the minds of conservative theorists, sap incentive and encourage dependency. By creating purchasing power without offsetting production, they contribute to inflation. Because the payments must be financed by federal borrowing, they help exert pressure on the capital markets and so raise interest rates and retard investment. The poor, in short, become less able as the country becomes poorer.

There is a substantial kernel of truth in the conservative position. One of the most alarming social statistics of recent decades is the fact that black and Hispanic girls account for more than half of the illegitimate births to teenagers in the country. A very large number of them go on welfare once their babies are born—almost half of black families overall are headed by single women, and a substantial proportion of them are on welfare. Liberals are wont to blame such statistics on the "economic crisis," but the data do not bear them out. The rates of illegitimacy and broken homes among blacks were much lower in the 1940s and 1950s, when blacks were much poorer than they are today. Since the liberalization of welfare standards in the early 1960s, the rate of black and Hispanic welfare dependency has grown steadily, regardless of overall improvements in black and Hispanic income, and regardless of whether black and Hispanic unemployment rates were moving up or down. For a generation of lower-class black and Hispanic girls, having a baby is an opportunity for an illusory independence. They can go on welfare in their own apartments with an annuity for the rest of their adult lives, and their boyfriends are able to escape completely the consequences of casual sexuality. It is hard to conceive of a social policy better calculated to keep an underclass permanently in dependency and poverty, whatever the good intentions of its liberal defenders.

But the conservative argument is misleading when it stresses the economic consequences of income support programs for working-age people, for the actual costs are relatively marginal. Of the roughly $250 billion the federal government spends each year on income support and related programs, about $150 billion is paid to the aged and disabled via the Social Security program, $50 billion is spent on Medicare coverage for the same aged and disabled, and only $50 billion goes to "welfare" as it is normally defined. The welfare payments include roughly $10 billion for food stamps, $10 billion for supplemental payments to the aged and disabled, and $10 billion for AFDC—Aid to Families with Dependent Children, the classic "welfare" program. The remaining $20 billion is spent on medical insurance for the poor, most of which, again, goes to the aged. The total "welfare" claim by people of working age is only in the $20 to $30 billion range. Doubtless there is waste and fraud in the program, but no one would claim that all or even most of the working-age welfare recipients should be ineligible. The vast majority of people on welfare really need it; and blacks are overrepresented on welfare largely, if not entirely, because they are poorer than other ethnic groups. The conservative arguments for welfare cuts, in other words, must be grounded almost solely on principle. Welfare for people of working age is not the cause of federal deficits or inflation, because, with federal deficits approaching $200 billion, the amount of money involved is simply too small to have those effects.

If conservatives have tended to overestimate vastly the costs of waste and fraud in welfare programs, the liberal program advocates have also done their best to confuse the debate. The "hunger lobby" greets any attempt to curtail the food stamp program with tales of swollen-bellied children in the Mississippi Delta, although surely some cuts could be made in a $10 billion program without immediately inducing starvation. The *New York Times* labeled a Reagan proposal to limit the Medicare program as an "attack on the poorest of the sick." Most Medicare recipients, in fact, are not poor, since everyone over sixty-five automatically qualifies for the program. The various lobbies for old people have fiercely resisted any attempts to restrict the growth of Social Security programs in the face of overwhelming evidence that the country's obligations to its retirees have vastly outrun its ability to pay for them. It is still too early to say whether the recent curtailment of future benefits will put the programs on a financially sound basis.

The conservative dream that a reduction in the public sector will restore a lost ethos of Jeffersonian self-reliance is no more grounded in reality than Dewey's or Rawls's hopes of engineering social justice and harmony. Short of breakthrough peace agreements with the Soviet Union, there is little hope of achieving major reductions in government spending, even if conservatives are successful in achieving some cutbacks in income transfer and social service programs. Conservative policy preferences in criminal justice and mental health, on the other hand, imply much higher levels of incarceration and institutionalization. Expanding prison space and bringing mental hospitals out of the mothballs will be immensely expensive, unless there is a return to the semibarbaric conditions that prevailed before the last phase of reform. Finally, there is accumulating evidence that the country has long deferred essential maintenance on its bridges, transit systems, and its highways. None of these is a private sector problem, and none can be addressed on the cheap.

A recent study of emerging agricultural problems illustrates the complex interplay of private and public sector roles. There is reason to worry about the long-term productivity of the U.S. grain belt because of declining water tables and increased soil erosion. Water tables are falling in part because government-subsidized irrigation schemes have encouraged wasteful patterns of water use. Farmers would conserve much more water if they had to pay its true cost. On the other hand, soil is eroding because the economics of the individual farm do not justify the costs of conservation measures. It is a problem like that of industrial pollution, where the profit-and-loss statement of the private firm does not adequately account for external or long-term costs. Maintaining the quality of the soil will probably require government enforcement of antierosion standards, while, on the other hand, extending the life of the grain-belt aquifers will require government withdrawal from subsidized irrigation programs. Most complex problems—ensuring adequate medical care, maintaining research and development in basic science, fostering export competitiveness, husbanding natural resources and ensuring adequate energy supplies, maintaining transportation and communication infrastructures—require some mix of public and private effort. The mix will vary with time and circumstances, and there is no sure path through the policy tangle.

John Kennedy's election as President in 1960 reflected the country's frustration with economic stagnation and declining international prestige, particularly as measured against the Soviet Union. The tired nostrums of Eisenhower's conservative advisers were an irritation. It was time for the country to be "moving again," and Kennedy's brand of technocratic pragmatism held out the straightforward and simple answers the voters were looking for. Twenty years later, the voting public was again wearied by economic woes and loss of international initiative to the Soviet Union; but by now the liberal prescriptions had become nostrums themselves, as shopworn and irrelevant in their own way as Eisenhower's had seemed in 1960. Ronald Reagan, from the opposite side of the political spectrum, won the presidency by offering a different set of simple answers, again promising to right all wrongs, this time by extirpating liberalism. There is no reason to expect that Reagan's panaceas will be any more successful than Kennedy's. The test of political maturity will be our ability to recognize the existence of complexity, and to formulate public and private policies in the sure knowledge only that outcomes will be uncertain and simple answers insufficient.

XI

MATURITY

When I was about twelve or thirteen, I often went to early morning Mass with my father. It was a wonderful way to start a day. The quiet luster of the priest's vestments, the burnished solidity of the gold altar plate, the first morning light through stained-glass windows gave a great sense of peace and calm. The buzz of the priest's Latin was hypnotic and mind-washing. There was just enough discomfort to heighten the effect. We knelt through most of the ceremony on wooden kneelers and, in those days, did not eat or drink before Mass. Breakfast put to flight the wispy beginnings of a headache. We approached the world with a slight moral edge for the rest of the day.

Thirty years later, I rise at about the same time in the morning, but now I jog—for the sake of an everlasting cardiovascular system rather than the safety of my immortal soul. The park where I run is an oasis in a clangorous city, rather as church was. There is the same sense of shared earnestness with my fellow joggers. The contemplative rhythm of running is one of its delights, and there is just enough discomfort to heighten the pleasure of the postrun shower and breakfast. And all early-morning runners, of course, start their day with just a slight moral edge over the rest of the world.

I suspect that there was much less change in the 1960s and 1970s than met the eye. As the recent resurgence of militant Christianity attests, the aggressive secularism of those decades was less of a permanent shift in outlook than is often supposed. Even the best educated and most secular classes merely substituted one set of religious rituals for another—jogging and mantras for conventional prayer; the obsessive tracking of success in "relationships" instead of a balance sheet of good and bad deeds; encounter sessions rather than religious retreats; the miracles of est in place of the cures at Lourdes.

At the grass roots, despite sharply declining attendance at traditional mainstream churches and synagogues, fundamentalist religion is flourishing as it has not done for decades. Somewhere between one-third and two-fifths of all Americans now consider themselves to be "born-again Christians," and it is no coincidence that both presidential candidates in 1980 professed a belief in an unadorned and simple Christianity. Herman Kahn's researchers at the Hudson Institute make the point that standard ways of tracking religious preferences—Catholic, Methodist, and so forth—fail to capture the distinction between fundamentalist and so-called transcendental religious belief. The mainstream churches that are proud of their freedom from doctrinaire theology, their emphasis on the social gospel, their rational and college-educated clergy, their liberal records on civil rights and Vietnam—those are the ones that have been losing adherents, while the gut-level sects have been gaining strength. It is still surprising to meet normal people—stockbrokers, for instance —who have been "slain by the spirit," that is, who regularly achieve such a state of religious ecstasy that they swoon, but it is becoming less so. A Catholic friend recently told me of a growing Catholic movement where she and the rest of the congregation were routinely "slain," saw visions, and spoke in tongues during Mass. The strength of the Creationist movement in science education, for all its regrettable obscurantism, attests to the durability of simple beliefs and simple values.

A major study by the National Institute of Mental Health has documented how little fundamental outlooks and beliefs have changed over the course of twenty years. Both in 1957 and 1976, NIMH researchers conducted massive field surveys of American households with a fifty-page questionnaire designed to elicit a picture of Americans' outlook on life and their future—how happy were they in their jobs, in their family lives, in their communities; were they anxious or optimistic about their futures; what values were most important to them; did they feel threatened or under siege? The original study was conducted to develop baseline data on Americans' mental health, and it was replicated in 1976 to document what the researchers expected would be massive changes in outlook and self-perception during the two decades. By their own admission, the researchers were "surprised" at the results, for as they report: "There is remarkable consistency in the way men and women respond to questions about their well-being in 1957 and 1976. *Overall, changes are small; often there is no change at all.*" (Italics in original.)

There *were* changes, to be sure, but most of them were minute. Interpersonal relations were somewhat more important to Americans in 1976 than in 1957;* the relational aspects of marriage—the opportunities for mutual support, for example—were ranked higher in importance by the later generation. Americans had become somewhat less inclined to describe success in terms of status and roles and somewhat more introspective about their success as parents or spouses. They were somewhat more willing to talk about fears and anxieties and more disposed to seek professional help in a personal crisis. There were several important changes in the self-perception of women. The percentage of women who derived their primary satisfaction from their job had risen sharply, although it was still far from a majority, and women were much less likely to feel that being single was a badge of personal failure.

What most surprised the researchers was that, overall, Americans were quite a contented lot in 1976, more or less as they had been in 1957. Despite the rising divorce rate, Americans were still remarkably family-centered; their families were by far the greatest source of personal satisfaction. They overwhelmingly preferred being married and were on the whole happy in their marriages, liked their children, tried hard to be good parents, and felt they were succeeding. They liked their jobs, thought they were demanding—interestingly, almost no matter what the jobs were—and thought they performed them competently. Other studies have produced similar results. A duplication of the famous Middletown study in 1977 showed that even over a span of fifty years, there had been strikingly little change. A majority of high school students, for instance, still regarded the Bible as a "sufficient guide to all the problems of modern life."

None of this comports with the picture of America that was the media staple of the 1970s—that of a people beleaguered by swirling change, by corrosive alienation in the workplace, by the collapse of the traditional family, by the turning away from the work ethic and the quest for personal expansion. It was a picture that existed, for the most

*Even some of these changes probably have more to do with styles of jargon than with substance. When hardheaded bankers meet to review loans, instead of saying, "Is the collateral sufficient to cover our loan?" they will typically say, "Are you 'comfortable' with the amount of collateral?" The very breadth of the conquest of the social worker's argot suggests that its substantive penetration is shallow.

part, in the minds of a self-regarding upper-middle-class elite, whose views were quite naturally those most likely to be reflected in television news shows or magazine columns. Daniel Yankelovich writes about the "search for self-fulfillment in a world turned upside down" in his book *New Rules* (1981), and defines the modern outlook as "exuberance shot through with anxiety . . . wilfulness coupled with a crippling sense of powerlessness . . . an odd sense of estrangement from the world." But Yankelovich himself concedes he is writing about only 17 percent (a suspiciously precise number) of the working population. His heroic assumption is that this highly selected subsegment will determine the outlook of the entire rest of the country—a pleasantly self-inflating conceit.

In his *Culture of Narcissism* (1979), Christopher Lasch writes that modern man is "plagued by anxiety, depression, vague discontents, a sense of inner emptiness." Work, according to Lasch, has lost its purpose. "Most Americans," says Lasch, "would still define success as riches, power, fame, but their actions show that they have little interest in the substance of these attainments." Instead of pursuing the traditional goals of capitalism, says Lasch, Americans now seek "glamour and the excitement of celebrity . . . public recognition and acclaim . . . because the dream of success has been drained of any meaning beyond itself." One must wonder who in the world Lasch is talking about. Most Americans might be puzzled to be told that they were working only for evanescent notions of narcissistic glory.

"Alienation in the workplace," a favorite topic of social science studies and White House conferences during the 1970s, appears to have been largely a figment of the collective imagination of professional problem-solvers.* When the 1976 NIMH survey did not turn up significant evidence of alienation, the authors reviewed a number of the earlier studies and found that "it is not always clear what data are being used to draw the dark conclusions. . . . Indeed, a careful reading of [a series of studies that claimed to find serious problems of alienation] . . . suggests that most American workers are not particularly dissatisfied with their jobs and do not find their work alienating." What the aliena-

---

*There are even, it seems, "long cycles" of worrying about alienation. In the 1920s, Dewey convinced himself that American productivity was lagging because "men's hearts, minds, thoughts, interests, are not *engaged* under the present system in the work which they are doing." He had a hatful of plans for industrial democracy and worker control to solve the problem, more or less the same solutions that his epigones came up with a half century later. The concept of worker alienation comes originally, of course, from Marx and Engels.

tion studies really show is how fervently foundation executives and sociology professors would have detested being assembly line workers.

Certainly, not all the dramatic changes of recent years are intellectual fictions. Sharp discontinuities in crime rates, divorce rates, and suicide rates all support the contention that the pace of change has been revolutionary. Yankelovich writes:

> Indeed, so far ranging are these . . . startling cultural changes that . . . a recurrent image comes to mind of . . . volcanoes and earthquakes . . . as American culture shift(s) relentlessly beneath us . . . creat(ing) huge dislocations in our lives. . . . Unlike most American women in the recent past, tens of millions of women no longer regard having babies as self-fulfilling. . . . In the nineteen-fifties a typical American family consisting of a working father, a stay-at-home mother, and one or more children was the norm. . . . It shocks most Americans to learn to what extent this norm has collapsed in a single generation. . . . Single households grew from 10.9% of all households in 1950 to 23% in the late seventies. . . . By the late seventies, a majority of women (51%) were working outside the home. By 1980, more than two out of five mothers of children age six or younger worked for pay.

But the same statistics give a rather different impression if they are viewed from a longer time perspective. For example, the rate at which women in their prime child-rearing years (twenty-five to thirty-four) worked outside the home rose steadily from 1900 to 1940 at an annual rate of about 1.2 percent. It was not at all uncommon for a working-class woman to take a job to help ends meet. My Irish grandmother worked as a cleaning woman much of her married life, and no one regarded it as particularly remarkable. When my *mother* went to work in the 1950s, on the other hand, it was the subject of much comment. Women were withdrawing from the labor force during the postwar nesting boom, and my mother was swimming against the social tide. (The priest regularly sermonized on Sundays about the moral dangers to a family with a working mother. We all kept our heads down.) Women's labor-force participation rates shot up sharply again after 1965, as Yankelovich notes, but the average rate of increase in the percentage of twenty-five-to thirty-four-year-old working women during the entire period after 1940 is, for all practical purposes, identical with the trend rate since the beginning of the century (1.25 percent for 1940 to 1975 compared to

1.22 percent for 1900 to 1940). One could argue, in short, that the 1950s were the aberration, not the 1960s and 1970s. Much the same point can be made about crime rates, divorce rates, and other measures of social disruption. All of the recent statistics look horrendous compared to the placid 1950s, but when the base for comparison is extended backward, the discontinuities fade away or disappear altogether.

Many of the statistical fluctuations that appear most striking relate fairly directly to demographics. With a large relative increase in young adults and older people, the increase in single-person households that Yankelovich lists among his volcanic changes is not very surprising. More fundamentally, because the number of young adults entering the labor force in the 1950s was so small, young men as a group did unusually well financially, particularly when compared to their fathers, who had the misfortune to be in their prime working years during the Depression. It was the economic success of young men that financed the mass move to the suburbs and allowed wives to stay home and concentrate on raising children. The contrast was painful when the enormously large cohort of young adults came crowding into the labor force during the 1960s and 1970s and found that getting ahead was an unexpected struggle. In the 1950s, when young workers were at a premium, the gap between the average wage paid to a new worker and an experienced worker narrowed perceptibly; and, predictably, it widened again in the 1960s and 1970s. With young men as a group in pinched circumstances —at least relative to the expectations they had built up during an affluent childhood—wives went back to work, marriage was delayed, and the birthrate dropped. The increase in young people, by itself, might have been expected to increase social tensions. Crime rates, divorce rates, suicide rates are all highest among young people. But, as Richard Easterlin suggests, when economic pressures were added to the pressures of a crowded birth cohort, all the indicators of social tension soared.

Disappointed young adults are a highly vocal minority and account for much of the impression of a "world turned upside down." In the 1976 NIMH study, college-educated young people were the one group that consistently expressed dissatisfaction with their jobs, because they weren't advancing fast enough. Almost all the case histories cited by Yankelovich in his *New Rules* are of disappointed young professionals. A college education used to be a sure ticket to economic success. During the glory days of the campus revolts, students flaunted their disdain for money and career precisely because they thought they could take them for granted. It was a shock to find they were just faces in the crowd when they finally entered the job market. The full dimensions of the problem are just now being felt in most large companies. The top-level jobs are filled by executives in their forties, who began their careers when competition was light, moved quickly up the corporate ladder, and expect to keep their jobs for another fifteen or twenty years. The ranks just below them are crowded with the baby boomers, now in their late twenties and early thirties, impatient for advancement, with high standards of consumption and no place to go, a sure recipe for frustration and intramural dissension.

A different kind of crowding lies behind the gloomy view of recent history favored by the upper-middle-class cultural elite. Since inflation pushed upper-middle-class salaries into the higher tax brackets and mass affluence created a national leisure industry, much of the advantage of being upper-middle-class has been stripped away. Now it's possible even for taxi drivers to take trips to Europe or the Caribbean. Tennis courts are noisy, crowded, or unavailable; squash is unaffordable; and ski resorts are mobbed with ladies on church bus tours, littering the lower slopes with their polyester-clad bodies—plenty there to make an elite feel alienated. Not surprisingly, people who advocate slower economic growth, or a "no-growth society," or who resist developing wilderness areas, are almost exclusively upper-middle-class. Whatever the long-run benefits of protecting the environment, restricting industrial growth is clearly not in the interest of the working class or the poor; and the attempt in the 1960s and the 1970s to link the environmental movement with efforts on behalf of blacks, women, or the underclass was simply meretricious. Because snowmobiles make "the winter forests screech with mechanical noise," Charles Reich decided there was a national spiritual crisis. But no matter how Reich universalizes his frustrations, it is unfortunately true that more people enjoy rollicking through the woods on mechanical cats or crowding into Yellowstone campgrounds than want to meditate on Thoreau during a solitary snowshoe trek. It is, nonetheless, depressing to be crowded, and the broadly-based affluence of the past several decades has made the elite feel very crowded indeed.

The twenty years from 1960 to 1980 can be put in perspective without trivializing them, for they were indeed a time of great stress and change. The urban riots, the campus revolts, the loss in Vietnam, Watergate and the resignation of Nixon, the first big OPEC price rise, inflation's first whirling out of control, were all crammed into the five-year period from 1968 to 1973.* But forces that had been set in motion long before made a disruption of the pleasant equilibrium of the 1950s inevitable. The children of the baby boom generation were becoming young adults. Blacks had moved en masse from the rural South to the cities. Sooner or later, a civil rights movement had to rattle the country's ossified social structure. Spin-offs like the women's movement necessarily followed. The unchallenged dominance of American smokestack industries had to end with the reindustrialization of Europe and the emergence of Asia as a first-class power. Rapid economic growth throughout the world strained natural resources. A global financial system that had been designed when America was the only economic power of consequence began to creak. The question is not whether there was stress and change, but whether it was, on balance, irremediably destructive of culture, values, and morals. Leaving aside the special pressures felt by upper-middle-class elites and young professionals, I think the gloomy case is very hard to make. It seems rather that the country survived a difficult period of transition with its basic strengths and institutions intact.

The list of positive achievements in the past two decades is immensely impressive. The pace of economic growth was the fastest in the entire history of the world. American family incomes increased by 50 percent in real terms, and the gains were broadly distributed across all income classes. There were three million fewer families in poverty in 1980 compared to 1960—even fewer if in-kind subsidies are included— and the percentage of poor families was cut in half to only 9.1 percent. The value of transfer payments to the poor and the aged more than quintupled, and the share of personal income devoted to transfer payments doubled. Although poverty was by no means eliminated—and in some relative sense never will be—the most vulnerable groups, older people and young children, were considerably more secure at the end of the period than they had been at the start. Although it is still fashiona-

---

*We shouldn't exaggerate, however. The two decades from 1960 to 1980 did see a lot of stress. But 1940 to 1960 suffered World War II and the Korean War; 1920 to 1940 saw the Great Depression; and 1900 to 1920, World War I. By comparison, 1960 to 1980 was a time of peace and progress.

ble to sneer at the progress made against poverty since 1960, rapid economic growth and generous transfer payments assured that it was greater than ever before.

The full weight of all the branches of government was enlisted to end official racial discrimination and segregation and finally to close a shameful three-hundred-year-old chapter in American history. Whatever one may think of the value of affirmative action programs and legislated integration, no government has ever done more to bring an oppressed minority into the mainstream. The fact that many whites still harbor racial prejudice and that blacks as a group are still on the lowest rung of the socioeconomic ladder demonstrates the magnitude of the problem, not the failure of the civil rights movement. The violent confrontations in Selma, Birmingham, and the Mississippi Delta, the explosions in Watts, Detroit, and Newark, the revolutionary fulminations of the Muslims, the black-leather swagger and dazzle of the Panthers, the upthrust clenched-fist shout for Black Power, were all part of a necessary rhetoric of change, a way of cauterizing the suppurating evil of racism and validating the epochal character of the social transformation that was under way.

The cathartic phase of the civil rights revolution is over now and—although many would disagree—I think blacks are safely embarked on the generational climb into the middle classes that has been negotiated by the white ethnic groups before them. The very ineffectiveness of continued government action to force the pace of social and economic integration—indeed, such efforts are probably now counterproductive —attests, in a perverse way, to the success of the efforts in the 1960s and 1970s. Whatever progress it is practicable to mandate has already been made, and blacks have begun to penetrate strongly and broadly into the middle classes. As the economy recovers, they can be expected to move ahead rapidly. A generation from now, I suspect, the peaceful revolution effected during two decades of concentrating on the civil rights of minorities, even taking the bleakest view of the confusions, false starts, and excesses that attended the movement, will be viewed as one of the great social successes of the century.

The women's movement enjoyed successes on a similar scale. In fact, women have progressed even faster because, as a group, they don't face the cultural and class barriers that stand in the way of progress for the great mass of blacks. As with blacks, lower-class women have yet to benefit from the emphasis on women's rights to the same degree as their middle- and upper-middle-class sisters.* Whereas the educated young professional woman now faces a dizzying plethora of choices—career? marriage? motherhood? all three?—the working-class mother still gets stuck with the dishes after a long day at her job. But even here, considering that the movement came broadly into public consciousness only some fifteen years ago, the progress has been remarkable. It is no longer unmasculine for even blue-collar "real men" to change diapers, to help with the housework, or to enjoy the tenderer pleasures of parenthood.

Prophets point to yesterday's events and call them trends. Like the "secular stagnation" theorists of the 1930s, who proved that the Depression would last forever, today's prognosticators of future gloom tend to project our present difficulties into the indefinite future. There is a stronger case, I think, for believing that the upheavals of the 1970s were a form of social and economic deck-clearing, opening the way for an era of extraordinary growth and peaceful progress. For one thing, the industrialized world seems nearly to have completed the expensive process of readjusting to higher energy costs. Less than a decade ago, an increase in production meant an even faster increase in the rate of energy consumption. The enormous capital investment in energy efficiency has reversed that relationship, and falling energy consumption has exposed the fragility of the OPEC cartel. In past decades, hungry independent drillers upset each price and production agreement put in place by the major oil-producers; now oil-rich countries in need of foreign exchange —Iran, Mexico, Nigeria, Norway, England—consistently undermine each OPEC attempt to maintain prices in declining markets. Most important, the speed with which the world economy acted to compensate for excessive petroleum costs, once governments dropped their subsidies and price controls, attests to a continued economic resilience that most economists thought had been lost long ago.

The dangers of energy disruptions are by no means past. A revolu-

*The leaders of the women's movement have seemed strikingly blind to the different life problems of the upper-middle-class movement leaders and the great bulk of working-class women. Even Betty Friedan, who has been more sensitive on this score than many other feminists, in a recent set of reminiscences lists the breakthrough achievements of the movement: " . . . the first woman to have a seat on the stock exchange, the first executive vice president of a major advertising agency, the nun who became a college president, the housewives who survived their own divorces and became labor arbitrators . . ." It is not much help to tell a middle-aged working-class woman whose husband has just left her that she should become a labor arbitrator. Her experiences are as different from those of the women Friedan lists as the experiences of a street black are from those of the black Ivy League law school graduate.

tion in Saudi Arabia, or even in a somewhat less critical producing country like Mexico, could throw the markets into turmoil overnight. The very speed of the market adjustment to high energy prices jeopardizes continued energy discipline. Falling real energy prices retard the process of bringing marginal supplies on line and reduce the profitability of investments in energy efficiency. Just a couple of years' worth of production of large energy-inefficient cars would impose an inflexible continuing claim on energy resources that would sharply increase our vulnerability. Already in 1983, the drive to convert Northeastern utilities to burn domestic coal instead of foreign oil is losing impetus. Only a crisis, it seems, can overcome regulatory obstacles to coal designed for a time when oil was the cheapest and cleanest energy resource available. Reducing the risk of repeating the experiences of 1973 and 1979 will probably require some form of continuing, but hopefully wise and forbearing, government intervention; a tax on foreign oil, reduced regulatory burdens on coal, and continued incentives for high-mileage cars are the obvious policies. But the prospects for successfully managing energy resources are brighter than they have been at any time since the OPEC cartel first became effective in 1973.

There is silver lining in the existence of the energy crisis itself, for it signals the end of the North-South division between wealthy industrialized nations and the impoverished rest of the world—the world picture that still dominates most of the debates in the United Nations General Assembly. Extremely rapid economic growth in countries like Brazil, Chile, Mexico, Ecuador, Korea, the Philippines, Taiwan, Indonesia, Malaysia, and India was an important reason for the global tightening of energy supplies. World real economic growth from 1960 to 1980 averaged a startling 7.3 percent per annum—the fastest in history—with the most rapid growth concentrated in the so-called Third World countries. Brazil is perhaps the paradigmatic case. Only twenty-five years ago, it was achingly poor, with a plantation agricultural economy, and a huge, illiterate, and unskilled population—a favorite subject for photographs in Christian missionary magazines. Without the benefit of an oil-find bonanza like Mexico's, Brazil for a generation has achieved growth rates that, year after year, rival those of Japan and Korea, Asia's economic superstars. It now exports more manufactured goods than commodities, is a leading exporter of machine tools and capital goods to West Africa, is a force in the U.S. small-airplane market, and recently exported its first oil rig. Brazil still has extremes of wealth and poverty, but a burgeoning middle class is firmly established and growing rapidly. The entire country radiates optimistic self-assurance; and the Brazilians I know have no doubt that they are about to assume their rightful place in the councils of the major nations of the world.

The success of the Brazils of the world is still precarious. A prolonged energy crisis or a sudden unraveling of the world's shaky financial system could undo years of progress. Most of the newly industrialized countries are in the process of a delicate transition from military or "authoritarian" governments to some form of middle-class democratic system of politics. Unexpected economic reversals could touch off sansculottes revolutions or a reversion to atavistic dictatorships. And economic progress is far from a universal phenomenon. Areas of the world like sub-Saharan Africa still seem as hopeless as ever. But the progress of the past twenty years has been so broadly based that it offers a realistic prospect of an emerging middle-class world economy, with strong links of trade and finance, and the shared cultural assumptions essential to stable prosperity and balanced world growth.

In the United States, the demographic forces that caused such disruption in the 1960s will have the opposite effect in the 1980s and 1990s as the baby boom cohort reaches mature adulthood. The same generation that wouldn't trust people over thirty will cast a jaundiced eye on anyone under forty. The student excesses of the 1960s may have been irrational, but they weren't crazy. Since there was sufficient social surplus to free the students at least temporarily from work and want, why not give free rein to their bursting impulses? The social surpluses and the bursting impulses have faded away at about the same time, and the change in outlook is already evident. The radicals of the 1960s, black and white, are for the most part living quietly bourgeois lives. The present thirty-year-old generation is intensely career-focused and settling down to marriage and parenthood. The campuses seem full of engineering students. Alcohol, it appears, may be replacing marijuana as the narcotic of choice—even unconsciousness will be respectable.

The economic consequences of a mature population are wholly favorable in the medium term.* The enormous increase in young workers during the 1970s reduced productivity and increased the unemployment rate because young people are such comparatively inefficient and unsta-

---

*The problems won't appear until the twenty-first century, when the baby boomers hit retirement age and bankrupt the Social Security system once and for all.

ble workers. By 1990, those same workers will be in their prime both as producers and as consumers. The implications for the private real estate market, for example, and for all the commercial spin-offs of a residential construction boom, are immense, particularly taking into account the low recent rates of housing production. It is entirely probable, in short, that the late 1980s and the 1990s will see the same kind of prolonged and stable expansion that marked the 1950s and 1960s. The potential for malign misfortune or grotesque mismanagement, of course, can never be underestimated; but after a long period of disruption and adjustment, the powerful underlying forces that drive the economy are all likely to be generating the positive momentum that can make any political leaders look like geniuses.

The stabilizing effects of an older population should extend far beyond the realm of economics. In the middle 1960s there was a subliminal, but almost tangible, moment when power shifted away from adults to young people. I knew a number of high school teachers in Trenton then, and almost overnight, it seems, they lost their self-assurance in the classroom. It was as if both they and the students realized at the same time that a teacher's authority in the classroom was a myth. The exaggerated fear students had always had of a teacher's wrath—or that of parents or of police for that matter—was groundless, actually foolish. A teacher couldn't force students to do anything, and the coercive punishments at his disposal were trivial.* In a physical confrontation, there was no question of who held the edge. Just a few years later, in fact, physical violence against teachers became a commonplace. As their status washed away beneath them like silt, most teachers, down deep, got scared; it showed in the classroom and reinforced their students' new sense of power. There was, I believe, a shift in the way young people and adults perceived the world, a change in their collective consciousness, in effect, that related directly to the shift in numbers and that happened more or less simultaneously, through the same sort of mysterious mechanism that tells lemmings when to start marching for the sea.

The country's collective consciousness should become a very grown-up one fairly soon, for a demographic shift of the same magnitude as that of the 1960s is already under way in the opposite direction. In 1975

---

*The "students' rights movement" wasn't the reason for the triviality of available punishment. The available punishments had been trivial for many years. When kids in decades past said, "My teacher will *kill* me if I don't get my homework done," they never believed it, of course. The exaggerated language and the mock terror were simply a way of reinforcing status and authority roles that were, on the whole, comfortable to wear. The belligerent students' rights movement, I think, was the result rather than the cause of student fractiousness.

young people—aged fourteen to twenty-one—held a 3:2 numerical advantage over adults aged thirty-five to forty-four; in 1990 the adults will hold a 3:2 edge over the kids, and the total number of young people will drop by about 20 percent. It should mark a decisive power shift back to adults. The tyranny that young people exercised over taste and culture in the 1960s will be a thing of the past. Teachers and school administrators should regain their psychological edge over their charges (this is already happening). Age-related social blights like violent crime should abate rapidly, for mugging requires quick reflexes and fleet feet. If the past is any guide, the drop in social disruption should be much sharper than the proportionate drop in the numbers of young people. The entire country should assume a rather tranquil and settled mien as it works its way past the hormonal surges of adolescence. It is not at all inconceivable that the 1990s will be a somewhat gray and conforming decade like the 1950s—Kondratieff would be delighted at the forty-year span involved—but a bit of dullness may be a welcome change.

The demographic shift in the black community will not be as sharp as that in the rest of the population, but it will still be substantial, and will be of immense importance to black progress. For one thing, as the black median age shifts upward, so will the skills, the job stability, and the earning power of black workers. Much more important, black adults should be able to regain control over the substantial minority of hoodlum youngsters who terrorize black neighborhoods and reinforce white racial stereotypes. Again, I think the early portents are favorable. Despite the recent recession, there are substantial middle-class black neighborhoods taking root, for example, near the area of Brooklyn where I live. Black politicians now typically list crime as their top priority issue, and working blacks are showing increasing impatience with their antisocial children. I have been told by black friends that resort to organized vigilantism, if not common, is becoming more frequent. An extended economic expansion, of course, is a prerequisite to substantial black progress. But a long period of growth, which I suspect is likely, will greatly reinforce black efforts to re-establish traditional systems of authority in their own communities;* and it is not unreasonable to expect

*The current national policy of subsidizing black teenage pregnancies is a major obstacle to achieving this optimistic scenario; but I don't know what can be done about it. One can only hope that as a middle-class worldview becomes dominant in black communities, welfare for working-age people will gradually regain the stigma it had before the "reforms" of the 1960s. Certainly, we should resist making the grants any more attractive (excepting some still below-subsistence Southern grant levels) to avoid repeating the experience of the 1960s when employment and the welfare rolls exploded at the same time. The comments here are focused on blacks, but I think more or less the same view may be taken of the future of Hispanics.

that by the mid-1990s, blacks will be a predominantly middle-class population, and that most of the major black-white issues will be behind us.

This is an optimistic scenario, and one could identify a host of reasons why things could turn out very badly indeed. If there is anything we should have learned over the past twenty years, it is that predictions are apt to be wrong. But since the factors predisposing toward positive outcomes seem at least as likely as any others, there seems to be little point in adopting a gloomy outlook.

What have we learned from the past twenty years, besides the inherent unreliability of soothsayers of all sorts? Drawing lessons from a generation's experience is a pretentious exercise, but it may be less so if the lessons themselves are modest ones.

We have learned, I think, the limits of our own bright ideas. It is fine to *claim* credit when things turn out well—whether the economy, foreign policy, or social programs—but it is quite another actually to believe that we deserve it. The principle applies in reverse. Since John Kennedy affected omnicompetence, we have, understandably, been inclined to blame our leaders for whatever goes wrong. In fact, the capacity of even a President to control outcomes is marginal at best, and his freedom of action to do evil is not much greater than his ability to do good. The real forces that govern the world—demographic surges, shifts in raw material balances, the emergence of a new social or ethnic consciousness—usually operate on deep levels of complexity that we only dimly perceive, or understand, if at all, only long after the event. In this respect, the long-wave theorists are assuredly right, but their theories have little predictive value. If there are long waves operating today, it is quite likely that we have no idea what they are.

The recognition that the most important events lie outside our control is a counsel of skepticism, rather than one of despair. Skepticism was the original spirit of American pragmatism, part of the open-minded acceptance that change, more often than not, was progress. Pragmatism means dealing with the world as it is, with an eye uncluttered by theory. The pragmatic instinct led us astray, I think, when it lost touch with its own insights. When the pragmatists, from Dewey to Kennedy, stopped being skeptical of each other, they slipped into a rationalist fascination with their own mental constructs, the "intellectualist" trap that James mocked. Conservative economists and intellectuals have recently demonstrated that they are just as prone to bumble into the same pitfall. One might have thought the lessons of rationalist arrogance had already been learned.

The dogmatic pragmatists also proved themselves slow to recognize moral imperatives, both in civil rights and in the Vietnam War. There is not much room for morality in a world reduced to mechanism. The experience of the later 1960s, however, shows that the moralist approach to politics has limits of its own. Moral concepts ring so grandly, and with such satisfying orotundity, that moral rhetoric can easily subsume moral reality. Pragmatism without moral sensibility leads to arid technocracy; and moralism that has lost contact with the real world is just self-righteous shrilling.

The loss of certainty—both technocratic and moral—in a single generation is not tragic. It is not even sad. Loss of certainty, in a way, is what maturity is all about. Coincidentally, as its obstreperous young generation from the 1960s passes into adulthood, the United States has become a mature country, ending finally an adolescence that lasted for roughly a half century. Maturity brings with it a consciousness of limits, to be sure, but there are compensations. A sense of limits can be grounded on an assured self-perception of formidable power. Respect for enduring values helps anchor a commitment to continued change and experiment. The complexity of events gives rise to neither hopelessness nor hubris, but inspires instead awe and delight at the wondrously unfolding patterns of the world.

BIBLIOGRAPHICAL NOTES

I. PRACTICAL MEN, PRACTICAL PLANS

The basic account of the 1960 presidential campaign is in Theodore H. White, *The Making of the President, 1960* (New York: Atheneum, 1961). The quote from Murray Kempton on p. 2 is from Murray Kempton, *America Comes of Middle Age* (Boston: Little, Brown, 1963), p. 283. The "end of ideology" argument is made by Edward Shils, "The End of Ideology?" *Encounter* 5 (November 1955):52–58; Daniel Bell, *The End of Ideology* (Glencoe, Ill.: The Free Press, 1960); and Seymour Martin Lipset, *Political Man, The Social Bases of Politics* (Garden City, N.Y.: Anchor, 1960). The predictions from Drucker and Burnham are in Lipset, *Political Man,* p. 414. "Other-directed" is a distinction used by David Riesman et al., *The Lonely Crowd: A Study of the Changing American Character* (New Haven: Yale University Press, 1950). The colorful background to the Philadelphia Republican machine is in Lincoln Steffens, *The Shame of the Cities* (New York: American Century, 1966). The Schlesinger quote on p. 3 is in Arthur M. Schlesinger, Jr., *The Big Decision: Private Indulgence or National Power* (New York: privately printed, 1960), p. 23. The T. H. White quote is in his *In Search of History* (New York: Harper & Row, 1978), pp. 492–493. The quote on Kennedy's character is from Schlesinger's *A Thousand Days* (Boston: Houghton Mifflin, 1965), pp. 114–115. Fairlie's criticisms are in Henry M. Fairlie, *The Kennedy Promise* (Garden City, N.Y.: Doubleday, 1973). For Nixon's self-characterization, see Richard M. Nixon, *Six Crises* (Garden City, N.Y.: Doubleday, 1962). Kennedy quote on ideology is in Henry J. Aaron, *Politics and the Professors* (Washington: Brookings, 1978), p. 167. The quote "Practical men . . . " is from John Maynard Keynes, *The General Theory of Employment, Interest, and Money* (New York: Harvest, 1966), p. 383. On pragmatism generally, see Morton G. White, *Pragmatism and the American Mind* (New York: Oxford University Press, 1972) and *Social Thought in*

America (Boston: Beacon Press, 1957). James's collected works have been recently issued by the Harvard University Press. I used his *Pragmatism* (Cambridge: Harvard University Press, 1975) and *Essays in Philosophy* (1978). Dewey's collected works are in the process of publication by the University of Southern Illinois Press. An extensive sample of his political writings are in J. Ratner, ed., *Characters and Events,* 2 vols. (New York: Holt, 1929). A synopsis of James's philosophy is in Bertrand Russell, *A History of Western Philosophy* (New York: Simon and Schuster, 1945), pp. 811–819, and of Dewey's philosophy, ibid., 819–828. A. J. Ayer's *Philosophy in the Twentieth Century* (New York: Random House, 1982) has a section on James's pragmatism on pp. 69–102. And see Morris Cohen, *Reason and Nature* (New York: Harcourt, Brace, 1931), for a contemporary critical view and T. R. Maitland, *The Metaphysics of William James and John Dewey* (New York: Philosophical Library, 1963). For the political link between pragmatism and progressivism, see Richard Hofstadter, *The Age of Reform* (New York: Vintage, 1955), and Ronald Steel, *Walter Lippmann and the American Century* (New York: Atlantic, Little, Brown, 1980). Dewey's quotes on James's zeal are from *Characters,* p. 111. James's "Give us . . . " is from *Pragmatism,* p. 62. Dewey's "Philosophy recovers itself . . . " is in White, *Social Thought,* p. 128. James's "either a concept . . . " is in *Pragmatism,* p. 98. Russell on pragmatism is quoted by Dewey in *Characters,* p. 542. James on "hypothesis of God" is from *Pragmatism,* p. 143. James's dichotomy between "tough-minded and tender-minded" is ibid., p. 12. I should note here that James viewed pragmatism as a middle course between the tough- and tender-minded, chiefly because the tough-minded view excluded his own interest in mysticism and parapsychology. But on virtually every other count, James was decidedly of the tough-minded view. "In this real world . . . " is ibid., p. 40. Note on the Big Dipper is ibid., p. 121. The relation between Veblen, Beard, Holmes, James, and Dewey is in White, *Pragmatism* and *Social Thought.* "Happy-go-lucky . . . " quote is in James, *Pragmatism,* p. 124. Holmes's "Life of law . . . " is in White, *Social Thought,* p. 13. Beard's comment on *Lochner* is ibid., p. 105. Holmes's *Lochner* opinion is in 198 U.S. 45 (1905). Dewey's praise of Holmes is in *Characters,* p. 105; on war experience, ibid., p. 755. Bourne quote is in White, *Pragmatism,* p. 169. For the modern attack on Beard, see Forrest McDonald, *We the People: The Economic Origins of the Constitution* (Chicago: University of Chicago Press, 1958), and for an evenhanded view, see Lee Benson, *Turner and Beard: American Historical Writing Reconsidered* (Glencoe, Ill.: The Free Press, 1960). A good example of the optimistic reformist writing of the "Chicago school" in the 1920s is Robert E. Park and Ernest W. Burgess, *The City* (Chicago: University of Chicago Press, 1925). Virtually the entire second volume of Dewey's *Characters* is given over to various schemes of social improvement. Dewey's quotes on economics are in *Characters,* p. 736. The standard life of Keynes is Sir Roy Harrod, *The Life of John Maynard Keynes* (New York: Norton, 1982). See also Robert Lekachman, *The Age of Keynes* (New York: Random House, 1966).

Keynes's *General Theory* is a better introduction than most commentaries. For Keynesian economics, see Axel Leijonhufvud, *On Keynesian Economics and the Economics of Keynes* (New York: Oxford University Press, 1968); a somewhat less technical exposition is in Brian Morgan, *Monetarists and Keynesians* (New York: Wiley, 1978). For the intellectual background to Keynesianism, see G. L. S. Shackle, *The Years of High Theory* (Cambridge: Cambridge University Press, 1967) and *Epistemics and Economics* (Cambridge: Cambridge University Press, 1972); also Joan Robinson, *Economic Heresies* (New York: Basic Books, 1971), and Adolph Lowe, *On Economic Knowledge* (New York: Harper & Row, 1965). The connection between Lippmann and Keynes is in Ronald Steel, *Walter Lippmann.* The Lekachman quote on p. 13 is from *The Age of Keynes,* p. 303. Keynes's quote on failure of classicism is from *The General Theory,* p. 33; the quotes on investor expectations are all ibid., chap. 12, "Long-Term Expectations"; on "socialization of investment" is ibid., p. 378; on "pyramid-building" is ibid., p. 129. On the growth of Keynesianism in the United States, see Herbert Stein, *The Fiscal Revolution in America* (Chicago: University of Chicago Press, 1969). The Keynes quote, "Oh, patriotic housewives . . . " is in Keynes, *Essays in Persuasion* (New York: Harcourt, Brace, 1932), p. 152. The intellectual smugness that accompanied the New Frontier's adoption of Keynesianism is exemplified in the last several chapters of Lekachman's *The Age of Keynes.* For anti-Communism among left-liberals, see, e.g., Norman Podhoretz, *Making It* (New York: Random House, 1967). Among the vast literature on Cold War background, I used, e.g., Adam Ulam, *Expansion and Coexistence* (New York: Praeger, 1968) and George F. Kennan, *Memoirs* (Boston: Little, Brown, vol. 1, 1967; vol. 2, 1972). For the impact of Sputnik, see Seymour Martin Lipset and Richard B. Dobson, "The Intellectual as Critic and Rebel: With Special Reference to the United States and the Soviet Union," *Daedalus* (Summer 1972):177. For Kennedy's militarism, see Fairlie, *The Kennedy Promise,* pp. 66–72. The Schlesinger quote on p. 20 is from Schlesinger, *The Big Decision,* p. 18. For the blurring of vigorous domestic and international policies, see also Schlesinger, *The Politics of Hope* (Boston: Houghton Mifflin, 1963).

II. THE POWER OF IDEAS

Almost everyone who worked for Kennedy wrote a book on his experiences. I used primarily Arthur M. Schlesinger, *A Thousand Days: John F. Kennedy in the White House* (Boston: Houghton Mifflin, 1965) and Theodore H. Sorensen, *Kennedy* (New York: Harper & Row, 1965). The quotes on pp. 22–24 are from Schlesinger, *A Thousand Days,* pp. 215, 120, and 213. Rostow's book is W. W. Rostow, *The Stages of Economic Growth: A Non-Communist Manifesto* (Cambridge: Cambridge University Press, 1961). On McNamara's Defense Department and the implementation of PPBS, see Robert S. McNamara, *The Essence of Security* (New York: Harper & Row, 1968); Alain Enthoven and

Wayne Smith, *How Much Is Enough?* (New York: Harper & Row, 1971); and Gregory Palmer, *The McNamara Strategy and the Viet Nam War* (Westport, Conn.: Greenwood Press, 1978). Thomas Schelling's *Strategy of Conflict* (Cambridge: Harvard University Press, 1960) is a good example of the work of the intellectual defense theorists. For extension of PPBS beyond the Defense Department, see Charles Schultze, *The Politics and Economics of Public Spending* (Washington: Brookings, 1968). McNamara's quote to Heller is from Schlesinger, *A Thousand Days,* p. 647. Economic and/or population data used here and in subsequent chapters come generally from U.S. Bureau of the Census, *Statistical Abstract, Current Population Reports,* and *Survey of Current Business* for the appropriate months or years. For accounts of Kennedy's economics, see Stein, *Fiscal Revolution;* Seymour Harris, *The Economics of the Kennedy Years* (New York: Harper & Row, 1964); Walter Heller, *New Dimensions in Political Economy* (Cambridge: Harvard University Press, 1966). The quote from Heller is ibid., p. 66. Schlesinger also devotes considerable space to economic issues in his *A Thousand Days.* The history of the implementation of Keynesian policies in the United States relies primarily on Stein, *Fiscal Revolution.* The Reston quote on p. 34 is ibid., p. 437. The counterexamples to Keynesian theory are ibid., pp. 320–348. For a summary of the Keynesian/Friedmanite dispute on the causes of the Depression, see Susan Lee and Peter Passell, *A New Economic View of American History* (New York: Norton, 1979), pp. 362–397. For the origins of the U.S. involvement in Vietnam, I used Robert Shaplen, *The Lost Revolution,* rev. ed. (New York: Harper & Row, 1966); Harold R. Isaacs, *No Peace for Asia* (Cambridge: MIT Press, 1967); and Leslie H. Gelb, *The Irony of Vietnam: The System Worked* (Washington: Brookings, 1979). The "recent evidence" cited on p. 40 is from Fox Butterfield, "The New Vietnam Scholarship," *New York Times Magazine* (Feb. 13, 1983). For the Kennedy predisposition toward involvement and the commitment to "flexible response," see Maxwell Taylor, *The Uncertain Trumpet* (New York: Harper, 1959); Townsend Hoopes, *The Limits of Intervention* (New York: David McKay, 1973); Roger Hilsman, *To Move a Nation: The Politics of Foreign Policy in the Administration of John F. Kennedy* (Garden City, N.Y.: Doubleday, 1967); and David Halberstam, *The Best and the Brightest* (New York: Random House, 1972). On the principles of guerrilla war, see Sir Richard Thompson, *No Exit from Vietnam* (London: Chatto and Windus, 1969). Dave R. Palmer's *The Summons of the Trumpet* (San Rafael, Calif.: Presidio Press, 1978), is a lucid history from a military point of view; and see Harry Summers, Jr., *On Strategy: A Critical Analysis of the Vietnam War* (San Rafael, Calif.: Presidio Press, 1982). See also the collections of essays in Anthony Lake, ed., *The Vietnam Legacy* (New York: New York University Press, 1976). A striking summary of Rostow's views is in W. W. Rostow, *The Great Transition: 25th Montague Burton Lecture on International Relations* (Leeds: Leeds University Press, 1967). The quote on Rostow's theories on p. 44 is from Hoopes, *Limits,* p. 20, and "mystic faith," ibid., p. 22. Rostow quote to Green Berets is in Fairlie, *The Kennedy Promise,* p. 132; the McNamara quote is in Hoopes, *Limits,* p. 19. The quotes on "élan," etc., on p. 46 are from Neil Sheehan et al., *The Pentagon Papers* (New York:

Bantam, 1971), pp. 84–85. The Schlesinger quote is from *A Thousand Days*, p. 341.

III. POLITICS AT THE EDGE OF MORALITY

For the origins of slavery and racism in the South, see Winthrop Jordan, *White Over Black* (Chapel Hill: University of North Carolina Press, 1968); Eugene Genovese, *Roll, Jordan, Roll* (New York: Vintage, 1976); and George M. Frederickson, *White Supremacy* (Oxford: Oxford University Press, 1981). The St. George Tucker quote is from Tucker's *Blackstone's Commentaries* (Philadelphia: Birch and Small, 1803), pp. 31–32. The economics of slavery is in Robert Fogel and Stanley Engerman, *Time on the Cross* (Boston: Little, Brown, 1974), and see "Slavery and the Southern Economy," in Lee and Passell, *A New Economic View*, pp. 154–186. For the background to the civil rights movement, see Gunnar Myrdal, *An American Dilemma*, 2 vols. (New York: McGraw-Hill, 1964); Charles Silberman, *Crisis in Black and White* (New York: Random House, 1964); and Harry Ashmore, *Hearts and Minds* (New York: McGraw-Hill, 1982). For Kennedy's position on civil rights, the most comprehensive study is Carl M. Brauer, *John F. Kennedy and the Second Reconstruction* (New York: Columbia University Press, 1977). Victor Navasky's *Kennedy Justice* (New York: Atheneum, 1977), is much more critical. Harris Wofford, *Of Kennedys and Kings: Making Sense of the Sixties* (New York: Farrar, Straus, 1980) is an insider's account, written by one disillusioned by the Kennedys' reserved commitment to the cause. And see Theodore H. White, *The Making of the President, 1960,* for civil rights and the 1960 campaign. For federal involvement in civil rights enforcement, see Foster Rhea Dulles, *The Civil Rights Commission, 1957–1965* (East Lansing: Michigan State University Press, 1968), and the U.S. Commission on Civil Rights, *Interim Report,* 1963; and *Federal Civil Rights Enforcement,* 1970 and 1971. The civil rights leadership's view of Kennedy is in Martin Luther King, "Equality Now," *Nation* 192 (Feb. 4, 1961):91–95; "Fumbling on the New Frontier," *Nation* 194 (Mar. 3, 1962):190–193; and "Who Is Their God?" *Nation* 195 (Oct. 13, 1962):209–210; and see his *Why We Can't Wait* (New York: Harper & Row, 1964). A critical view of Kennedy's judicial appointments is in Victor Navasky, *Kennedy Justice*, pp. 243–276; and Alexander Bickel, "Civil Rights," *New Republic* (Dec. 15, 1962):11–16. The story of the civil rights struggle in the South is drawn from Victor Navasky, *Kennedy Justice;* Howard Zinn, *SNCC: The New Abolitionists* (Boston: Beacon Press, 1965); and James Forman, *The Making of Black Revolutionaries* (New York: Macmillan, 1972). The two latter books have little patience with the dilatoriness of the Kennedy administration. See also Robert Williams, *Negroes with Guns* (Chicago: Third World Press, 1973). A defense of the administration's strategy is in Burke Marshall, *Federalism and Civil Rights* (New York: Columbia University Press, 1964). The *Screws* case is found in *Screws* v. *U.S.,* 425 U.S. 91 (1945). The argument of the critics of the Justice Department's cautious approach was borne out when the Supreme Court, in effect, overruled *Screws* in *U.S.* v. *Guest,* 383 U.S. 745 (1966). For the principles of civil disobedience, see Martin Luther King, "Letter from a Birmingham Jail," *Christian Century* 80 (June 12, 1963):767–773; Robert T. Hall, *Morality and Civil Disobedience* (New York: Harper & Row, 1971); and Howard Zinn, *Disobedience and Democracy* (New York: Random House, 1968). The classic statement is in Henry David Thoreau, *On the Duty of Civil Disobedience* (New York: New American Library, 1960). John Rawls's formulation is in *A Theory of Justice* (London: Oxford University Press, 1973), p. 364; and his "each person must decide . . . " quote is ibid., p. 389. The quotations from Howard Zinn are in *Disobedience,* pp. 108–111. For Thoreau's quirkiness, see, e.g., his *Civil Disobedience,* p. 232, and for Emerson and Brown, see David Potter, *The Impending Crisis, 1848–1861* (New York: Harper & Row, 1976), pp. 213–214 and 360–361. The black migration data is from U.S. Bureau of the Census, *A Statistical History of the United States: From Colonial Times to the Present* (1976). For the change in the black mood, see James Baldwin, *The Fire Next Time* (New York: Dial, 1963), and Eric C. Lincoln, *The Black Muslims in America* (Boston: Beacon Press, 1961).

IV. REVOLTS AND REVOLUTIONS

The story of the baby boom generation is told in Landon Jones, *Great Expectations: America and the Baby Boom Generation* (New York: Coward, McCann and Geoghegan, 1980), and see the extensive list of sources cited therein. Richard Easterlin, *Birth and Fortune: The Impact of Numbers on Personal Welfare* (New York: Basic Books, 1980), outlines the "Easterlin hypothesis" and includes a provocative statistical appendix. Arthur M. Schlesinger, Sr., "The Tides of National Politics," in *Paths to the Present* (New York: Macmillan, 1949), presents an early argument for the impact of marginal demographic changes. The concept of a "generation" in the sense of a group of people with a shared cultural experience is a recent one, stemming from the writings of Karl Mannheim and José Ortega y Gasset. See the collection of essays entitled "Generations," *Daedalus* (Fall 1978). The sociology and history of rock is in Simon Frith, *Sound Effects: Youth, Leisure and the Politics of Rock and Roll* (New York: Pantheon, 1981). The quote on "Sergeant Pepper's" is cited in Landon Jones, *Great Expectations,* p. 84. For an analysis of crime rates and citations to the most recent research, see Charles Silberman, *Criminal Violence, Criminal Justice* (New York: Random House, 1978). Marvin Wolfgang's studies of crime and youth are summarized in Wolfgang, "Crime in a Birth Cohort," *Proceedings of the American Philosophical Society,* 117 (October 1972):5. The quote from Clark Kerr is in Landon Jones, *Great Expectations,* p. 86. A personal history of the events of Berkeley is in Sarah Davidson, *Loose Change* (Garden City, N.Y.: Doubleday, 1977). See also Milton Viorst, *Fire in the Streets* (New York: Simon and Schuster, 1979). The titles of the *Nation*'s annual campus surveys indicate the speed of the change in mood: "Careful Young Men," Mar. 9, 1957; "Class of '58 Speaks Up," May 17, 1958; "Tension Beneath the Apathy," May 16, 1959; "Rebels with a Hundred Causes," May 16, 1961; and "Integration and Survival," May 19, 1962. For an introduction to existentialism, see Ernst Breisach, *Introduction to Modern Existentialism* (New York: Grove Press, 1962), and Kurt Rudolf Fisher, "The Existentialism of Nietzsche's Zarathustra," *Daedalus* (Summer 1964). Also Jean-Paul Sartre, *Being and Nothingness* (New York: Citadel, 1956); Will Heuber, ed., *Four Existentialist Theologians* (Garden City, N.Y.: Doubleday, 1958); and Gabriel Marcel, *The Mystery of Being* (Chicago: Regnery, 1962). The quote from Sartre on p. 77 is from Jean-Paul Sartre, *Essays in Existentialism* (New York: Citadel, 1974), p. 36, and the one from Albert Camus is in *The Myth of Sisyphus and Other Essays* (New York: Knopf, 1955), pp. 89–90. Camus's novel *The Stranger* captures the existentialist mood as well as any. Note the importance of the theme of isolation and alienation in the "Port Huron Statement," the original manifesto of the Students for a Democratic Society, reprinted in *Papers, 1958–1970* (Glen Rock: Microfilming Corp. of America, 1977). For a summary of empiricism and positivism, see A. J. Ayer, *Philosophy in the Twentieth Century.* James's "Does Consciousness Exist?" is in his *Essays in Radical Empiricism* (Cambridge: Harvard University Press, 1976), pp. 3–20. For Russell's views, see his "The Philosophy of Logical Analysis," *History of Western Philosophy,* pp. 828–836. For radical positivism, see A. J. Ayer, *Language, Truth, and Logic* (New York: Dover, 1952). For Wittgenstein, see A. J. Ayer, *Philosophy in the Twentieth Century,* pp. 108–167; and Anthony Kenny, *Wittgenstein* (London: Pelican, 1975), is a brief introduction. Stanley Cavell, "Existentialism and Analytical Philosophy," *Daedalus* (Summer 1964), is an interesting juxtaposition. The quotation from Ryle comes from Gilbert Ryle, *The Concept of Mind* (London: Penguin, 1976), p. 219. An example of the simplistic approach to artificial intelligence is David Hawkins's "Design for a Mind," *Daedalus* (Summer 1962). Dewey's *Democracy and Education* (New York: Macmillan, 1916) was only the most well known of a number of his books on education; see Richard Hofstadter, "The Child and the World," *Daedalus* (Summer 1962), for a summary of his influence. The quote on managing schools is from Joseph Ratner, ed., *John Dewey: Philosophy, Psychology, and Social Practice* (New York: Putnam, 1963), pp. 308–309; quote on the *Gosplan* from *Characters and Events,* p. 418. The first quotation from Skinner is in B. F. Skinner, *Beyond Freedom and Dignity* (New York: Bantam/Vintage, 1972), pp. 167 and 169; and the second is cited by Erik H. Erikson, *Dimensions of a New Identity* (New York: Norton, 1974), p. 66. For descriptions and analyses of the "counterculture," see: Erik H. Erikson, *Dimensions;* Kenneth Keniston, *Young Radicals: Notes on Committed Youth* (New York: Harcourt, Brace, 1968); Theodore Roszak, *The Making of a Counter Culture* (Garden City, N.Y.: Doubleday, 1969); Daniel Yankelovich, *The New Morality* (New York: McGraw-Hill, 1974); and Edgar Z. Friedenberg, *The Anti-American Generation* (New York: Transaction Books, 1971). The quotes from Leslie Fiedler and James Silver on p. 82 are in *Reflections on Rebellion: Northwestern University Student Symposium on Rebellion* (Evanston, Ill.: Northwestern Student Symposium 1965), pp. 15 and 62. The "academic" quotation is from F. Davis, "Why All of Us Might Be Hippies Someday," in Friedenberg, *The Anti-American Generation,* p. 65. The quotations from Reich are in Charles Reich, *The Greening of America*

(New York: Random House, 1970), pp. 18–19, 152–153, and 305. For the Austrian student movement, see Carl E. Schorske, "Generational Tension and Cultural Change: Reflections on the Case of Vienna," *Daedalus* (Fall 1978): 111–122. The quotation from Friedenberg is in his *Anti-American Generation,* p. 15. The Reich quotation on the suburbs is from *The Greening of America,* pp. 8–9. The quote from Goodman is in Paul Goodman, *Growing Up Absurd* (New York: Random House, 1960), p. 241; and from Silver in *Reflections on Rebellion,* p. 15. For a sense of the personal crises that motivated some of the academic allies of the student radicals, see the painful details laid bare by Reich in Charles Reich, *The Sorcerer of Bolinas Reef* (New York: Random House, 1976). The Riesman quote is in David Riesman, *Abundance for What? and Other Essays* (Garden City, N.Y.: Doubleday, 1964), p. 50. Reich on technology is in *The Greening of America,* p. 10; and see Herbert Marcuse, *One-Dimensional Man* (Boston: Beacon Press, 1964); and Paul and Percival Goodman, *Communitas* (New York: Vintage, 1960). For the small numbers of the student radicals and the predominant conservatism of students, see Seymour Martin Lipset, "Students and Politics in Comparative Perspective," *Daedalus* (Winter 1968): 1–20, and *Passion and Politics: Student Activism in America* (Boston: Little, Brown, 1974), pp. 63–64. For the view from the suburbs, see Herbert Gans, *The Levittowners* (New York: Vintage, 1969).

V. TWO WARS

For the history of the war on poverty, see Robert A. Levine, *The Poor Ye Need Not Have Always With You* (Cambridge: MIT Press, 1970); and Daniel Patrick Moynihan, *Maximum Feasible Misunderstanding* (Glencoe, Ill.: The Free Press, 1969). For the civil rights connectedness, see Kenneth Clark, *Dark Ghetto: Dilemmas of Social Power* (New York: Harper & Row, 1965); and Charles Silberman, *Crisis in Black and White* (New York: Random House, 1964). For black sensitivities, see Lee Rainwater and William Yancey, *The Moynihan Report and the Politics of Controversy* (Cambridge: MIT Press, 1967). For the varying interpretations of the impact of education on income, see Christopher Jencks, *Inequality: A Reassessment of the Effect of Family and Schooling in America* (New York: Basic Books, 1972). For the antipoverty program in New York, see my *The Cost of Good Intentions: New York City and the Liberal Experiment, 1960–1975* (New York: Norton, 1980). The books cited on self-criticism are John Keats's, *The Crack in the Picture Window* (Boston: Houghton Mifflin, 1956), and William H. Whyte, *The Organization Man* (New York: Simon and Schuster, 1956). The quotation from the Joint Commission on Mental Health is from J. Veroff et al., *The Inner American: A Self-Portrait from 1957 to 1976* (New York: Basic Books, 1981). The summary of the development of the mental health and social service profession draws on my own experiences as a mental health and social services administrator. For juvenile delinquency theories, see Ian Taylor et al., *The New Criminology: For a Theory of Social Deviance* (London: Routledge & Kegan Paul, 1973), and A.M. Platt, *The Child Savers* (Chicago: University of Chicago Press, 1969). For a case history of a social work solution in search of a problem, see Gilbert Steiner, *The Futility of Family Policy* (Washington: Brookings, 1981). Henry J. Aaron's *Politics and the Professors* contains a good discussion of the rationalist approach to social problem solving. The discussion of Vietnam relies heavily on Leslie Gelb, *The Irony of Vietnam*. See also Herbert Schandler, *The Unmaking of a President: Lyndon Johnson and Vietnam* (Princeton: Princeton University Press, 1977), and Lyndon Johnson, *The Vantage Point* (New York: Popular Library, 1971). For the military's frustrations, see William Westmoreland, *A Soldier Reports* (Garden City, N.Y.: Doubleday, 1976), and U. S. G. Sharp, *Strategy for Defeat* (San Rafael, Calif.: Presidio Press, 1978). The quote from Lodge is in Leslie Gelb, *The Irony of Vietnam*, pp. 135–136; the quote from Warnke is ibid., p. 139; and Gelb makes the point that there is no compromise in civil wars. The running Johnson-Lippmann discussion is in Ronald Steel, *Walter Lippmann*, pp. 555–570. For the argument that the liberals were not deceived on the war, see Ian Maitland, "Only the Best and the Brightest?" *Asian Affairs*, 3 (March/April 1976):263–271, and Henry Fairlie, "We Knew What We Were Doing When We Went into Vietnam," *Washington Monthly* (May 1973), p. 7. The poll of New Hampshire McCarthy voters is cited in Richard Scammon and Ben Wattenberg, *The Real Majority* (New York: Coward McCann, 1970), p. 91. For the North's military tactics, see Dave R. Palmer, *Summons of the Trumpet;* Harry Summers, Jr., *On Strategy;* and Vo Nguyen Giap, *How We Won the War* (Philadelphia: Reconstruction Publications, 1976). Giap's quote is ibid., p. 52. The story of the post-Tet troop request is in Gelb, *The Irony of Vietnam*, pp. 173–174. A brief account of the impact of the antipoverty programs on welfare is in my *The Cost of Good Intentions*, pp. 67–71 and 185–188. For a careful assessment of the impact of Vietnam on inflation, see Otto Eckstein, *The Great Recession* (Amsterdam: North Holland, 1978), p. 142.

VI. VIOLENCE

A chronology of the violent events of the 1960s is in Milton Viorst, *Fire in the Streets;* and see the sources previously cited for events in the South. Northern riots are chronicled in *Report of the National Advisory Commission on Civil Disorders* (New York: Bantam, 1968). The quote from Nietzsche on p. 116 is in R. J. Hollingdale, *Nietzsche* (London: Routledge & Kegan Paul, 1973), p. 119. The quotations from Sorel are from his *Reflections on Violence* (Glencoe, Ill.: The Free Press, 1950), pp. 78 and 277; and see the discussion of Sorel in Isaiah Berlin, *Against the Current: Essays in the History of Ideas* (New York: Penguin, 1982), pp. 296–332. Sartre's quotation on the Algerian war is from his introduction to Frantz Fanon, *The Wretched of the Earth* (New York: Grove Press, 1968), p. 21. A caustic analysis of Sartre's glorification of violence is in Raymond Aron, *History and the Dialectic of Violence: An Analysis of Sartre's Critique de la Raison Dialectique* (Oxford: Blackwell, 1975). The classic indictment of dilettantish intellectual toying with violence is Julien Benda, *Treason of the Clerks* (New York: Norton, 1962). The Mailer quote on the psychopath is from Norman Mailer, *Advertisements for Myself* (New York: Putnam, 1959), p. 347. For a discussion of Fanon, see Edmund Burke III, "Frantz Fanon's *The Wretched of the Earth,*" *Daedalus* (Winter 1976). The quote from Fanon is from *The Wretched of the Earth,* pp. 35 and 37. The quotations from Eldridge Cleaver are from Robert Scheer, ed., *Eldridge Cleaver: The Post-Prison Writings* (Palo Alto, Calif.: Ramparts Press, 1973), pp. 29 and 35. Other basic works are Eldridge Cleaver, *Soul on Ice* (New York: McGraw-Hill, 1968); George Brectman, ed., *Malcolm X Speaks* (New York: Grove Press, 1966); George Jackson, *Soledad Brother: The Prison Letters of George Jackson* (New York: Coward, McCann, 1970); Angela Davis, *Angela Davis: With My Mind on Freedom, An Autobiography* (New York: Bantam, 1975). Also see Charles Silberman, *Criminal Violence, Criminal Justice.* For the riots, see Edward Banfield, *The Unheavenly City Revisited* (Boston: Little, Brown, 1974), and the extensive sources cited therein. For the reanalysis of the riot commission data, see Abraham Miller et al., "The New Urban Blacks," *Ethnicity* 3 (December 1976):338–367; and Anthony Oberschall, "The Los Angeles Race Riot of August 1965," *Social Problems* 15 (Winter 1968):330–356. For New York City's management of riots, see my *The Cost of Good Intentions,* pp. 74–78. A detailed chronicle of the Newark riot is in Governor's Select Commission on Civil Disorder, *Report for Action* (State of New Jersey, 1968). The quotation on p. 124 is from Tom Wolfe, *Radical Chic and Mau-Mauing the FlakCatchers* (New York: Farrar, Straus, 1970), pp. 7–8. The quotation from Mailer is from *Advertisements,* p. 341. For writing on prisons, see Jessica Mitford, *Kind and Unusual Punishment* (New York: Knopf, 1973), and Tom Wicker, *A Time to Die* (New York: Times Books, 1975). The quote from the white radical is in Robert Scheer, *Eldridge Cleaver,* p. 190. For the events at Columbia, see James Kunen, *The Strawberry Statement: Notes of a College Revolutionary* (New York: Random House, 1969); and Barry Gottehrer, *The Mayor's Man* (Garden City: Doubleday, 1975). The Dwight Macdonald quotation appears in the *New York Review of Books* (July 11, 1968): 42. The account of the Black Panther trial in New Haven is drawn from Gail Sheehy, *Panthermania: The Clash of Black Against Black* (New York: Harper & Row, 1971).

VII. NIXON

The brief portrait of Nixon here is distilled from a number of sources. I consulted, among other books and articles, Richard Nixon, *Six Crises* and *R.N.: Memoirs of Richard Nixon* (New York: Grosset & Dunlap, 1978); Theodore H. White, *The Making of the President, 1960; The Making of the President, 1968* (New York: Atheneum, 1969); *The Making of the President, 1972* (New York: Atheneum, 1973); and *Breach of Faith* (New York: Harper & Row, 1975); Garry Wills, *Nixon Agonistes* (New York: New American Library, 1970); Jules Witcover, *The Resurrection of Richard Nixon* (New York: Putnam, 1970); Bruce Mazlish, *In Search of Nixon* (New York: Basic Books, 1972); Fawn Brodie, *Richard Nixon: The Shaping of His Character* (New York: Norton, 1981); William Safire, *Before the Fall* (New York: Tower Books, 1975); Henry

Kissinger, *The White House Years* (Boston: Little, Brown, 1979) and *Years of Upheaval* (Boston: Little, Brown, 1982); and Joe McGinniss, *The Selling of the President, 1968* (New York: Pocket Books, 1970). The two quotations on p. 130 are cited in Henry Kissinger, *The White House Years,* p. 504. The Haldeman quote is in Theodore H. White, *Breach of Faith,* p. 171. When I started this chapter, I wanted to avoid indulging in psychohistory, but I'm afraid the temptation in Nixon's case was irresistible. The brief psychological portrait represents my own view, but it is inevitably influenced by Kissinger, Mazlish, and Wills. Nixon's *Foreign Affairs* article is "Asia After Vietnam," *Foreign Affairs* 46 (October 1967):111–125. The "revisionist" accounts of Nixon's visit with student protesters are in Bruce Mazlish, *In Search of Nixon,* p. 134, and William Safire, *Before the Fall,* pp. 202–212. Mailer's encounter with the Nixon daughters is in Norman Mailer, "Miami Beach and Chicago," *Harper's* (November 1968). The section on "the real majority" draws primarily from Richard Scammon and Ben Wattenberg, *The Real Majority,* and Ben Wattenberg, *In Search of the Real America* (New York: Doubleday, 1976). The quote from Jack Newfield is in Scammon and Wattenberg, *The Real Majority,* p. 244; the quote from Galbraith is in Mazlish, *In Search of Nixon,* p. 22; the quote on the Dayton lady is in Scammon and Wattenberg, *The Real Majority,* p. 71. The story of Nixon's anticrime program is summarized in "Nixon: the First Year of His Administration," summarized in *Congressional Quarterly,* 1969. See the *Congressional Quarterly* reports for summaries of the remaining years. Charles Hamilton's point on black political maturity is in Charles Hamilton, "The Patron-Recipient Relationship and Minority Politics in New York City," a paper delivered at the 1978 annual meeting of the American Political Science Association. The data on Nixon's social initiatives is drawn primarily from Daniel Patrick Moynihan, *The Politics of a Guaranteed Income* (New York: Random House, 1973). The quotation "among presidents . . . " is on p. 542. The quote from Richard Rovere is ibid., p. 268. A sample of the left-liberal and social worker view of Nixon is in Alan Gartner et al., *What Nixon Is Doing to Us* (New York: Harrow, 1973). I have drawn the account of the Child Development Act from the *New York Times.* A *Times* editorial on Sept. 10, 1971, enthused that the program would be "a universal, multi-service program for children of all economic strata." For Kissinger's view of foreign policy, see his *The White House Years* and *Years of Upheaval,* and *American Foreign Policy* (New York: Norton, 1969). See also Bruce Mazlish, *Kissinger* (New York: Basic Books, 1976), and Peter Dickson, *Kissinger and the Meaning of History* (New York: Cambridge University Press, 1973). For the "European" view of foreign affairs, see also Irving Kristol, "Consensus and Dissent in U.S. Foreign Policy," in Anthony Lake, ed., *The Vietnam Legacy,* pp. 80–101. Both Townsend Hoopes, *The Limits of Intervention,* and Leslie Gelb, *The Irony of Vietnam,* include useful appendices on the Nixon-Kissinger policy in Vietnam. The story of Kissinger's secret negotiations with the North Vietnamese was told first by Tad Szulc, "Behind the Ceasefire Agreement," *Foreign Policy* 15 (Summer 1974):21–69. The story of the North's consistent reliance on conventional military tactics is in Leslie Gelb, *The Irony of Vietnam,* Dave R. Palmer, *The*

Summons of the Trumpet, and Harry Summers, *On Strategy,* as well as in Kissinger's memoirs. The quotations from General Dung are in Harry Summers, *On Strategy,* pp. 136–137. The senatorial and newspaper reactions to the Cambodian foray are in Henry Kissinger, *The White House Years,* pp. 1190–1191. Shawcross's indictment is in William Shawcross, *Sideshow: Kissinger, Nixon, and the Destruction of Cambodia* (New York: Pocket Books, 1979). The Kissinger quotation on p. 149 is from *Years of Upheaval,* p. 369. Seymour Hersh's *The Price of Power: Kissinger in the Nixon White House* (New York: Summit Books, 1983) paints a portrait of a Kissinger utterly without redeeming virtues—alternatively a venal fool or an obsequious schemer. Probably without intending it, by so denigrating Kissinger, Hersh magnifies Nixon's role in guiding foreign policy. On the whole, I don't find the Hersh portrayal credible, dark and depressing as the underside of the Nixon White House undoubtedly was. Hersh, for example, even begrudges the administration credit for the opening to China; he interprets it primarily as a ploy in Kissinger's quest for personal ascendance. There is much to find fault with in the Nixon-Kissinger foreign policy, and Hersh overlooks nothing; but the appropriate standard of comparison, I would suggest, is not an academic ideal constructed *ex parte* with a decade's hindsight, but contemporary standards of achievement. If the first-term Nixon-Kissinger record in foreign affairs is compared with those of the Kennedy, Johnson, Ford, Carter, or Reagan administration, it is, without question, outstanding. Hersh's account of the aftermath of the North's 1972 offensive is in ibid., pp. 503–528. For Watergate, the most objective view, I think, is Theodore H. White, *Breach of Faith.* A measure of the liberal hatred of Nixon is Anthony Lewis's review of White's book in the *New Yorker* (Aug. 11, 1975), p. 81. Lewis excoriates White for implying that Nixon had *any* redeeming social virtues. See also Carl Bernstein and Bob Woodward, *All the President's Men* (New York: Simon and Schuster, 1974) and *The Final Days* (New York: Simon and Schuster, 1976); Elizabeth Drew, *White House Journal* (New York: Random House, 1975); and R. W. Apple et al., *The White House Transcripts* (New York: Bantam, 1974). For the press role in Watergate, see *The Columbia Journalism Review.* Virtually every issue between 1973 and 1976 has at least one article arguing the press's responsibility on Vietnam and Watergate and/or the alleged elitist character of the "national press." For a defendant's view of the Watergate prosecutions, see Maurice Stans, *The Terrors of Justice* (New York: Everest, 1978). The quote on the Rebozo prosecution is ibid., pp. 68–69. I am indebted to Evan Davis, who was an assistant to John Doar and in charge of the cover-up portion of the House impeachment investigation, for helping me sift through the Watergate charges. Also see Leon Jaworski, *The Right and the Power* (Pleasantville, N.Y.: Reader's Digest Press, 1977).

VIII. THE COLLAPSE OF THE KEYNESIAN CONSENSUS

A detailed analysis of Nixon's economic problems is in Otto Eckstein, *The Great Recession.* A comprehensive analysis of America's economic problems in a global context is in David Calleo, *The Imperious Economy* (Cambridge: Har-

vard University Press, 1982). Robert Zevin, *The Greater Good* (Boston: Houghton Mifflin, 1983), contains a wealth of data and a comprehensive analysis of
recent inflation. For wage-price controls, see John Dunlop, *The Lessons of
Wage-Price Controls: The Food Sector* (Cambridge: Harvard University Press,
1977). For a review of inflation and current economic theory, see James Trevi-
thick and Charles Mulvey, *The Economics of Inflation* (Glasgow: Martin Rob-
ertson, 1975), and Brian Morgan, *Monetarists and Keynesians.* For surveys of
current economic policy and inflation from generally opposing political view-
points, see the series of essays published each year by the Brookings Institution,
Brookings Papers on Economic Activity (Washington: Brookings, various years),
and those by the American Enterprise Institute, *Contemporary Economic Problems* (Washington: AEI, various years). The former are generally somewhat left
of center and the latter right of center. For a summary of Friedman's views,
see Milton Friedman, *Dollars and Deficits: Living with America's Economic
Problems* (Englewood Cliffs, N.J.: Prentice-Hall, 1968). For a summary of
Kuznets and Kondratieff cycles, see Robert Zevin, *The Greater Good.* Walt
Rostow's analysis of long cycles in the world economy is in W. W. Rostow,
The World Economy: History and Prospect (Austin: University of Texas Press,
1978), pp. 103–304 and 625–643. Keynes's long-term view cited on p. 168 is in
the *General Theory,* p. 376. On the dollar glut, see David Calleo, *The Imperious
Economy,* and the extensive sources cited therein. Martin Mayer, *The Fate of
the Dollar* (New York: Times Books, 1980), also chronicles U.S. dollar policy.
The statistics I cite on Eurodollars and the volume of lending to developing
countries are drawn from Calleo, Zevin, and various internal publications of the
Chase Manhattan Bank. They are accurate only as orders of magnitude. Because of the supranational character of the global dollar buildup, there are as
yet no data that can be cited with total confidence. A consortium of the major
banks and the international lending agencies is currently working on the data
problem. For the New York City financing crisis, see my *The Cost of Good
Intentions.*

IX. THE HEAVENLY CITY OF THE LIBERAL PHILOSOPHERS

Ronald Dworkin, *Taking Rights Seriously* (Cambridge: Harvard University
Press, 1977), and Thomas Sowell, *Knowledge and Decisions* (New York: Basic
Books, 1980), are good recent statements of the current philosophic positions
on the left and right respectively. The phrase "Life is a swallow . . ." is R. H.
Tawney's. The quotations from Tawney are in *Equality* (New York: Barnes &
Noble, 1965), pp. 47 and 165. The Rawls quote on natural talents is in *A Theory
of Justice,* p. 72. Dworkin on liberty is in *Taking Rights Seriously,* pp. 267 ff.
The Rawls quote "Any doubt . . . " is in *A Theory of Justice,* p. 520; "social
arrangements . . . " is ibid., p. 144. Public school desegregation data are in U.S.
Civil Rights Commission, *Desegregation of Public Schools,* 1979. Lester Thu-
row's book is *Poverty and Discrimination* (Washington: Brookings, 1969). A
summary of the events in Boston can be found in the case record, *Morgan* v.
Kerrigan, 401 F. Supp. 216 (1975). The data on blacks, discrimination, and

ethnicity-related social characteristics are drawn from Walter Williams, *The State Against Blacks* (New York: McGraw-Hill, 1982), pp. 19–33 and 53–66; and Thomas Sowell, *Knowledge and Decisions,* pp. 256–260. An analysis of race as a rational proxy for other variables is in Henry Aaron, *Politics and the Professors,* pp. 16–64. The quote from *A Dream Deferred* (Washington, D.C.: The Center for the Study of Social Policy, 1983) is on p. 23. The data on black SAT scores appears in Harry Edwards, "Educating Black Athletes," *Atlantic* (August 1983): 31–35. A summary of prison reform efforts is in Robert Martinson, "What Works?: Questions and Answers about Prison Reform," *The Public Interest* 35 (Spring 1974): 22–53. For the progress of various ethnic groups in the United States, see Daniel Patrick Moynihan and Nathan Glazer, *Beyond the Melting Pot* (Cambridge: MIT and Harvard, 1963) and Thomas Sowell, *Ethnic America* (New York: Basic Books, 1981). For a contemporary despairing view of the "Wild Irish," see Pauline Goldmark, ed., *West Side Studies* (New York: Russell Sage, 1914). A recent view of the changing attitudes of younger women toward feminist militancy is in Susan Bolotin, "Voices from the Post-Feminist Generation," *New York Times Magazine* (Oct. 17, 1982). For a compendium of ethnic differences, see Thomas Sowell, *Ethnic America* and *Knowledge and Decisions.* The data on Polish-American IQs is in *Ethnic America,* p. 281. The quote "disprove the popular . . . " on p. 198 is ibid., p. 88. The quotation on the Constitution is cited in Alexander Bickel, *The Supreme Court and the Idea of Progress* (New York: Harper & Row, 1970), p. 14. For a conservative criticism of the recent trend in judicial decisions, see ibid., and Raoul Berger, *Government by Judiciary: The Transformation of the Fourteenth Amendment* (Cambridge: Harvard University Press, 1972). The Supreme Court cases cited are *Mapp* v. *Ohio,* 367 U.S. 643 (1961); *Brown* v. *Board of Education,* 347 U.S. 494 (1954); *Milliken* v. *Bradley,* 418 U.S. 779 (1971); *Reynold* v. *Sims,* 377 U.S. 533 (1964) (for Warren quote on representation); *Roe* v. *Wade,* 410 U.S. 113 (1973); *Griswold* v. *Connecticut,* 381 U.S. 479 (1965); and *Paris Adult Theater* v. *Slater,* 413 U.S. 49 (1973) (for Brennan quotation). The federal court rule on "racial mixing . . . " is cited in Thomas Sowell, *Knowledge and Decisions,* p. 262; the J. Skelly Wright quote is in Alexander Bickel, *The Supreme Court,* p. 106; the quotation on *Roe* is in Lawrence Trube, "The Supreme Court 1972 Term—Foreword: Toward a Model of Roles in the Due Process of Life and Law," *Harvard Law Review,* vol. 87, no. 1, p. 3. The newspaper column on cable television was in the *Wall Street Journal* (Dec. 20, 1982). The quotation on Locke is from Carl Becker, *The Heavenly City of the Eighteenth Century Philosophers* (New Haven: Yale University Press, 1932), p. 65. Becker's view of the philosophes has been superseded by, for instance, the work of Peter Gay, but it is apposite to the point I want to make about Rawls and Dworkin. Alexander Bickel uses Becker the same way in his *The Supreme Court.* On the moral issues of human experimentation, see the essays collected in *Daedalus* (Spring 1969) under the title "The Ethical Aspects of Human Experimentation." The quotation from Keynes on immoralism is in Friedrich Hayek, *Law, Legislation, and Liberty* (Chicago: University of Chicago Press, 1973), vol. 1, p. 25. Keynes's comment on *The Road to Serfdom* is in Sir Roy Harrod, *The*

Life of John Maynard Keynes, pp. 436–437. Burke's writings are conveniently assembled in R. Hoffman and P. Levack, *Burke's Politics* (New York: Knopf, 1959). The "wisdom without . . . " quote is ibid., p. xvii. Hayek's *Law, Legislation, and Liberty* is a recent statement of his views; and see Isaiah Berlin, *Against the Current,* for another modern criticism of philosophic and political rationalism.

X. RATIONALISM RESURGENT

On the 1976 and 1980 elections, see Kandy Stroud, *How Jimmy Won* (New York: Morrow, 1977); Bruce Mazlish and Edwin Diamond, *Jimmy Carter* (New York: Simon and Schuster, 1979); Theodore H. White, *America in Search of Itself* (New York: Harper & Row, 1982); and Jeff Greenfield, *The Real Election* (New York: Summit, 1982). For the dispute between monetarists and Keynesians, see the sources cited in previous chapters. The discussion of the problems of implementing theoretical monetarism is drawn primarily from day-to-day accounts in the business press and from various internal publications of the Chase Manhattan Bank. The American Enterprise Institute's *Contemporary Economic Problems* series has a number of essays, particularly those by Philip Cagan, on practical monetarism. Thurow's view of regulation is in Lester Thurow, *The Zero-Sum Society* (New York: Basic Books, 1980). Notable recent statements of simplistic economic conservatism are Milton and Rose Friedman, *Freedom and Capitalism* (New York: Harcourt Brace Jovanovich 1980), and George Gilder, *Wealth and Poverty* (New York: Basic Books, 1981). An account of the bureaucratization of most large American businesses is in Thomas Peters and Robert Waterman, *In Search of Excellence* (New York: Harper & Row, 1982). A compendium of statistics on the current military balance and a detailed discussion of the problem of making dollar/ruble comparisons is in John Collins, *U.S.-Soviet Military Balance,* 7 vols. (Congressional Research Service, 1980), and see James Fallows's *National Defense* (New York: Random House, 1981). A pessimistic view of U.S. vulnerability is in Norman Podhoretz, *The Present Danger* (New York: Simon and Schuster, 1981). The statement about the U.S. missile-firing failures is from a conversation with Herman Kahn. For black and Hispanic illegitimacy rates, see the summary in the *New York Times* (Oct. 26, 1982). The statistics on social spending in the federal budget are drawn from Joseph Pechman et al., *Setting National Priorities: The 1982 Budget* (Washington: Brookings, 1981). The *New York Times* Medicare quotation appeared in an editorial on Feb. 7, 1983. The agricultural policy illustration is in Sandra Batie and Robert Healey, "The Future of American Agriculture," *Scientific American* 248:2 (February 1983):45–53.

XI. MATURITY

For a sour view of contemporary spiritual fads, see Shiva Naipaul, *Journey to Nowhere* (New York: Simon and Schuster, 1981). The figures on "born-again" Christians were developed at the Hudson Institute; they were recounted to me in a conversation with Herman Kahn. The NIMH study is Joseph Veroff et al., *The Inner American.* The quotation is ibid., p. 542. The Middletown restudy is reported in Howard Baker, "Changes in Family Life in Middletown, 1924–1977," *Public Opinion Quarterly* (Spring 1980): 17–36; the quotation is from p. 24. The quotes on p. 229 are from Christopher Lasch, *The Culture of Narcissism* (New York: Norton, 1979), pp. 13 and 59. The "alienation" quote is from J. Veroff et al., *The Inner American,* p. 242. The "Indeed, so far ranging . . . " quote is from Daniel Yankelovich, *New Rules* (New York: Random House, 1981). For more information on the lack of data to support the "alienation" hypothesis, see Rosabeth Kantor, "Work in a New America," *Daedalus* (Winter 1978):50–53. Dewey's interest in alienation is in *Characters and Events,* p. 752. Tom Wolfe skewers agonized intellectuals in "The Intelligent Coed's Guide to America," *Mauve Gloves* (New York: Farrar, Straus, 1976), pp. 107–125. The data on women working are from the statistical appendix in Richard Easterlin, *Birth and Fortune.* The quotation from Charles Reich is in *The Greening of America,* p. 95. The quotation from Betty Friedan is in her "Twenty Years After," *New York Times Magazine* (Feb. 27, 1983):55. For a bullish view of the future of the world economy, with which I basically agree, see Herman Kahn, *The Coming Boom* (New York: Simon and Schuster, 1982). The optimistic view of Brazil is based on several visits to the country and a number of conversations with Brazilian bankers. An English compendium of current Brazilian economic data, *Doing Business in Brazil,* is published by Banco Lar do Brasileiro, a subsidiary of the Chase Manhattan Bank.

INDEX

abolitionist movements, 49, 66
abortion, 202–3, 206
Acheson, Dean, 38
Adams, Sam, 66, 67
affirmative action programs, 190, 192, 234
Affluent Society, The (Galbraith), 30
Agnew, Spiro, 87, 152, 153, 156, 207
agriculture, 171–72, 217, 225
Aid to Families with Dependent Children
    (AFDC), 107, 223–24
    see also welfare system
Allen, Lewis, 61
Alliance for Progress, 23
All the President's Men, 154
American Dream, The (Mailer), 114
anectine treatment, 196–97
Armies of the Night, The (Mailer), 76, 112
Augustine of Hippo, 205
auto industry, 167, 170–71, 217, 218
Ayer, A. J., 79

Baker, Bobby, 151
Baker, Ella Jo, 59
Baldwin, James, 69
Ball, George, 101
Banfield, Edward, 118
banking system:
    dollar removed from gold standard and,
        176–77
    Federal Reserve money restrictions and,
        215–16

foreign loans and, 177–81, 216, 218
inflation as useful in, 166–67
inner-city investment by, 190–91
long-term investment and, 162–63
money as created by, 161n
unregulated interest rates and, 217
Bao Dai, 39, 40, 41
Barnett, Ross, 55
Bay of Pigs, 42
Beard, Charles, 7, 8, 9n–10n
Beatles, 70, 73
Beauvoir, Simone de, 76, 113
Becker, Carl, 205
Beckett, Samuel, 76
Bell, Daniel, 2
Bell, David, 31
Benda, Julian, 114
Bentham, Jeremy, 7
Berkeley, 75, 87, 109–10, 112
Berlin crisis (1961), 33, 42
Beyond Freedom and Dignity (Skinner),
    80–81
big business interests, 217–18
Black Panthers, 65, 69, 110, 115, 124, 128
blacks:
    affirmative action programs as harmful
        to, 192
    anticrime programs and, 138–39, 239–40
    college enrollment of, 187, 189–90
    crime rates and, 116–17, 138–39, 188,
        197, 239

259

blacks *(cont.)*
  enslavement of, 48–50
  family disintegration among, 90, 92, 141,
    190, 223
  Kennedy's appointments of, 53–54
  median age of, in upward shift, 239
  middle-class assimilation of, 234–35, 240
  Northern migration of, 68–69, 233
  vs. other ethnic groups' progress, 191,
    197–98
  poverty among, 34, 187, 190, 233–34
  racism of, 125–26
  "real majority's" view of, 137–39
  rioting by, 114–23
  social and economic success of, 187–88,
    191–92
  Southern remigration of, 187
  stereotypes of, 49–50, 125, 192, 197,
    239
  welfare dependency and, 107, 138, 190,
    223–24
  West Indian vs. native American, 191
  working-class vs. lower-class, 188–89,
    191
Bond, Julian, 59
Boston, Mass., 189
Bourne, Randolph, 9, 47
Bradlee, Benjamin, 129, 154
Brazier, James, 57
Brazil, 172
  economic development in, 167, 236–37
  inflation in, 162
  loans taken by, 177–79
Bretton Woods agreement (1944), 12, 176
Brezhnev, Leonid, 132
Brown, H. Rap, 67
Brown, John, 67
Brown v. *Board of Education,* 8, 51, 52,
  201
Buber, Martin, 76
Bundy, McGeorge, 23
Burke, Edmund, 207, 208
Burns, Arthur, 33, 158
Burt, Cyril, 184

Cambodia, 147–48, 152, 219
Campbell, Cull, 58
Camp David accord, 211
Camus, Albert, 66, 76, 77–78
Cannon, Howard, 57
Carmichael, Stokely, 69, 110–11, 116
Carswell, G. Harrold, 131
Carter, Jimmy, 132, 177, 182, 210–11

Castro, Fidel, 210
Chaney, James, 64
Chatfield, Jack, 57
Chicago, Ill., 112, 127, 134, 137
  University of, 5, 10
  see also monetarism
Child Development Act (1971), 143
China, People's Republic of, 38, 40
  Ho Chi Minh and, 38–40, 99, 145
  U.S. relations with, 131, 132, 145, 147,
    151, 219
Christmas bombing (1972), 150
Church, Frank, 101
Churchill, Winston, 11–12, 39–40
cities, *see* urban centers
Civil Rights Act (1957), 52
Civil Rights Act (1964), 64
Civil Rights Commission, 54
civil rights movement, 48–69, 134, 198,
  232, 234
  abolition movements before, 49, 66
  anticrime programs and, 138–39
  black separatism and undermining of,
    111
  blacks' violence and, 114–16, 123
  civil disobedience as tactic of, 65–68
  civil rights laws as emasculated and, 63
  gradualist approach to, 56, 67
  legalism in aftermath of, 185–86
  moral issues involved in, 65–68
  in North, 68–69, 90, 93–94
  poverty highlighted by, 89–90
  "real majority's" view of, 137–39
  Southern brutality and, 64
  Southern judicial obstructionism and,
    56–57, 64
  standardized educational tests and,
    189–90
  violent vs. nonviolent, 66–67, 69
  violent white reaction to, 55, 57–64
  youth revolution and, 69, 75, 84
Clark, Jim, 62–63
Clark, Joseph, 101
Cleaver, Eldridge, 69, 115–17
Coffin, William Sloane, 112
Cohen, Morris, 67
Columbia University, 126
Communism, 17–21
  containment policy toward, 43
  expansion of, 18–19, 38, 42, 102
  see also Soviet Union
Community Mental Health Act (1962), 97
Connor, Bull, 55

conservatism, 212–25
  failures of, 182–83, 208
  income support as viewed by, 222–24
  money supply as economic focus of, 213–15
  traditions valued by, 156, 207–8, 228
CORE (Congress of Racial Equality), 55, 75, 119
Cost of Living Council, 158–59
Council of Economic Advisers, 31–37
  see also "new economists"
Cox, Archibald, 154
Crack in the Picture Window, The (Keats), 96
Crawford, James, 58
creationist movement, 212, 227
crime, 74, 116–17, 138–39, 188, 197, 230
Culture of Narcissism (Lasch), 229

Days of Rage, 127
Dean, James, 71
Defense Department, U.S., 24–30
  bureaucratic structure of, 24
  interservice competition in, 24–25
  McNamara's budget for, 26
  McNamara's management of, 24–30
de Gaulle, Charles, 132, 175
Democratic Convention (1968), 112, 137
Democratic party:
  anti-Communist strategies as creation of, 18
  étatisme in, 29
  Keynesian economics in, 33
demonstrations, 64, 109–10, 123–28, 133–35
  "sit-ins," 51
  "teach-ins," 109
Depression, Great, 12–13, 15, 36, 83, 205, 206, 214
deregulation, economic, 217–19
Detroit, Mich., 106–7, 111, 122, 201
Dewey, John, 5–11, 24, 47, 224, 240
  on social engineering, 8–11, 224
Diem, Ngo Dinh, 39, 41–42, 102, 145
Dien Bien Phu, battle of (1954), 39–40, 46, 103
Dillon, Douglas, 24
divorce rates, 74, 228, 230
Doar, John, 60, 64, 154
dollar, 158, 172–81
  Eurodollars, 177–81
  overvaluing of, 173–76
  speculative dealing in, 174–76

Douglas, Helen Gahagan, 129
Douglas, Paul, 33
Dream Deferred, A, 188, 189–90
Drift and Mastery (Lippmann), 6
drugs:
  abuse of, 90, 92, 125, 128, 237
  as countercultural phenomenon, 81, 85
  exclusionary rule and dealers of, 200
  prisoners administered with, 196–97
  psychoactive, discovery of, 96–97
Dulles, Allen, 24
Dulles, John Foster, 18, 39–41
Dung, Van Tien, 147
Dunlop, John, 159
Dworkin, Ronald, 67, 182, 184–86, 204–5

Easterlin, Richard, 73–74, 169, 231
Eastertide offensive (1972), 146
Eastland, James, 52, 54, 57
Economic Consequences of Mr. Churchill, The (Keynes), 11
Economic Consequences of Peace, The (Keynes), 11
Economic Interpretation of the Constitution, An (Beard), 7, 9n–10n
Eden, Anthony, 39–40
education, 181
  aging population and, 238–39
  "Black English" movement in, 125
  blacks' performance in, 189–90, 197–98
  black stereotypes in, 192
  creationist movement in, 212, 227
  desegregation of, 8, 51, 52, 185, 186–89, 201, 206
  gender-integration of, 193
  mechanistic theories applied to, 80–81, 88
  PPBS applied to, 28
  prayer as issue in, 199n
  quality of, vs. desegregation, 188
  role of, in antipoverty programs, 92–93
Eisenhower, Dwight D., 1, 3–5, 187
  anti-Communist policy of, 42, 43
  civil rights and, 51, 52
  defense budget under, 26, 43
  Defense Department secretary under, 24
  economic conditions under, 30, 33, 35–36, 43
  presidential power as viewed by, 24
  Vietnam conflict and, 39–40, 41, 42, 44
Employment Act (1946), 33
"end of ideology" theorists, 2, 4

energy crisis:
  economic vulnerability and, 218, 235–36
  oil embargoes and, 160, 162, 170–72,
    177–79, 235–36
  recession and, 211, 218, 236
  U.S. military planning and, 219–20
England, 185
  legal system in history of, 199
  long-term investment in, 163
  long wave cycles as seen in, 168–69
  Vietnam involvement of, 39–40
Enke, Stephen, 25
Enthoven, Alain, 25, 26
environmental movement, 134
Equality (Tawney), 184
Erikson, Erik, 82
Ervin, Sam, 154
Eurodollars, 177–81, 216
Europe:
  Communist expansion in, 18, 19, 38
  defense spending in, 165, 219
  existentialism in, 76–78, 183
  inflation in, 175–76
  intellectual disillusionment in, 77–78
  national planning in, 31
  postwar economic recovery in, 15,
    173–75
  overvalued dollar in, 174–76
  Soviet military buildup in, 221
Evers, Medgar, 60
existentialism, 76–81, 183
  violent aspects of, 113–15

Fairlie, Henry, 4, 102
Falwell, Jerry, 212
Family Assistance Plan, 132–33, 139,
    140–43
family court system, 98
Fanon, Frantz, 114–15
Farrell, Greg, 93
Faubus, Orville, 51
Federal Bureau of Investigation (FBI):
  civil rights movement and, 60, 61–62
  Hoover's appointment to, 24
Federal Reserve Bank, 161n
  monetarist policies of, 214–16
Fiedler, Leslie, 82
Fire Next Time, The (Baldwin), 69
Flaming Dart bombing program, 99
Ford, Gerald R., 182, 210–11
Forman, James, 58–59, 62, 124–25
Forrestal, James, 24

France, 38, 219
  Vietnam involvement of, 38–41
Frankfurter, Felix, 199
Freedom Day (1963), 62
Freedom Rides, 54–55, 56
Free Speech Movement, 75, 87
Friedan, Betty, 87, 235n
Friedenberg, Edgar Z., 84–85
Friedman, Milton, 36, 163–64, 182, 213–15
Frye, Marquette, 110
Fulbright, William, 57, 101, 102

Galbraith, John Kenneth, 4, 29, 31–37,
    129, 135
  on antipoverty programs, 90–91
  on Eisenhower's economic policy, 33
  equality as viewed by, 184
  as "new economist," 31–37
  social spending urged by, 30, 34
Gandhi, Mohandas K., 66, 67
Gans, Herbert, 87
Gelb, Leslie, 102, 145
*General Theory of Employment, Interest,
    and Money, The* (Keynes), 12–13
Geneva conference (1954), 39–40
Giap, Vo Nguyen, 103–4, 145–46
Ginsberg, Allen, 112
gnomes of Zurich, 174–76
gold reserves, U.S., 158, 174–77
Goodman, Andrew, 64
Goodman, Paul, 84–85, 86–87
Gordon, Kermit, 23, 31
government bonds, 161n
Great Society:
  failure of, 9
  as Johnson's "beautiful woman," 105
  Model Cities program and, 105–6
  social-engineering bias in, 10
  see also War on Poverty
Greening of America, The (Reich), 82–83
Griswold v. *Connecticut,* 203
Growing Up Absurd (Goodman), 85
Gruening, Ernest, 101
Guyot, Lawrence, 59

Halberstam, David, 37, 101
Haldeman, H. R., 130
Hampton, Fred, 128
Hansen, Bill, 58
Hardy, John, 58
Harrington, Michael, 18
Harris, Fred, 142
Harris, Seymour, 31, 32

Harvard Business Review, 29
Hatcher, Andrew, 52, 53
Hauge, Gabriel, 33
Hayden, Tom, 126, 128
Hayek, Friedrich, 182, 207–8
Hegel, Georg Wilhelm Friedrich, 79–80, 113
Heidegger, Martin, 76, 114
Heller, Walter, 27, 31–37
Hiss, Alger, 129
Hitch, Charles, 25, 26, 28
Ho Chi Minh, 38–47, 98–108, 143–51
  Communist support of, 38–39, 99, 145
  French support of, 41
  negotiations eschewed by, 99–101, 145
  U.S. bombing programs and, 99–100, 102–4
  see also Vietnam War
Hoffman, Abbie, 112, 127, 128
Holland, Arthur, 95
Holmes, Oliver Wendell, 6, 8
homosexual rights, 136
Hoover, J. Edgar, 24, 60
How to Pay for the War (Keynes), 12, 14–15
Hume, David, 7, 67, 78
Humphrey, George, 33
Humphrey, Hubert, 112, 124, 134
Hurst, E. H., 61
Husserl, Edmund, 77
Huston, Donald, 155
Hutton, Bobby, 116–17

income, wages and:
  of blacks, 187–88, 191–92, 234–35, 240
  governmental freeze on, 158–60, 162
  labor demands for, and inflation, 163–65, 167
  mass affluence and, 232
  rapid increases in (1960–1980), 233
  of women, 198
inflation, 157–68
  automatic stabilizers and, 166
  "cost-push," 161–62
  damaging effects of, 162–63
  definition of, 160–61
  demand-management policies in, 163–64
  "demand-pull," 161–62
  dollar recycling and, 161*n,* 178
  under Eisenhower administration, 30, 35
  as embedded in economy, 164–72
  food price increases and, 159–60, 166, 171–72

government budget deficits and, 163*n*
government policy and, 165–66
under Kennedy administration, 32
long business cycles underlying, 168–72
long-term investment and, 162–63, 166–67
new credit creation and, 161
1970 recession and, 158
oil embargo and, 160, 162, 170–71, 177–79
positive effects of, 162, 166–67
severe recession and, 218
stagflation, 158
Vietnam War and, 108, 157, 165
wage and price controls used against, 158–60, 162
wages in, 158–59, 163–65, 167
Innis, Roy, 126
Iran hostage crisis, 211
Irish immigrants, 191, 197

Jackson, George, 125
James, William, 5–10, 79, 240
Japan:
  defense spending in, 165
  industrial competition from, 167
  inflation in, 162
  lawyers in, 185
  overvalued dollar in, 174–76
  postwar economic development in, 173–75
Jaspers, Karl, 76
Jefferson, Thomas, 49, 184
Johnson, Lyndon B., 1, 10, 21, 89–108, 134, 151
  antipoverty programs under, 10, 34, 89–98, 104–8, 139
  civil rights movement and, 52, 65
  draft deferment canceled by, 111
  economic policy under, 31, 108, 157, 165
  PPBS applied by, 27–28
  riots investigated by, 117–18
  South courted by, 52
  Vietnam involvement and, 41, 98–108, 112
  wrongdoings of, exposed, 155
Justice Department, U.S.:
  civil rights violations and, 55–57, 60–64
  juvenile delinquency programs and, 91
juvenile delinquency, 91, 92, 95, 98

Kahn, Herman, 20, 25, 227
Kattenburg, Paul, 101

Keats, John, 96
Kefauver, Estes, 52
Kempton, Murray, 2
Kennan, George, 18
Kennedy, Edward (Ted), 154
Kennedy, Jacqueline, 22, 97
Kennedy, John F., 1–5, 22–47
  aides chosen by, 23–24
  assassination of, 65
  bureaucracy as concern of, 24
  cabinet appointments made by, 24
  Catholicism of, as issue, 53
  civil rights movement and, 48, 51–57,
    61, 64–65
  Communism as viewed by, 17–21, 37
  economic policy under, 30–37, 108
  "flexible response" policy of, 42–43
  Keynes's appeal to, 16–17
  McCarthy and, 17–18
  military buildup under, 20–21, 27, 32,
    149
  popular appeal of, 2–4, 34
  poverty as concern of, 89, 139
  pragmatic style of, 3–5, 183
  presidential power as exercised by,
    22–24, 29
  Reagan compared with, 212, 225
  social spending under, 30, 32
  on U.S.-Soviet economic competition,
    18–20
  Vietnam involvement and, 41, 44–47,
    66–67, 149
  as war hero, 23
  wrongdoings of, exposed, 155, 210
Kennedy, Robert, 17, 76, 101, 134
  assassination of, 112
  civil rights movement and, 52, 53,
    55–57, 60, 64
  see also Justice Department, U.S.
Kent State, 128, 149
Kenyatta, Charles 37X, 126
Kerner Commission, 117–18
Kerr, Clark, 75
Keynes, John Maynard, 10–17, 168, 214
  on economy as intelligible, 12–13
  government spending recommended by,
    14–16
  increasing influence of, 16–17, 31–35
  on long-term growth, 168
  on long-term investments, 162–63
  on moral responsibility, 207–8
  "new economists" influenced by, 31,
    33–36, 37

Khmer Rouge, 148, 149, 219
Khrushchev, Nikita, 1, 19, 42
Kierkegaard, Søren, 77
King, Coretta, 53
King, Martin Luther, Jr., 1, 51, 53, 60,
    112, 118
  antiwar address of, 112
  on civil disobedience, 65–66, 69
King, Martin Luther, Sr., 53
King, Mrs. Slater, 58
Kissinger, Henry, 101, 131, 143–51
  on Cambodian invasion, 148
  on collapse of South Vietnam, 149, 150
  international politics as viewed by, 144
Knowledge and Decisions (Sowell), 182
Knowles, William, 18
Kondratieff, Nicolai, 168, 169, 239
Kondratieff long waves, 168, 169–72, 173, 208
Korea, South:
  industrial competition from, 167
  loans taken by, 177–79
Korean War, 30, 35, 39–40, 170
Ku Klux Klan Act, 63
Kuznets, Simon, 168
Kuznets cycle, 168–69

labor:
  standard contract for, 164–65
  wage controls and, 158–60, 162
  wages demanded by, 163–65, 167
  white vs. black, 189–90, 218–19
Laffer, Arthur, 216n
Laffer curve, 216–17
Laing, R. D., 76
Landrum, Phil, 141–42
Lang, Fritz, 81
Lansdale, Edward, 41, 44–45
Laos, 42, 149
Lasch, Christopher, 229
Le Duc Tho, 146
legal system, 185–86, 198–205
  arbitrary decisions involved in, 201
  blacks as lawyers in, 192
  dangers of legalism in, 203–4
  exclusionary rule in, 200
  glut of lawyers in, 185
  personal or factional influences in,
    199–200, 205
  realism movement in, 6, 8
  Southern obstructionism in, 56–57, 64
  women as lawyers in, 192–93
  see also Justice Department, U.S.;
    Supreme Court, U.S.

leisure industry, 232
"Letter from a Birmingham Jail" (King),
   65–66
Lewis, John, 59, 61, 69
liberal political philosophy, 183–209
   antidemocratic strain in, 28–29, 193
   collapse of, 108, 157, 180–81
   equality as viewed in, 183–84, 197
   legalistic character of, 185–86, 198–205
   single-variable policy analysis and, 189,
     197–98, 206, 212
   see also pragmatism, liberal
Lindsay, John, 135, 142
Lingo, Al, 62
Lippmann, Walter, 6, 34, 101
Lipset, Seymour Martin, 2
Lochner v. *N.Y.,* 8
Locke, John, 7, 67, 78, 205
Lonely Crowd, The (Riesman), 96
"Long Waves in Economic Life, The"
   (Kondratieff), 168–69
Lynd, Theron, 58

McCarthy, Eugene, 101, 102, 134, 142, 211
McCarthy, Joseph, 17–18
Macdonald, Dwight, 126
McGovern, George, 101, 135, 142, 211
McGrory, Mary, 133
McNamara, Robert, 23, 24–30
   "flexible response" policy of, 42–43
   PPBS developed by, 24–30
   public style of, 27
   rationalized policy processes and, 25–26
   war experience of, 23, 25
Madison, James, 202
Mailer, Norman, 76, 112, 114, 125, 133
Maitland, Ian, 102
Malcolm X, 69, 116
management techniques:
   forecasting, 31, 36
   McNamara's contribution to, 24–30
   new trends in, 217*n*
   pragmatic liberalism and changes in, 24
   rationalized policy processes and, 24–25
Mandarins, The (Beauvoir), 113
Mao Tse-tung, 38, 115, 116
Marcel, Gabriel, 76
March on Washington (1963), 64
Marcuse, Herbert, 86, 88, 193
Marshall, Burke, 60–61
Marshall, George, 18
Marshall, Thurgood, 53–54, 185
Marshall Plan, 18, 23

Martin, Louis, 53
Mathews, Zeke, 57
media:
   blacks as portrayed in, 50–51
   civil rights movement in, 109
   demonstrations geared toward, 127–28
   Kennedy's call to Coretta King and, 53
   Kennedy's tax reductions in, 34
   "new economists" as portrayed in,
     32–33, 35
   New Politics and manipulation of,
     134–35, 136
   Nixon and, 132, 152–54
   political wrongdoings as fashionable in,
     153, 210
   rioting in, 118, 127
   social upheaval as portrayed in, 228–29
   Vietnam War as portrayed in, 46, 101–2,
     145, 146–48, 149
   youth counterculture as portrayed in, 82,
     87
Medicaid, 92, 107
Medicare, 223–24
Menninger, Karl, 10
mental health system, reform of, 96–97, 98,
   224
Meredith, James, 55
Middletown study (1977), 228
Milliken v. *Bradley,* 201
Mississippi, University of, 54–55
Mississippi Summer (1964), 60, 75
Mitchell, Clarence, 54
Mitchell, John, 155
Mitford, Jessica, 125
Model Cities program, 105–6
monetarism, 163–64, 213–15
   foreign-exchange rates in, 216*n*
   market adjustments under, 215–16
   markets as viewed in, 214
   rationalist assumptions in, 214–15
Monetary History of the United States
   (Friedman), 214–15
"Moral Equivalent of War," 211
moral issues, morality:
   in civil disobedience, 65–67
   in civil rights movement, 65–68
   conservative, 156, 207–9
   legalism and, 185–86, 203–4
   liberal political philosophy and, 65,
     67–68, 108, 183–84, 207–8
   logic of pragmatism vs., 65, 67–68,
     75–76, 108, 207–8
   in policy-making, 47, 144

moral issues *(cont.)*
  rationality applied to, 183–84
  scientific discoveries and, 206
  traditional values and, 207–8, 228
  youth movement and established
    standards of, 75, 81–86, 88, 207,
    231–32
Morris, Michael, 70, 137
Morse, Wayne, 101
Moses, Bob, 59, 61, 64
Moynihan, Daniel Patrick, 90, 131, 133,
  139, 141–42
My Lai massacre, 149
Myth of Sisyphus, The (Camus), 77–78

Nash, Diane, 59
National Black Power Conference (1967),
  111
National Bureau of Economic Research,
  168
National Institute of Mental Health
  (NIMH), 96–97, 227–29
National Welfare Rights Organization, 142
Neblett, Chico, 62
Neshoba assassinations, 64
Newark, N.J., 69, 94–95, 111, 118–23
New Economic Policy (1971), 158–60
"new economists," 31–37, 168
  Kennedy's hesitancy with, 33–34
  policy differences among, 34
  rationalist character of, 36–38
  statistics and forecasting used in, 31, 36
  tax reductions and, 35
Newfield, Jack, 76, 135
New Frontier:
  ascendance of intellectuals in, 23–29
  ideology involved in, 23–24
  rationalist approach in, 36–38, 47
  spirit as characterized in, 7, 13, 22
  see also Kennedy, John F.
New Politics, 134–36
New Republic, 6, 101
New Rules (Yankelovich), 229, 231–32
Newton, Huey, 69, 115–16
New York City, N.Y., 28, 94, 111–12, 157,
  202
  crime rate in, 117, 138, 188
  defaulting of, 180–81
  demonstrations in, 111–12, 126–27
  "Open Enrollment" experiment in, 190
  rioting in, 118
New York Times, 101, 129, 139, 147–48,
  154

Nietzsche, Friedrich, 77, 84, 113
Nixon, Richard M., 1–3, 30, 39, 129–56,
  210, 222
  anticrime program proposed by, 138–39
  antipoverty program of, 132–33, 139–43
  defense spending under, 151
  dollar removed from gold standard by,
    12, 176–77
  economic policies under, 151, 157–60,
    176–77
  environmental programs under, 151
  international politics as viewed by, 144
  media relations of, 132, 152–54
  personality characteristics of, 1, 4,
    130–33, 139, 207
  public style of, 129–30, 207
  social progress as viewed by, 133–34,
    144
  Vietnam withdrawal and, 135, 143–51
Northern states:
  blacks in, 52, 68–69, 187
  Irish immigrants in, 191, 197
  racial tension in, 69, 90, 93–94
  urban decay in, 90
NSC-68 memorandum, 43
nuclear warfare, 20, 220–22
  deterrence needed in, 222
  first strike capability in, 220–21
  north-south trajectories in, 220
  old-line military wisdom in, 27

obscenity laws, 204–5, 206
oil embargoes, 160, 162, 170–72, 177–79,
  235–36
OPEC price cartel, 171–72, 177–79,
  235–36
Operation Marigold diplomatic assault
  (1966), 100
optimistic progressivism, 133
Organization Man, The (Whyte), 96

Park, Robert, 10
Parks, Rosa, 51
Peirce, Charles, 79
Phillips, Ulrich B., 50
population, aging trend in, 237–40
population growth, 68, 71–74
  of blacks, 68–69
  in Kuznets cycle, 169
  low-birth vs. high-birth cohorts and,
    73–74, 231
  postwar baby boom, 71–74, 232, 233,
    237–40

population growth *(cont.)*
  university populations and, 84
  youth movement and, 71–74, 231–32
pornography, 204–5, 206
poverty:
  of blacks, 34, 187, 190, 233–34
  Nixon's programs for, 132–33, 139–43
  of older white women, 92, 96, 140, 233
  overall decrease in (1960–1980), 233–34
  Reagan's view of, 212, 213
  of single-parent families, 190
  "structuralists" on, 34
Poverty and Discrimination (Thurow), 188
Powell, Adam Clayton, 94
pragmatism (Dewey and James), 5–11, 183
  constitution interpreted in accordance
    with, 7, 9n–10n
  in global politics, 19–21, 144
  Keynesian thought and, 10–11, 16–17
  philosophers responsible for, 5–8
  rationalism rejected in, 7
  society as viewed in, 9–10
  truth and usefulness linked in, 6–7
Pragmatism (James), 5, 6
pragmatism, liberal:
  antidemocratic bias of, 28–29, 193
  civil rights movement and, 56, 65
  educational policies based on, 80–81, 88
  equality as viewed in, 184, 197
  facts eclipsed by theory in, 7, 9, 36–38,
    47, 207–8, 240–41
  legal system influenced by, 6, 8
  monetarism and, 214–15
  morality vs. arid logic of, 65, 67–68,
    75–76, 108, 207–8
  "new economic" management and, 31,
    32–33, 36–38, 47, 215
  optimism inherent in, 32–33, 205
  radicals' view of, 75–76, 86, 88
  reductionist strain involved in, 78–80, 183
  simplistic models common in, 189,
    197–98, 206, 212
  social engineering in, 8–11, 224
  see also liberal political philosophy
presidential election of 1960, 1–5
  civil rights issue in, 48, 51–53, 54
  economy as issue in, 29–30
  issues generally lacking in, 1–2, 4
  Keynesian ideas and, 16
  Northern black vote in, 52
Presley, Elvis, 73
Price Commission, 159
Price of Power, The (Hersh), 146n

Prison Letters (Jackson), 125
prison system, 150, 224
  blacks in, 125
  Menninger's reforms in, 10
  rehabilitation programs in, 193–97
  social work profession and, 97
Pritchett, Laurie, 61
Program Planning and Budget System
    (PPBS), 26–30
  in antipoverty programs, 93
  failure of, 29
  Johnson's application of, 27–28
  theory of, 25–27
psychoactive drugs, 96–97

racial discrimination, 186–93, 205
racism, 48–69, 186–93
  black, 125–26
  blacks' violent reaction to, 115
  class conflict and, 90, 193, 206
  cognitive dissonance at heart of, 50
  ethnic differences and, 197–98
  in Northern cities, 69, 90, 93–94
  political liberalism and, 182
  recession and, 218–19
  upwardly mobile blacks and, 192–93
  see also civil rights movement
Radford, Arthur, 39
RAND (Research and Development)
    Corporation, 25
Rangel, Charles, 126
Rawls, John, 66, 67, 182, 183–86, 205, 224
Reagan, Ronald, 212–25
  academic theorists as advisers of, 212
  economic policies under, 213–19
  military buildup under, 32, 219–22
  popular appeal of, 212
  social welfare systems under, 222–26
  traditional value systems represented by,
    182, 209
Real Majority, The (Wattenberg and
    Scammon), 136–38
Reasoner, Harry, 82
Rebel Without a Cause, 71
Rebozo, Charles (Bebe), 154
recession:
  automatic stabilizers and, 166
  dollar speculation and, 175–76
  international trading and, 218–19
  oil price increases and, 211, 218, 236
  under Reagan administration, 213–19
"Recession, Great" (1974–1975), 160, 171,
    177

Reeves, Frank, 53
Reflections on Violence (Sorel), 113
Reich, Charles, 82–85, 107, 193, 232
religion:
    fundamentalist movements in, 212,
        226–27
    mainstream, 226–27, 228
    school prayer issue and, 199*n*
research and development expenditures,
    217–18
Reston, James, 34
Ridgway, Matthew, 40, 44
Riesman, David, 86, 96
riots, 117–23
    contagiousness of, 118
    "frustration" theory of, 117–18
    "message" expressed in, 122–23
    profile of blacks in, 118
Rockefeller, Nelson, 92
Roe v. *Wade,* 202–3
Rolling Thunder bombing program,
    99–100, 109
Rostow, Walt, 23–24, 43–44, 170
Roszak, Theodore, 82
Rovere, Richard, 140
Rowan, Carl, 53
Rubin, Jerry, 112, 127
Rusk, Dean, 24
Russell, Bertrand, 6–7, 79
Russell, Richard, 52
Ryle, Gilbert, 80

Sartre, Jean-Paul, 76, 113–14
Saulnier, Raymond, 33
Savio, Mario, 75
Scammon, Richard, 136–37
Schelling, Thomas, 25
Schlesinger, Arthur, Jr., 2–4, 129
    equality as viewed by, 184
    on Kennedy as president, 22, 32
    on military hardware production, 20–21
    "new economists" and, 31–37
    social spending urged by, 30, 34
    on Vietnam involvement, 46
Schwerner, Michael, 64
Seale, Bobby, 69, 115–16
Segretti, Donald, 155
Shawcross, William, 148
Sheehan, Neil, 101
Sherrod, Charles, 59
Shils, Edward, 2
Shriver, Sargent, 53, 70, 91–92
Shultz, George, 158

Sideshow (Shawcross), 148
Silver, James, 82, 85
Six Crises (Nixon), 4
Skinner, B. F., 80–81, 88
slavery, 48–50
Smith, John, 119
social progress, Puritan vs. optimistic views
    of, 133
social science:
    Dewey on, 8–9
    social engineering and, 91
Social Security, 140, 166, 219, 223–24
social work profession, 91, 97–98, 142
Sorel, Georges, 113
Sorensen, Ted, 35, 55
Southern Christian Leadership Conference
    (SCLC), 59
Southern states, 51–65
    civil rights accepted in, 59
    Family Assistance Plan opposed in,
        141–42
    Freedom Riders attacked in, 55
    school desegregation in, 186–87
    segregationist judges appointed in,
        56–57, 64
Soviet Union, 17–22
    Afghanistan invaded by, 211
    agriculture in, 172, 222
    Carter's relationship with, 132, 211
    Dewey on education in, 80
    economic growth in, 30–31
    economic uncertainty in, 222
    Eisenhower's policy toward, 43
    Eurodollars and, 177*n*
    grain imports concealed by, 159–60
    first strike potential of, 220–22
    Ho Chi Minh's reliance on, 38–39, 99,
        145
    U.S. détente with, 131, 132, 145, 147,
        151
    U.S. economic competition with, 18–19,
        31, 212, 225
Sowell, Thomas, 182, 192
Sputnik satellite, 19
*Stages of Economic Growth, The: A
    Non-Communist Manifesto* (Rostow),
    44
stagflation, 158
Stalin, Joseph, 18, 19, 38, 168, 169
Stein, Herbert, 158
Stennis, John, 52
stock market, "Kennedy crash" in, 34

Student Nonviolent Coordinating
   Committee (SNCC), 57–65, 123
 antiwar sentiment in, 111
 founding of, 59–60
 nonviolence rejected by, 66–67
 revolutionary change in, 110–11
 white violence toward, 57–65
Students for a Democratic Society (SDS),
   109–11, 119–20
Supreme Court, U.S., 185–86, 199–205
 abortion decision of, 202–3
 obscenity decision of, 204
 on school desegregation, 8, 51, 52, 201
Sutton, Percy, 126

Taking Rights Seriously (Dworkin), 182,
   204–5
Tawney, R. H., 184, 193
taxes:
 federal, on poor, 140
 investment in relation to, 216–17, 218
 negative income, 141
 1962 package, 35
 1964 reductions in, 34–35
 service and public employment contracts
   and, 164–65
Taylor, Maxwell, 43–44
Tet offensive (1968), 101, 103–4, 112,
   145–46
Theory of Justice, A (Rawls), 182, 183–86
Third World:
 bank loans to, 177–81, 216, 218
 economic growth in, 236–37
 revolutions as threat to, 219, 237
 Rostow on, 44
Thompson, Sir Robert, 44
Thoreau, Henry David, 66, 67
Thurow, Lester, 188, 217
Tillich, Paul, 76
Time, 10, 32
Tobin, James, 31
Tonkin Gulf Resolution, 102
Travis, Jimmy, 58, 61
Treason of the Clerks (Benda), 114–15
Trenton, N.J., 93–95
Truman, Harry S, 38
Tucker, St. George, 49
Turner, Bessie, 58

Uncertain Trumpet, The (Taylor), 44
unemployment:
 of black teenagers, 187, 190
 of baby boom, 74, 169, 237–38

 under Eisenhower administration, 30
 under Kennedy administration, 31
 "natural rate" of, 163–64
 in 1970 recession, 158
 oil embargo and, 160
 in overheated economy, 157
United Nations, 220, 236
urban centers:
 black migration to, 68–69, 233
 black rioting in, 111, 117–23
 crime rate increases in, 116–17, 138–39,
   188, 197
 growth of federal aid to, 140
 inner-city, bank investment in, 190–91
 Irish ghettos in, 191, 197
 poverty in, 90, 105–6
 see also specific cities

Vietnam War, 29, 37–47, 98–108, 143–51
 background of, 38–43
 ceasefire in, 145
 as civil war, 100
 "compellence" theory of bombing in,
   99–100, 205
 cost and casualties in, 105
 Eisenhower and, 39–40, 41, 42, 44
 French-American cooperation in, 39–40
 Johnson and, 41, 98–108, 112
 Kennedy and, 41, 44–47, 67–68, 149
 media coverage of, 46, 101–2, 145,
   146–48, 149
 negotiated settlement required in,
   100–101
 North Vietnamese cynicism suggested in,
   145–46
 pragmatic decision-making in, 9, 28, 99
 protest demonstrations against, 102,
   109–12, 128, 135
 Saigon captured in, 145, 147
 Southern insurgency in, 42
 Taylor-Rostow fact-finding mission in,
   43–44
 U.S. authority undermined after, 152
 U.S. degradation felt after, 150–51
 U.S. right-wing reaction to loss in,
   101–2
Voorhis, Jerry, 129
Voting Rights Act (1965), 64

wage and price controls, 158–60, 162
Walter, Francis, 18
Ware, Charlie, 62
Warnke, Paul, 100

War on Poverty, 10, 89–98, 105–8, 134
 civil rights leaders in, 111
 failures of, 95–96, 98, 105–8
 juvenile delinquency as issue in, 98
 poverty as viewed in, 95–96, 98, 106,
  139
 pragmatic approach in, 91–93, 205–6
 urban emphasis of, 92
 welfare dependency increases after,
  107–8, 138
Warren, Earl, 8, 199, 202
Washington, D.C., antiwar demonstrations
 in, 64, 109–10
Washington *Post,* 101, 129, 148, 154
Watergate, 102, 131, 132, 150–56
 media role in, 152–54
 Nixon's adversaries and, 153–54
 public outcry in, 150–51
Wattenberg, Ben, 136–38
Watts, N.J., 118–22
Weaver, Robert, 53, 54
Weinberg, Jack, 75
welfare demonstrations, 127, 134
welfare system, 166, 181, 203
 conservative politics and, 222–24
 increasing dependency on, 107, 138, 190,
  223–24
 reforms in, 136, 138, 140–41
Westmoreland, William, 104
Wharton, Clifton, 53
White, Theodore H., 3, 4, 152
"White Negro, The" (Mailer), 114
Whyte, William H., 96
Wicker, Tom, 152
William of Occam, 78
Williams, William Appleman, 18
Wittgenstein, Ludwig, 79
Wolfe, Tom, 124
women:
 black, 190, 223
 college education of, 97
 family as moral responsibility of, 230

job discrimination and, 198, 205
 in law and finance, 192–93
 pornography and, 204–5
 self-perception changes in, 228
 in social work profession, 97
 white older, poverty of, 92, 96, 140, 233
 working vs. nonworking, 230–31
women's movement, 87, 136, 198, 233
 lower-class women unaddressed by, 87,
  234–35
Wood, John, 58
World War II, 8, 10
 government investment in, 15
 peacetime economy developed after, 23,
  173–75
 racial barriers broken in, 51
Wretched of the Earth, The (Fanon),
  114–15
Wright, J. Skelly, 202*n*

Yankelovich, Daniel, 82, 229–31
Yeoman, Sol, 58
Youth International Party (Yippies), 112
youth movement, 70–76, 81–88
 antiwar demonstrations held by, 102,
  109–12, 128, 134, 135
 civil rights movement and, 69, 75, 84
 on college campuses, 71, 75, 81–88, 134
 counterculture of, 81–85
 economic power of, 72–73
 established values challenged by, 75,
  81–86, 88, 207, 231–32
 existentialism as appealing to, 78
 historical precedents for, 70–71
 limited extent of, 87, 228–29
 money and career rejected by, 232
 radicalism in, 84–88, 207
 self-importance felt in, 72–73
 social influence of, 70–71, 78, 82, 239

Zellner, Bob, 58
Zinn, Howard, 62, 66–67

About the Author

Charles R. Morris is a graduate of the University of Pennsylvania and the University of Pennsylvania Law School. He was assistant budget director of New York City and director of the city's welfare and Medicaid programs. He was also secretary for social and health services in Washington State, where he administered the state's prison, mental health, welfare, and health systems. For two years he was a consultant to the British Home Office, working on improving the police's prosecution and management of cases in the British lower courts. Most recently, Mr. Morris was a vice president of the Chase Manhattan Bank, where he was responsible for, among other things, the bank's global cash-management services and the managing of export and import banking services for U.S. corporate customers. He is currently a principal in an investment and management firm specializing in the health industry. His first book, *The Cost of Good Intentions: New York City and the Liberal Experiment—1960–1975,* was chosen one of the ten best books of 1980 by the *New York Times Book Review.* Mr. Morris makes his home with his wife and three children in Brooklyn, N.Y.